MW00996649

JCE understands teachers and students and kno━━━━━━━━━n. We have been helping teachers since 1924, and we are ready to help you. As our contribution to the professional development of new faculty, JCE offers anyone currently in the first or second year of teaching a two-year subscription (or subscription extension) for the regular one-year price. If you qualify, or if you want to give a subscription to a colleague who qualifies, you can take advantage of this offer in either of the two ways below. Choose **A** or **B**.

A. Just send an email to **jce@chem.wisc.edu** with the words "two-for-one offer" in the subject field. Give the name and postal address of the person who is in the first or second year of teaching and the date on which that person's teaching appointment began. We will take it from there. We will send you payment information.

B. Fill in the attached card (*please print*); return the card to us. We will send you payment information. The subscription will begin after payment has been received.

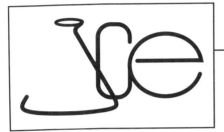

Journal of Chemical Education

Journal of Chemical Education, Department of Chemistry, University of Wisconsin–Madison, 1101 University Avenue, Madison, WI 53706-1396; phone: 800/991-5534 (U.S.) or 608/262-3033; fax: 608/265-8094; email: jce@chem.wisc.edu

JChemEd.chem.wisc.edu

Clip or tear along the dotted line.

Clip or tear along the dotted line.

• Recipient Mailing Information

Name of New Teacher _____   Date teaching appointment began _____

Institution/Department _____

Mailing Address _____

City _____   State/Province _____   Country _____   ZIP/Postal Code _____

• Donor Mailing Information (if different from above)

Name of Donor _____   Email Address _____

Institution/Department _____

Mailing Address _____

City _____   State/Province _____   Country _____   ZIP/Postal Code _____

Journal of Chemical Education
Department of Chemistry
University of Wisconsin—Madison
1101 University Avenue
Madison, WI 53706-1396

Survival Handbook for the New Chemistry Instructor

Survival Handbook for the New Chemistry Instructor

Edited by

Diane M. Bunce
Department of Chemistry
The Catholic University of America
Washington, DC 29964

Cinzia M. Muzzi
Physical Sciences Department
Truckee Meadows Community College
Reno, NV 89512-3999

Prentice Hall Series in Educational Innovation

Upper Saddle River, NJ 07458

Library of Congress Cataloging-in-Publication Data

Survival handbook for the new chemistry instructor / Diane M. Bunce, editor, Cinzia M. Muzzi, editor.
    p.   cm.
Includes bibliographical references.
ISBN 0-13-143370-9
  1. Chemistry—Study and teaching (Higher) I. Bunce, Diane M. II. Muzzi, Cinzia M.

QD40.S87 2004
540'.71'1—dc22

2003058247

Editorial Assistant: Jacquelyn Howard
Executive Editor: Kent Porter Hamann
Editor in Chief, Science: John Challice
Vice President of Production and Manufacturing: David W. Riccardi
Executive Managing Editor: Kathleen Schiaparelli
Assistant Managing Editor: Beth Sweeten
Production Editor: Edward Thomas
Manufacturing Manager: Trudy Pisciotti
Manufacturing Buyer: Alan Fischer
Marketing Manager: Steve Sartori
Marketing Assistant: Larry Grodsky
Copy Editor: Barbara Booth
Production Assistant: Nancy Bauer
Art Director: Jayne Conte
Cover Designer: Lisa Boylan

© 2004 Pearson Education, Inc.
Pearson Prentice Hall
Pearson Education, Inc.
Upper Saddle River, NJ 07458

Pearson Prentice Hall ® is a trademark of Pearson Education, Inc.

Printed in the United States of America

10 9 8 7 6 5 4 3 2 1

ISBN 0-13-143370-9

Pearson Education Ltd., London
Pearson Education Australia Pty., Limited, Sydney
Pearson Education Singapore, Pte. Ltd.
Pearson Education North Asia Ltd., Hong Kong
Pearson Education Canada, Ltd., Toronto
Pearson Educación de Mexico, S.A. de C.V.
Pearson Education—Japan, Tokyo
Pearson Education Malaysia, Pte. Ltd.

Other Titles in the Prentice Hall Series in Educational Innovation

Chemistry ConcepTests: A Pathway to Interactive Classrooms
By Clark R. Landis, Arthur B. Ellis, George C. Lisenky, Julie K. Lorenz, Kathleen Meeker, , and Carl C. Wasmer
0-13-090628-X

The Ethical Chemist
By Jeffrey D. Kovac
0-13-141132-2

Peer-Led Team Learning: A Guidebook
By David K. Gosser, Mark S. Cracolice, J.A. Kampmeier, Vicki Roth, Victor S. Strozak, and Pratibha Varma-Nelson
0-13-028805-5

Peer-Led Team Learning: A Handbook for Team Leaders
By Vicki Roth, Ellen Goldstein, and Gretchen Mancus
0-13-040811-5

Peer-Led Team Learning: General Chemistry
By David K. Gosser, Victor S. Strozak, and Mark S. Cracolice
0-13-028806-3

Peer-Led Team Learning: General, Organic, and Biological Chemistry
By Pratibha Varma-Nelson and Mark S. Cracolice
0-13-028361-4

Peer-Led Team Learning: Organic Chemistry
By J.A. Kampmeier, Pratibha Varma-Nelson, and Donald Wedegaertner
0-13-028413-0

Science and Its Ways of Knowing
By John Hatton and Paul B. Plouffe
0-13-205576-7

Writing Across the Chemistry Curriculum: An Instructor's Handbook
By Jeffrey Kovac and Donna Sherwood
0-13-029284-2

CONTENTS

INTRODUCTION AND OVERVIEW

SECTION I: REFLECTIONS ON PAST EXPERIENCE

SECTION II: GETTING STARTED

SECTION III: PEDAGOGY AND CLASSROOM INSTRUCTION

SECTION IV: TESTING AND ASSESSMENT

SECTION V: CAREER AND PROFESSION

FOREWORD

The problem with being a new instructor is that there seems to be an endless number of details to attend to. Some of these are involved with just settling into a new position, but the majority has to do with the prospect of teaching.

> *Teaching seems as if it should be easy. After all, we have been the recipients of teaching for some 20 years. Why, we might even have had experience teaching as an assistant or lecturer in graduate school. How hard could it be? We know the material. We know what the students should be taught to be as successful as we are. Everyone else in the department seems to know how to do it. They don't seem too stressed. It is just a question of putting one foot in front of the other or, in this case, one fact in front of the other.*

Matter of fact, you may have some definite ideas on how to improve the teaching you will do compared to that of some of your former instructors. Perhaps you plan to introduce the use of technology to help illustrate your lectures (PowerPoint, diagrams) or to deliver homework assignments or quizzes (Web pages, e-mail, WebCT, Blackboard). You might be planning to use live demonstrations to illustrate the excitement of chemistry. You have a lot of ideas. You're up to the challenge. You might want to just check on a few details before that first class. It might be useful to sit with a colleague and bounce some of your ideas around and ask some specific questions on how to set up some parameters of your course. That's the idea behind *this* book. Reading this book is comparable to sitting down with a colleague in the department and talking through some ideas or gaining some pointers on how to avoid common pitfalls. We think it is a *must* read for anyone who is facing teaching on his/her own for the first time (or second or third)!

In order to judge the potential usefulness of this book, it might be wise to understand how it came to be. The book is the result of a new instructor's search for help in understanding her successes and the need for improving her teaching. She wanted to engage others in this discussion—experts who might have some suggestions, and peers who were struggling as she was. Cinzia Muzzi first saw a need to provide information for new instructors during her second year of teaching. She suggested to the Division of Chemical Education's executive committee that a symposium on the topic be organized. This sounded like such a good idea that Diane Bunce volunteered to help Cinzia organize the symposium. Pertinent topics were selected, authors invited, and the symposium entitled "Survival 101 for the New College Chemistry Instructor" was launched at the 2001 American Chemical Society meeting in Chicago. Audience attendance was substantial for the full-day symposium. An informal survey of the participants showed that in addition to new faculty members, graduate students and "seasoned" two- and three-year veterans attended in substantial numbers. At the urging of some of the participants, the symposium was expanded and offered again in the summer of 2002 at the Biennial Chemical Education Conference in Bellingham, Washington. Here, the three-day symposium was equally well received. This led Cinzia and Diane to believe that there was an ongoing need for the information that was being presented at the symposium, so they got to work planning this book. Each author in this book was happy to share his/her expertise on a specific area. The purpose of each chapter is not to be an academic treatise on a particular topic but rather to be, as the book title suggests, a "how to" manual. *Practical* and *useful* are the words we hope that you will agree describe each chapter and its references. It should be obvious after reading this book that everyone goes through ups and downs in teaching, no matter how "expert" one is. Many of the same issues the new instructor faces at the beginning of his/her career are experienced by veterans when they teach a new course or face a new population of students. The important things to remember are to keep the goal of teaching in the forefront—to help students truly understand chemistry, not just memorize a laundry list of isolated facts and figures. The emphasis is on how the instructor can help this learning take place within the student, not how knowledgeable the instructor is. Teaching is about the learner. The teacher's ego should not be the most prevalent aspect of the exchange. As you read this book, keep in mind that time spent on organizing your course may free you to spend the majority of your time with students dealing with the chemistry concepts, not with details such as the due date of the next assignment.

We feel that this book can be used two ways—as an afternoon's read to get an overview of the issues that should be addressed as you *prepare to teach* or as a reference to answer specific questions that have arisen *as you teach*. There are many perspectives on the teaching process offered in this book. Bryan May (Chapter 1) suggests that you "teach with a purpose" and treat your students as "intellectual peers who just do not have some of the specific knowledge and skills you do." John Todd (Chapter 2) shares some of the things that can go wrong with the first teaching experience and proves beyond a shadow of a doubt that one can recover from a misstep. Cinzia Muzzi (Chapter 3) traces her search for understanding the difficulties students were having in her class through the learning-style literature. The results will help all instructors view the disconnect between teachers and students differently. Christina (Tina) Bailey offers some very practical advice on what purpose a course syllabus should serve (Chapter 4) and what questions to consider when selecting a textbook for your course (Chapter 5). Mary Flekke and Carmen Gauthier (Chapter 6) share specific suggestions on how to engage other resources on campus, like the library, to help enrich students' experiences in chemistry. Diane Bunce (Chapter 7) uses typical student comments to explain the difficulties students experience in chemistry and what the instructor can do to help. Saundra McGuire (Chapter 8) emphasizes how important it is to specifically teach students how to study. Her practical approach to this problem will be a great help for teachers and students. John Kotz (Chapter 9) describes how his course is organized utilizing on-line homework assignments, worksheets and CDs in recitation, computer-assisted lectures, and student surveys. Norbert (Norb) Pienta (Chapter 10) offers some practical advice on how to organize courses that utlize technology in the learning process. Statements such as "Students having a computer only ensures that they know how to turn it on" seem to say a lot. Julianne Smist (Chapter 11) discusses the use of small groups in chemistry. Advice ranges from how to determine the composition of each group to roles that can be assigned to group members. Susan Nurrenbern (Chapter 12) outlines how to introduce the use of small groups slowly into a chemistry course and how to address conflicts that can arise with such a method. William Robinson and Eunyoung Hurh (Chapter 13) introduce new instructors to the use of conceptual questions, including suggestions on how to write them. I. Dwaine Eubanks (Chapter 14) describes and gives examples of what goes into writing good multiple choice questions. Thomas Greenbowe and Kathy Burke (Chaper 15) explain the difference between norm- and criteria-referenced grading practices, and the difference these approaches can have on course statistics. John Moore, Elizabeth Moore, Jon Holmes, and Mary Saecker (Chapter 16) describe in detail all the information that is available to help new instructors teach chemistry in the *Journal of Chemical Education* print and on-line versions. Dawn Del Carlo (Chapter 17) offers practical advice on how to apply for that first (or subsequent) academic position. Richard Jones (Chapter 18) outlines the differences between teaching in a four-year and two-year college. Christina (Tina) Bailey and Philip Bailey (Chapter 19) offer advice to new instructors on how to prepare for an academic review, including what information to include and the roles the dean and other senior faculty play in the process. And finally, in "One Last Word" Diane and Cinzia put their two cents in on what this all means to the new instructor.

Diane M. Bunce
Cinzia M. Muzzi

I

REFLECTIONS ON PAST EXPERIENCE

1

Reflections on First Teaching Experience

Bryan May
Department of Science
Central Carolina Technical College

Abstract

In this chapter we will consider what you should expect and what you need to do before you ever walk into your first class. What kind of goals will you set? How will you achieve your goals? What concerns do students bring to class, and how can those concerns be addressed? What can you do to ensure that your students actually learn? This chapter focuses on general chemistry, as almost all instructors will teach general chemistry during their careers. As you begin reading, you should start to ask yourself questions about your approach to teaching.

Biography

This is the part where I am supposed to tell you why I am an expert and therefore qualified to write this chapter. Well, I am not an expert. In fact, the longer I teach, the more questions I have about teaching and learning that I cannot answer. By the time I retire, I am afraid that I will have so many unanswered questions that I will know nothing!

I graduated from Methodist College in Fayetteville, NC, with a bachelor's degree in chemistry and business administration. During my time at Methodist, I played and taught tennis, which is where I really started to learn about teaching. When you are 19 and people are paying a lot of money for an hour of your time, you had better teach them something! I taught a year of high school chemistry before starting graduate school at the University of South Carolina. While in graduate school, I taught physical chemistry lab. After earning a master's degree in chemistry, I started teaching at Central Carolina Technical College in Sumter, SC, where I have served as a chemistry instructor for over six years and as chairman of the Department of Science during the last year.

What will your classes look like?

As you begin to prepare for your first teaching assignment, it is important for you to stop and consider what your classes are going to look like. How large will your classes be? Will they be composed of traditional college students? What are the meeting times? Is there a recitation section? Will you be teaching lecture and lab? The answers to these questions will guide your approach to teaching the class.

There is no such thing as a "typical" general chemistry class, but there is some information that indicates that general chemistry classes are smaller than most people would expect. Seventy-eight percent of all colleges and universities have less than 5000 students, and 40 percent of all colleges and universities have less then 1000 students (Snyder, 2001). Over 44 percent of all undergraduates are currently enrolled in a two-year college, and over 50 percent of all undergraduates have taken classes in two-year colleges. The student-to-faculty ratio at two-year colleges is 18 to 1 (Phillippe, 2000). The Occupational Safety and

Health Administration (OSHA) recommends that lab sections have a student-to-instructor ratio of not more than 24 to 1. In other words, almost all instructors will do a lot of teaching in small classes, which means you will have a chance to interact with your students on a personal level.

Most general chemistry classes will be composed of students from a variety of academic programs, and they will bring a wide range of ability and preparation to class. In 1998 there were almost 1.2 million bachelor's degrees awarded, but only 32.6 percent of these degrees were in science and engineering. Only 1.3 percent of these degrees were in the physical sciences, of which 0.91 percent were degrees in chemistry. Another 5.1 percent of all bachelor's degrees were in engineering, but only 0.56 percent were chemical engineering degrees (Hill, 2001).

While there is not a "typical" general chemistry class, I believe that most instructors teach in small classes, or at least in small lab sections. A small class size will allow you to get to know your students and really get to understand them. Many, if not most of your students, are not science majors. This will likely be their only exposure to the physical sciences.

What do you want your classes to accomplish?

I must confess that for the first few years of my teaching career I never considered what I wanted my students to take from my class. I followed the course outline in the syllabus and worked hard to help my students learn the material, but I never set goals for my students. I suppose that I wanted them to learn some chemistry, but I am really not sure what that means. My blissfully ignorant state came crashing down one afternoon while reading a paper on writing assignments by Stanley Sunderwirth. In the conclusion Sunderwirth wrote, "The most important skill you can learn in college is to communicate clearly and to think critically" (Sunderwirth, 1993, p. 474).

I can remember sitting there for what felt like an hour with my head spinning! It suddenly occurred to me that I had been teaching without any purpose! I believe Sunderwirth's statement is correct. No matter what career your students enter, they will be required to solve problems and communicate with others. Many of your students will never use chemistry in their careers, so specific aspects of general chemistry may be of little to no use to them. Unlike other courses, the material in general chemistry does offer students a chance to develop critical-thinking skills.

Once you have pondered Sunderwirth's statement for a while, you will be better prepared for the inevitable question from your students: "Why do we need to know this?" It is okay to let students know that a specific detail from class may not be important to their future. This class only serves as one piece of their overall education, but they will be asked to solve difficult problems and think in terms of abstract concepts—skills that will help them in any field. These are the challenges that make chemistry difficult to teach, but this is also what makes chemistry valuable to students.

The first day of class I always ask students what they hope to get out of the chemistry class. Most students say they are in class to get a passing grade, and some of the ambitious students may even specify that they want a good grade. Since I do not accept these answers, students will then typically say things like, "We need to know the material." I try to help students understand that they will not be paid for their knowledge (unless, of course, they are a contestant on a game show) but they will be paid to solve problems and communicate with others. In general, the more difficult the problem you solve, the more you will be paid. By setting a broad overall goal for the class, I eliminate many questions and concerns from students about specific material that we cover.

I have another primary goal for all of my classes that I do not readily admit to students. Since many students have had little chemistry and may never take another chemistry class, I see this as my one chance to help them appreciate what chemistry is and the positive impact it does have in their lives. Much has been made in the literature about the negative image of chemistry, and I do believe that it is our responsibility to share some examples where chemistry has improved our quality of life (Adams, 2001).

Chemistry has certainly improved society over the years, but it is important that we direct our students' attention to the future. General chemistry is an ideal opportunity to introduce students to some of the challenges that we face as a society and to discuss how chemistry is helping to solve these problems or how it is still searching for solutions to some questions. The perception that chemistry is a mature and stagnant discipline is obviously not true, and we can help our students see the bright future of chemistry. Chemistry will only prosper if we can continue to recruit some of the best and brightest of our students. These students are attracted to chemistry if they see that they can make a positive impact and that there are opportunities for a productive and rewarding career (Breslow, 1997).

What else do you want to accomplish with your class?

We live in a complex world that is changing at an ever faster pace. Society faces many challenges that can only be solved by science. Our students will be the leaders of tomorrow, so we do need to educate them to be good citizens. This does not mean that they should have all of the answers when they leave our class, but that they should be able to consider a problem logically and arrive at a reasonable conclusion as well as articulate these same problems and conclusions. If people had a basic understanding of science, much of the pseudoscience prevalent today would be recognized for what it is. Since our students will be the leaders of tomorrow, it is important that they be able to make logical decisions about difficult problems.

The United States is suffering from a shortage of teachers, especially science teachers. It is important to recognize that many of our future elementary, middle school, physical science, and even some chemistry teachers will not take many college chemistry courses. It is important to have teachers that understand what science is and how it is important to society. If a teacher does not have a passion for science, it is less likely that the students will have a positive impression of science.

Obviously we want to give all of our students a solid foundation in general chemistry, but in particular we need our future science and engineering majors, as well as teachers, to be prepared for upper-level classes. One technique that I use to engage my students in the learning process is to discuss some of the different pedagogical techniques that I can use to teach a particular concept. Chemistry is a subject that can easily be taught by a variety of methods, and teachers normally intertwine multiple methods in their teaching. This should allow students to consider a concept from multiple perspectives, developing a deeper understanding. Unfortunately, as we bounce from approach to approach, many students do not make the natural connections and view our instruction as incoherent. For example, students commonly struggle with the abstract nature of chemistry. We expect students to be able to move between the atomic scale and the molar scale as well as to describe a system both symbolically and mathematically. When I introduce the mole concept in my courses, we discuss how students commonly struggle to relate these difficult concepts. Later in the course, when we introduce the kinetic-molecular theory, I will revisit these same issues. This reassures students that the difficulties they are facing are normal. By making students aware of how they and their classmates learn, I hope they will gain a deeper understanding of the concepts covered in my class.

I always try to make my students aware that my instruction can and does shape their understanding of the concepts we cover in class. For example, as I begin the first lecture on gases, I perform a demonstration for the students. I take an open paint can and set it on a Bunsen burner. After a few minutes I cap and remove the can. I then take a second paint can, place a small amount of water in the can, and place it on the burner. After a few minutes I cap and remove the can. The entire time, I continue with my lecture. My only comment about the demonstration is that it will take a while, but I want them to observe what happens. After a few minutes the can with air will make some popping noises, while the can that had the water in it collapses. I then have the students explain their observations in a question-and-answer format. By performing the demonstrations simultaneously, the students easily recognize the difference in the two systems and they are able to explain why the can with water collapses while the can with air undergoes a much less dramatic change. Students gain insight into Charles' law, the difference between gases and liquids, as well as into phase transitions. I then explain that some teachers use the demonstration with water in the can to illustrate Charles' law. We then discuss why teachers would use this demonstration (the consensus is that it is cool to watch) as well as the significance of presenting incorrect information in class.

Finally, I have students dissect poor questions to see how the question could be improved to better measure understanding. I assign students to work in small groups where they are assigned some problems. For each problem, the group must provide a solution and explain why this problem does not adequately measure every skill concept. As you will see in the following examples, I am defining a poor question as a question that can be answered correctly without a correct solution.

What is the theoretical yield of carbon dioxide when 10g of propane is burned in an oxygen atmosphere?

$$C_3H_8 + 5O_2 \rightarrow 3CO_2 + 4H_2O$$

A correct solution would require a student to convert 10g of propane to moles, then convert moles of propane to moles of carbon dioxide, and finally to convert moles of carbon dioxide back to grams. Since propane and carbon dioxide both have a molar mass of 44 g/mol, it is possible to get the correct answer without performing the gram-to-mole and mole-to-gram conversions. This question can only confirm that a student understands that propane and carbon dioxide occur in a 1:3 ratio.

What is the theoretical yield of $AlCl_3$ if 10g of Al and 10g of HCl are reacted?

$$2Al + 6HCl \rightarrow 2AlCl_3 + 3H_2$$

This problem requires a similar three-step solution to the problem above. Since the ratio of Al to $AlCl_3$ is 2:2, a student can solve this problem without understanding the molar ratio. If 10g of Al are converted to moles and then converted back to grams of $AlCl_3$, a student can arrive at the correct answer.

Students need a strong conceptual understanding to recognize instructional flaws and to propose possible improvements. I use these three techniques throughout the semester. I am not only trying to help students gain a better conceptual understanding but to introduce them to some of the nuts and bolts of teaching.

I have observed teachers who set some goals (probably unconsciously) that are not appropriate. New teachers bring enthusiasm to the classroom, which is great, but sometimes they can go too far. New instructors have a tendency to think that once they have helped their students see what chemistry is, they will all decide to become chemists. They bring an evangelical mind-set to the classroom, where they will convert the ignorant heathens to chemistry! Obviously our job is not to push students into any discipline, but to point them in the direction they want and need to go.

Your first teaching job is a real shift from what you have been doing as a graduate student or as a postdoc. Before, you were focused almost exclusively on research, but now you will probably be asked to focus most, if not all, of your energy on teaching. You will have to consciously change your priorities. Research may still be important, but if you are primarily a teacher, this must be where you place most of your effort. Consider what Roald Hoffman said at the Nobel Centennial Symposium: "Whatever success I have, I owe to my teaching. Research and teaching are inseparable. I became a better researcher because I had to teach beginning classes. The desire and obligation to teach others leads to greater creativity of research."

What are some student concerns?

Almost every student brings some concerns and baggage into your class, and yes, it can feel like every student is actually bringing multiple unique concerns. In reality, most concerns students have can be broken down into a few broad categories: intimidation by the instructor and the material, self-confidence, and communication barriers. If you are aware of some of the common concerns that students have, you will be better prepared to address them during the semester. By simply acknowledging student concerns, you will many times disarm the students and thus help them overcome these obstacles. Sometimes the first step in addressing a concern is having it acknowledged as being real. This is a role the instructor can play, but the instructor should go further and help the student solve their problems or assist them in getting help from someone such as a counselor or doctor, who can help if the problem is outside the range of the instructor's expertise.

The first challenge that you will encounter in your general chemistry class is intimidation. While not every student is intimidated, enough of them will be that it is better to go in with the mind-set that your entire class is nervous about learning chemistry. The reality is that many students do not feel competent in chemistry and they perceive a great chasm that separates you from them. Do not consider acknowledging their attitudes as a defeat. It is an opportunity. It is easy to exceed low expectations!

Students are intimidated by chemistry because it is perceived to be difficult. Many students have weak math and critical-thinking skills. They will struggle in class, and at times you may feel more like a remedial math teacher than a chemistry teacher. However, most students are actually capable of performing well in class, but they have probably not developed the study skills, the logical or critical-thinking skills, and the discipline necessary to succeed. Many strong students were able to coast through high school, and they will likely be challenged for the first time in general chemistry. Rather than acknowledging and addressing their own shortcomings, students simply use the excuse that chemistry is hard. My most effective work as a teacher occurs during my office hours with these students. These are the students who will come to you and say, "I have studied and studied, and I just don't get it!" I do not spend my time tutoring these students, but I ask them questions about their study habits. Once I have a feel of a student's study skills and learning style, I can then begin to teach the student how to become a better learner.

Obviously there is no simple method to help every student that you encounter, but a majority of these students simply need to learn to study. They spend time memorizing definitions and going over the problems that we have covered in class. I first encourage them to work on understanding the concepts we cover in class. Students should always try to answer the question, "What is the point of this material?" A great place for students to check their understanding is by answering the conceptual questions at the end of chapters in almost every textbook. I do encourage students to begin problem solving by using the problems we have covered in class. Students should write down the questions and problems that we have covered in class and try to solve them sometime later (when they have forgotten the answers!). They should consult their notes or quizzes only when they have finished. I also provide my students with a list of problems in their text that they can solve and then check their work. The performance of these "weak" students will improve dramatically when they actually start solving problems instead of looking over the problems in their notes.

Another type of student intimidated by chemistry is the student who is actually capable but is convinced that they are not capable of doing the work. There are many reasons that students feel this way. You will encounter women who feel that chemistry is for men, minorities who feel chemistry is for whites, as well as people from poor, rural areas who feel that they cannot compete with affluent students who have strong secondary educations. These students are the most frustrating because everything is in place for them to succeed except confidence.

There are three approaches that I have built into my teaching style to address these students. First, I try to make class fun and laid back. I use a lot of demonstrations, and I try to engage my students every step of the way. Many times a student will learn a great deal of material without even realizing that it should have been hard! I try to identify the weak students and the students who lack confidence at the beginning of the class. I am constantly asking my students questions, but I tailor the questions to the student. I try to ask questions that the student can answer. If they do not know the answer, I will rephrase the question or break it down into smaller, easier questions. This forces the student to succeed. Finally, I try to provide perpetual positive reinforcement to these students. When a student that is struggling answers a question correctly, I praise them in the middle of class. This public approval really does boost student confidence. I am most satisfied as a teacher when these students start to believe in themselves and begin to realize their potential.

It will not take long for you to realize that communication barriers exist between you and your students. There are countless reasons that these barriers exist between students and a chemistry instructor. Demographic differences such as race, age, sex, and socioeconomic background shape each of us. You must be constantly aware that your students come from a different world than you and they will see the world differently than you do. This does not make them wrong, only different. This different perspective is what makes diversity such a valuable asset to any type of group.

The last barrier that I want to mention is probably the biggest barrier between students and instructors, but it is the easiest to remedy. In many cases instructors do not have good communication skills. Many instructors feel pressure to sound scientific and to have all of the answers. I have often heard students say something like, "I guess she is a good teacher; she is just so smart, she can't break things down to our level." You should set a goal to never have a student say this about your teaching. Obviously your communication skills and your knowledge of chemistry are independent of each other. H. G. Wells said, "The reader for whom you write is just as intelligent as you are but does not possess your store of knowledge, he is not to be offended by a recital in technical language." Try to treat your students as intellectual peers that just do not happen to have some of the specific knowledge and skills that you already possess.

By the way, if you felt like the quote in the previous paragraph was awkward because I used she as the pronoun, you on some level believe the stereotype that science teachers are men. It is impossible not to let your own biases and experiences influence your performance in class.

The interaction of students and instructors is not at the root of all communication barriers that students may encounter. Many students cannot understand their textbooks and lack the skills to use this resource effectively. Students tend to read a chapter from beginning to end like you might read a novel. I want you to realize that students will have difficulty with their text and you will need to address this with your classes. Many students have never really needed a text, and you will need to spend some time early in the semester teaching your students how to use their text. The basic framework of a general chemistry course is established in the lecture and laboratory sessions. While the text is not the primary source of information, students should use their text as a reference when they are not comfortable with a concept. The text also serves as a source of questions, problems, and solutions for students to use when studying.

As an instructor, you do not have all the answers, so don't try to deceive your students into thinking that you do. It is a valuable lesson for students to learn, and yes, some of them still see you as this omniscient being who has come to share your infinite wisdom with them. Not only do we not have all of the answers but the act of doing research is actually our striving to generate answers (or even to refine the questions). Many times in class a student will ask what they think is a harmless question, but they really have no idea what they are asking. Early in the first semester of my general chemistry class, we cover isotopes and we interpret some simple mass spectra. Without fail a student will ask how a mass spectrometer works. I would guess that 99 percent of the students that ask this question do not know what they are asking, and if they did, they would not have asked. Many instructors feel obligated to answer every question asked in class. If you can answer this question in detail, that's nice, but all you may accomplish is to bore your class. The students do not have the background to understand a detailed account of how a mass spectroscope works at this point in their chemical careers. When you are faced with these types of questions in class, always try to remember the level of the class. General chemistry is just an introductory class, so you cannot cover everything in chemistry. Even though I will not answer these difficult questions, I want my students to ask them. I view these questions as an indication that the students are beginning to understand the concepts and that they are trying to construct a big picture. I hope that by not answering them, I will tap into their basic curiosity and plant seeds that will grow and bloom in later courses.

If you do have the rare student that really does want to know, take time with that student after class or in your office. These students are a lot of fun to work with, and these are also the students that we will want to recruit as chemistry majors. A little personal attention and a push in the right direction will go a long way toward helping these students choose a career in chemistry without turning off the others in class.

Students are always concerned, and I believe rightly so, about doing busy work. As instructors, we should strive to emphasize what is really important for students to learn. For example, do your students need to memorize the entire periodic table, or do you really want them to understand and learn how to use a periodic table? I am amazed at how many of my students memorized the entire periodic table in high school. I always respond to these students with a question like, "What is the molar mass of tantalum?" Obviously none of the students can remember the answer. I am willing to bet that most of you reading this do not know the answer either. It is 180.9479 g/mol. Do not waste your student's time and energy on unnecessary memorization, but strive to teach them how to use and understand the tools in chemistry, such as the periodic table.

I do not want my students to memorize definitions and facts about chemistry or to solve problems with algorithmic solutions. I want my students to be able to think critically and independently to solve problems. The topics we cover in general chemistry include some of the tools that are necessary for students to understand and solve the basic problems that we introduce. John Moore explores this idea in detail in a column entitled "Teaching for Understanding" (Moore 2002, p. 775).

There is a great deal of evidence that suggests that students are not learning what we teach. For those of you who have not taught yet, you will realize this the first time you cover something basic, like temperature conversions or unit conversions. I am amazed at how many students in advanced math classes still have trouble performing simple algebraic functions like temperature or liter-milliliter conversions. Paul Jasien considered this phenomenon in a recent paper that should be required reading for science teachers at all levels (Jasien and Oberem 2002). The following quote is quite telling in regards to our entire education system: "Although the ability to correctly answer algorithmic problems typically found in the introductory chemistry course may lead to a passing grade, the foundations of heat and temperature were quite shaky in the individuals we examined in this work. There appears to be no correlation between the number of college-level physical science courses and the ability to correctly answer basic questions related to thermal equilibrium." In other words, even though we teach heat and temperature over and over, our students do not typically learn these basic concepts. There are several physical science topics that students study in middle school, high school, and again in college. If students actually learned the basic concepts, we would not have to revisit the same topics again and again in our own classes.

So how do we break the cycle and produce students that have truly learned chemistry? I have to confess that I do not know the answer. Actually, I do not think there really is a simple answer, but there are a lot of things that we can do to improve student learning. First, every student has a unique learning style. Chemistry is a subject that can easily be taught with multiple teaching methods such as lecture, group work, demonstrations, and laboratory work. Try to incorporate as many teaching methods as possible into your class so you can reach a larger proportion of your students.

Are Students Learning?

Testing is a skill that every teacher should always strive to improve. The first question you need to ask about every question you ask is, "Does a correct answer to this question demonstrate that a student understands the material?" It is easy to ask questions that do not test what students have truly learned. For example, we can ask a straightforward factual question such as "What is an acid?" Typically the answer we are looking for is some specific answer that was covered in class. Does reciting a specific definition really demonstrate student comprehension of what an acid is?

Probably the most common and certainly the easiest testing pitfall that chemistry teachers fall into is the use of quantitative problems. A student can algorithmically solve almost any problem that you ask, but this does not demonstrate that learning has occurred (Moore 2001, p. 855). Instead of just asking students to calculate a free-energy value, have them also interpret the meaning of this free energy value.

Many questions appear to measure student understanding, but on closer inspection they may only be a partial indication of conceptual understanding. Consider the following limiting reactant question:

What is the limiting reactant when 25g of zinc and 20g of hydrochloric acid are reacted?

$$Zn + 2HCl \rightarrow ZnCl_2 + H_2$$

A student may get the answer correct without performing the correct calculations. If they simply remember that the limiting reactant is the reactant that will be consumed first, they may choose hydrochloric acid, which is the correct answer. While the student might know the definition of a limiting reactant, they do not understand the concept. The concept of limiting reactant is based on amount of reactants at the molar level and it is dependant on the molar ratio of products to reactants. We can better pinpoint the student difficulty by changing the starting amounts. This problem could be improved by simply changing the starting amounts to 20g of zinc and 20g of hydrochloric acid. If a student says that both reactants are the limiting reactants we know they are not moving from the mass to the molar scale.

In chemistry it is easy to stack multiple concepts into one question, which can make it difficult to determine which concepts the students do and do not understand. Consider the following question:

A mole of a gas at 0° C and 760 mmHg is heated to 20° C, and the pressure is held constant. What will the new volume be?

To solve this problem, students first must recognize that the question relates temperature and volume. They must remember that Charles' law is based on absolute temperature, so Celsius values must be converted to Kelvin, and they must know that the molar mass of any gas at 0° C and 1 atmosphere (760 mmHg) is 22.4 L. A student must possess all of this knowledge to correctly calculate the new volume. I do not think this is a bad question, but you must be aware of what concepts or skills you want a question to measure. If you simply want to measure how well a student understands the relationship between temperature and volume, you could ask them to describe what would happen to the volume when the temperature is raised. If you do want a mathematical solution that demonstrates a student's comprehension of Charles' law, remove some of the required peripheral knowledge. Provide the temperature in Kelvin, or give the formula to convert Celsius to Kelvin as well as the molar volume of a gas. The most effective method of measuring how well a student understands Charles' law would be to use multiple questions with varying levels of difficulty. Many students could describe what happens to the volume as the temperature, but fewer students will be able to solve the problem given above.

I do not pretend to be an expert on testing. Measuring the conceptual understanding of students is an inexact science at best, one that you can never truly master. I want you to always be aware of what concepts you want your students to learn and try to design questions that will measure this understanding. By simply reflecting on what skills and knowledge a student must possess to answer a question, you will write better questions.

Is there anything else I need to do to get ready for class?

There are several simple instructional-management ideas that you should implement as you prepare for class. First, set up a calendar for the semester. At the least, be able to tell your class when each major assignment will be due during the semester. For example, I may not know exactly what material will be on test #2, but I know that test #2 will occur on a specific day at a specific time. This not only helps students plan their workload in your course but it really makes your job easier. A calendar will eliminate almost every excuse students have concerning missing a test, test preparation, etc. Students may forget to study for a test (and yes, some of them will), but with an announced course calendar the responsibility is their own.

You will also need to prepare a syllabus that includes an outline of topics covered in the class, your grading system, and any specific assignments you are giving during the semester. In many cases you will have a syllabus in place from your department. If you do need to create your own syllabus, I recommend you use old syllabi from your institution as well as other schools as a guide. The more detail you can provide, the better. The syllabus is a contract between you and your students, but it should also serve as a guide to your specific course. Students really appreciate a good syllabus because it lays out how the class will work and what will be expected of them, but you will also reap rewards from a good syllabus. A good syllabus allows you to spend class time working on chemistry instead of handling classroom-management issues.

A common complaint from students is they feel that they will never use chemistry once they get out of the course. While you know this is obviously not true, it is difficult to help general chemistry students appreciate the relevance of chemistry. You should strive to incorporate real-world examples of chemistry throughout your class to help address this issue. For example, a majority of students have mixed Clorox and ammonia cleaners at some point. I bring up this example early in class because students understand that this combination is a mistake (usually from personal experience), and the chemistry is easily understandable in a first-semester class. I use this simple example to plant the seed that chemistry is important and that they should strive to understand chemical issues in their own lives. In my course, we consider real-world examples in areas such as nutrition, medicine, and the environment. The July 2002 issue of the *Journal of Chemical Education* featured several articles with an emphasis on real-world concepts that ranged from athletics to food to warfare.

Conclusion

Chemistry is a difficult subject, but it does not deserve as bad a reputation as it often has. Many of our students fear chemistry and are convinced that they do not like it. You will realize how wonderful teaching chemistry is when you begin to reach these students. There is no better feeling than when a student has realized that chemistry is "cool" or that they are capable of understanding the material in your course and become confident enough to continue in chemistry. Teaching is about building relationships with your students, and chemistry is a great vehicle to help you connect with your students by guiding them to a realization of their potential.

Bibliography

Adams, D. (2001). What's in a name? *Nature, 411,* 408–409.

Breslow, R. (1997). *Chemistry Today and Tomorrow: The Central, Useful, and Creative Science.* Washington, DC: American Chemical Society.

Herron, J. D. (1996). *The Chemistry Classroom: Formulas for Successful Teaching.* Washington, DC: American Chemical Society.

Hill, S. T. (Ed.) (2001). *Science and Engineering Degrees: 1966–98* (NSF 01-325). Arlington, VA: National Science Foundation.

Jasien, Paul & Oberem, G. E. (2002). Understanding of elementary concepts in heat and temperature among college students and K–12 teachers. *Journal of Chemical Education, 79,* 889–895.

Moore, J. (2001). Testing, testing. *Journal of Chemical Education, 78,* 855.

Moore, J. (2002). Teaching for understanding. *Journal of Chemical Education, 79,* 775.

Phillippe, K. (Ed.) (2000). *National Profile of Community Colleges Trends and Statistics.* *3rd ed.* Washington, DC: Community College Press.

Snyder, Thomas & Hoffman, C. (Eds.) (2001). *The Digest of Education Statistics.* Washington, DC: Claitors Publishing Division.

Sunderwirth, S. (1993). Required writing in freshman chemistry courses. *Journal of Chemical Education, 70,* 474–475.

2

Teaching College Chemistry:
The View From a Newcomer to the Field

John Todd
Department of Chemistry
Bowling Green State University

Abstract

I am not an expert instructor, so I cannot share any advice or tips from any sort of an expert perspective. Rather, I thought I would share some experiences I had teaching my first college chemistry classes and the most important lessons I learned as a result. I have four premises that guide the experiences I will relate in this chapter. First, learning is an internal, personal process of constructing ideas, schemata, and explanations of observations rather than the direct transfer of knowledge from one person to another (constructivism). Second, this process is difficult, lengthy, and often uncomfortable for the person undergoing it. Therefore, third, one of the best ways teachers can facilitate this process is to provide a structured, supportive learning environment for their students. The best way to do this is to maximize the connections between the student and teacher. Finally, the reverse is also true: If students feel disconnected and alienated from their teacher, they will not undertake constructivist learning, reverting to the easier, more familiar and comfortable processes of rote memorization, algorithmic problem-solving techniques, and cramming. Next, I attempt to show how several policies and practices I implemented in my first several classes have affected my students' learning, both for the better and for the worse. Finally, I attempt to show that no matter how badly a teaching experience may start off, persistence and reflection about one's practices can lead to better teaching in the end.

Biography

I received my B.S. degree in biochemistry from the University of Tennessee at Knoxville in 1994 and my Ph.D. degree in biochemistry from Northwestern University in 1999. While at Northwestern I became interested in teaching at the college level and researching chemistry education after attending a Biennial Conference in Chemical Education at Waterloo, Ontario, in the summer of 1997. I participated in the Preparing Future Faculty program at Northwestern, through which I was exposed to constructivism, gained some experience teaching college students, and interacted with a mentor who was also interested in college teaching. After graduating, I studied chemistry education research for a year as a postdoctoral fellow at the University of Wisconsin at Madison (UW). My mentor was a good chemistry teacher and a leader in the field of chemistry education research from whom I learned a great deal about effective college teaching. In addition, while at UW I took classes in educational psychology and statistics and studied the effects of technology on student learning. After a year at UW I accepted a position as an assistant professor of chemistry at Bowling Green State University (BGSU).

Premises: Constructivism

My guiding theory for education is the dominant theory guiding modern educational research: constructivism. Constructivism holds that learning is *not* the direct transfer of intact knowledge from one person to another. Rather, learning is an internal, very personal process of constructing ideas based on the learner's past and current experiences. Imagine that structures in the teacher's mind are broken down into a stream of data (words in lecture, text in books and lecture notes, a series of experiences undergone in lab, etc.) that are transmitted to the student. The student, in turn, accepts these streams of input and integrates them into structures in his or her own mind (Maslow 1954; Herron 1996).

Unfortunately, the structures erected in the student's mind are not exact copies of those in the instructor's mind. There are several reasons for this. First, students' minds are not blank slates that teachers are free to write new knowledge upon. Every student comes equipped with preexisting knowledge structures that serve as the foundations that new structures based on the experiences in class must be built upon. All of these preexisting structures are different, and some (many? most?) of them may be incorrect. Second, the experiences the teacher is providing are not the only streams of input entering the students' sensory apparatus. Simultaneously there are many other streams of input and sources of modification of the input, such as physical or mental discomfort, a sunny day outside the classroom, disruptive classmates, etc. Therefore, in many cases in order for correct learning to take place, structures that have already been constructed in the learner's mind in the past that are not accurate reflections of scientific theory must be modified, partially removed, or completely torn down in order for correct structures to be erected in their place.

Premises: How the learning environment can aid or hinder constructivist learning

My second premise is that this process is difficult, time consuming, and often very uncomfortable for the person undergoing it. Take a moment to read the last sentence of the previous paragraph again: "Structures that have already been constructed in the learner's mind … must be modified, partially removed, or completely torn down in order for correct structures to be erected in their place." These structures that I am talking about are schemata, explanations, and experiences that we use to understand the world we experience around us. Everything that we see, feel, or experience in any way is interpreted through the lens of these mental structures we have built in the past to explain similar phenomena. Now, for a teacher to ask that a student's mechanism for understanding the world be modified, altered, or torn down and replaced with something new is surely a terrifying thing for a student to experience.

Therefore, my third premise is that one of the best ways teachers can facilitate this process is to provide a structured, supportive environment within which the students feel comfortable enough to reexamine their mental structures and are willing to modify them in any necessary ways. In turn, one of the best ways to form a supporting environment is to maximize the number and quality of the connections between the teacher and the students (Cole & Todd 2003). Finally, the reverse of this final premise is also true: If students feel uncomfortable in their classroom experience; in particular, disconnected and alienated from their teacher; they will not dare to undertake constructivist learning, reverting to the easier, more familiar and comfortable but ultimately less efficient and meaningful learning processes of rote memorization, algorithmic problem-solving techniques, and cramming.

First teaching experience: Chemistry 125

Chemistry 125 is the first semester of general chemistry at BGSU. It is a large enrollment class with over 200 students in a large lecture hall. Since this was my first time teaching, I decided not to stray from the examples of instructors I had observed in the past. I wanted to employ techniques that I had seen work in other classes. Therefore, I organized the class in a traditional manner, with three lectures, a recitation, and a lab each week. However, I did introduce several innovative components that I had seen used effectively in other classes and that I thought would enhance the students' learning experience. I made extensive use of demonstrations in the lectures. I used PowerPoint presentations projected from a laptop computer for several of the lectures, and I used the course organization software program WebCT. WebCT stored the students' grades and made them available at any time, had a bulletin board feature that students could use to post messages to the class or to the instructor at any time, and had a quizzing function that I used for weekly homework assignments. My research at UW had involved on-line homework assignments (Cole & Todd 2003), so I brought those assignments to BGSU. I thought that with only slight modification, in a similar class with nearly identical subject matter and students in a similar situation, they would work as effectively at BGSU as they did at UW.

After all my preparation, on the first day of class I felt ready to go. I had a detailed PowerPoint presentation loaded on my laptop, I planned to connect to the Internet to demonstrate to the students how to use WebCT, and I had overheads and demonstrations planned. Instead of delivering a well-rehearsed lesson plan that day, however, I received a vivid lesson in the fine art of improvisation. When I was interviewing at BGSU, I had been informed that all the lecture halls had Internet connections, and I could see a booth that I assumed was occupied by consultants who were there to help lecturers who were having difficulty with the technology. When I arrived at the lecture hall that day, however, I discovered that I had no idea how to connect to the Internet or plug my laptop into the lecture hall's projection system; the booth I had noticed earlier was empty. Fortunately, there were overhead transparencies left on the projector by the previous teacher, and I had an overhead pen, so I improvised a presentation on the overhead instead and let the students go early. I have heard many people say that the way the first class goes and the impression the students have of the teacher on the first day can have a large effect on the way the class goes during the rest of the term; I cannot see how the impression I made that first day could have led to constructivist and integrated learning.

This would merely have been a minor embarrassment, except that the problems didn't stop there. I had planned to use the students' birthdays as initial passwords for them to access WebCT. With all the preparations I was having to make before the class got started, I put off getting this information from the registrar and discovered the first week of class that instructors were not allowed access to students' birthdays. Unfortunately, I had composed and printed out the syllabus already, so I had to switch the initial passwords to their student ID and inform the students of the change orally in class. This took time and was still a source of confusion for the students several weeks later; many students could not connect to WebCT during this time. With homework assignments assigned and due every week, this was understandably stressful for the students, even though I extended deadlines and gave them the opportunity to make up the work.

The problems continued from there. One feature of the on-line homework was feedback on students' answers, both right and wrong, directing them to sections in the textbook where they could find additional explanations and similar problems. The homework problems were written for a different textbook than the one the students were using. This meant that the feedback pointed to incorrect sections of the textbook, and in many cases the feedback was just plain wrong. I tried to correct this as I went along on an ad hoc basis, but the students pointed out to me that the discrepancies in the feedback required a more systematic and thorough review in order to correct them. I eventually had to set aside a couple of hours every week to review in detail every single homework problem assigned that week to ensure that it was free of error and pointed to the correct section in the textbook we were using. In the meantime, this was a source of stress that was not conducive to the sort of constructivist learning I was trying to promote in my class.

I thought that my postdoctoral advisor at UW organized the material in his class in an especially effective way, so I based my lesson plans on the order of topics that he followed. Again, however, since the textbooks were different, the order of topics differed substantially from the one used at UW and the one I was using at BGSU. The order of topics in the first five weeks of my class came from Chapters 1, 2, 3, 2, 3, 2, 24, 4, 2, 3, 4, 3, 4, 3, and 4. There was a common thread running through all of these jumps in the text, and I tried to make the connection plain in my lectures. But the students only heard my explanation once, in the lecture. When they were sitting in their dorm rooms with their textbooks studying on their own, the common thread was not apparent to them. Not being able to find the links between ideas we were discussing in class added to their discomfort and distress and again impeded the constructivist learning I was trying to foster.

The University of Wisconsin is a premier institution in the Big 10; the students are of a very high caliber and ability. On the other hand, many of the students at BGSU are first-generation college students who do not have the preparation of the student body at UW. So when I based my exam questions on those I had seen my advisor at UW use, my students at BGSU struggled with them and scored significantly lower than the UW students. Their difficulty and resulting lack of confidence were compounded by my grading system, in which I did not set concrete percentages or point cutoffs for A's, B's, etc., but instead held that back to the end of the semester. On the advice of my department chair, I planned to devise a grading scale at the end of the semester because of my lack of teaching experience and inability to predict how well the students would perform on my assessments. By scoring so low on the exam and then not knowing how final grades would be computed, students were never certain of what grade they would receive and naturally began to expect the worst.

As you might expect, these problems led to student discontent, and this was the source of yet another problem. I did not always promptly answer e-mail I received from students for several reasons. First, when I started the class, I expected that I would be overwhelmed by e-mail from the 200 students enrolled in the course. Therefore, I tended to answer e-mails immediately only if they were urgent or I could quickly and easily formulate a response them. Second, I have a natural tendency to procrastinate, so I would often let an e-mail sit in my inbox for several days, telling myself I would deal with it later. Third, as time went on, the nature of the e-mails began to change, and I began telling myself, "I won't even dignify that with a response!" It certainly was not conducive to my own confidence and willingness to undergo constructivist learning about teaching to be receiving responses like this. And of course, not receiving responses from the teacher was another wedge separating me from the students, increasing their fear and discomfort and decreasing the likelihood of constructivist learning.

So what was the result? Images of nuclear bomb explosions, riots in the streets, and the dangling bodies of lynching victims come to my mind when I recall my feelings during this time. I am exaggerating slightly, of course, but I literally felt that I was going to be sued by my students, wind up in court, and make the evening news across the country. The department chair and even the dean of the college received numerous phone and e-mail messages and office visits from students complaining about Dr. Todd and his Chem125 class.

The students saw me as capricious, arbitrary, unreliable, and unresponsive to their concerns. They felt out of control and insecure. These perceptions and emotions were exactly the opposite conditions as those I described above as being necessary for constructivist learning. As a result, besides blaming me for their lack of success, the students relied on other learning patterns: rote memorization, cramming, disconnected learning, etc. I am certain that some learning was going on, but not as much as I would like and certainly not the integrated constructivist learning I was aiming for.

Adjustments

So what did I do? After meetings with the department chair, I changed several of my policies. I began responding promptly to every single e-mail I received. I found that it took far less time than I had imagined. It does not take very much time to respond to six or so e-mail messages in a morning, and students are satisfied with an honest "I'll think about that and get back to you." This tells the students that you have received and heard their message, and when you actually do get back to them, they know that they will get a thoughtful response to their question or concern.

I met with several of the students who were my most outspoken critics on the WebCT bulletin board and e-mail. I acknowledged that there were considerable problems in the class and asked for their input on how to restructure the situation to address their concerns. I established the ground rule that they were free to criticize me, but they had to do so in a civil way and restrict their language and manner appropriately. I was especially concerned about and forbade their "flaming" other students in the course who were defending me, and I pleaded with them to be patient and act in a civilized manner. One student in particular was very gratified that I chose to speak to her and became one of my strongest supporters for the remainder of the course. (Just the other day she stopped by my office to say hi. She is interning as a nurse at a local teaching hospital and is taking organic chemistry in the chemistry department.)

For the rest of the course I followed the textbook much more closely. My original plan did follow the order of chapters closely, but after the experience of the first half of the semester, I certainly was not about to try topics out of order. Nevertheless, I found that there were still ample opportunities to make connections between different sections of the book, and the students were much more comfortable when they knew which section would be covered next. As I mentioned above, I began setting aside time each week to carefully edit the homework assignments the students would have the next week, making sure that the feedback pointed to correct places in the textbook and was correct. As a result, the number of complaints about the homework dropped dramatically.

I cannot say that Chem125 in the fall of 2000 was a great success as a result of these modifications. The students, because of their discomfort and unease, were unwilling to undergo the constructivist learning I had tried to foster. But viewing myself as a constructivist learner, these experiences became the foundations for new and expanded schemata, especially about the need for connections between teacher and students (Palmer 1998).

Other classes I have taught since then have been more successful as a result of the lessons I learned. I taught Chem125 in the summer of 2001 and again the following fall. I followed the book closely, made sure all the materials I used were accurate and integrated with each other, and went out of my way to elicit and respond to student feedback and concerns. These all seem like simple things to do, and a fair question is why I did not do them at first. I think there are two reasons. First, as a first-time teacher, there were a multitude of things to remember, and so inevitably some of the obvious things to do slipped out of my mind. Second, before I took this position at BGSU, I had heard many stories about how busy new assistant professors are, and so I was extremely jealous of my time. All the solutions I outlined above take time to implement, and I think I felt at the beginning of the fall 2000 term that I couldn't spare the time to attend to them. As I discovered, however, not taking the time causes many more problems that take up even more time to solve with a less effective final result than dealing with them from the outset. As a result of implementing these solutions, however, the semesters have gone much more smoothly, and students seem to have struggled with the chemistry and not with me.

Second teaching experience: Chemistry 127

Some of these problems returned, however, when I taught Chemistry 127, the second semester of general chemistry, during the spring of 2002. This was the first time I had taught second-semester general chemistry, and therefore some of the problems I have described above returned. I think this is because every new class is a different situation and requires experimenting and trial and error to construct a working model of how the class should operate smoothly. Even if you have been successful in other classes, starting a new class in many ways sets you back at the beginning, and you get the chance to make all new mistakes in the new class.

This certainly happened to me, starting early in the semester. I get very frustrated when students focus on things that I consider trivial but that appear important to them. For example, students often asked me to return to a previous overhead so they could write down all the details when I thought they had had plenty of time to write down the important information. I lost my temper with my students at one point early in the semester, and I think that that outburst adversely affected the class the rest of the semester since the students felt less comfortable asking me questions in class or asking for help that they needed. I think this reluctance applied to any problem they had in the class, not just asking me to leave an overhead up for a longer time. This applies especially to students who visited me in my office. When they arrived at my office, they were at their most vulnerable, having admitted that they didn't "get" it and needing outside help. Nothing justifies being impatient or abrupt with someone who visits me in my office, no matter how many times I have covered similar problems in class or elsewhere, but I fear I was just that on several occasions when students came to me. Fear and disconnection with the instructor, again, impaired the integrated constructivist learning I was trying to foster in the class.

My postdoctoral advisor at UW had used an American Chemical Society (ACS) standardized full-year exam for the final exam of second-semester general chemistry, so I planned to do the same. When an instructor uses one of the ACS standardized exams, they add that instructor's class data to a national database and provide the instructor with free statistical comparisons to the other students in the database. Therefore, I hoped to obtain objective information about how my students compared to other chemistry students nationwide and also some information about my teaching. This was disastrous. ACS exams had not been used at BGSU for many years, and I failed to discuss this with anybody on campus before putting it into effect. The students thought it was unfair that I was announcing that a comprehensive exam would be given at the end of the semester, even though I made the announcement several weeks ahead of time, giving them ample opportunity to review first-semester material. They still complained about the exam when I changed it to one that covered only the second semester. Their main objection here was that there was material on the exam that had not been covered in class. Even though I assured them that those questions would not be graded, they did poorly on the exam and I did not get the information I wanted.

A more subtle problem that I have only begun to discern since observing other teachers' classes in a variety of disciplines on campus has to do with differing expectations of the pace of classes. As a chemistry student at the University of Tennessee, I "got" chemistry very easily. I needed little time for review and was able to quickly incorporate new concepts into the chemistry concepts I already had. My experiences at Northwestern and UW, both highly respected institutions in the Big 10, reinforced this experience. As a result, I set a fairly fast pace to the class. I set aside little time for review of previously covered material, expecting the students to do this on their own outside of class. I never released grading keys, reasoning that students would learn more effectively by interacting with me and their fellow students to construct the correct answers on their own. Other classes I have observed at BGSU have led me to suspect that the students expect a more leisurely pace to the classes, with ample time for review. After quizzes and exams, instructors often set aside entire lecture periods to review common mistakes on the assignments and discuss the correct solutions. There is certainly nothing wrong with either approach, but I think the difference between my and my students' expectations led to conflict and disconnection impeding constructivist learning.

Finally, as I described above, I had been using relative grading scales, examining the distribution of student points at the end of the semester and assigning cutoffs to give approximately 10 percent of the students A's, 10 percent D's and F's, and the rest B's and C's. I had not been using an absolute scale on the advice of my department chair, because of my lack of experience in setting appropriate point cutoffs. The students were uneasy with not knowing exactly where they stood in the class and questioned this process repeatedly the whole semester.

Again, the causes of the students' discontent go back to what I outlined before. When I was not encouraging questions, students did not feel comfortable enough to examine and alter their mental structures. Surprising them with a new exam format in the middle of the semester, especially one that would be comprehensive through first- and second-semester general chemistry as I originally planned, did nothing to help this. Not receiving reviews of the material and the correct answers on their assignments, in their minds, prevented them from learning from their mistakes and further drove home the wedge between us. Finally, not knowing at any time what grade they were earning in the class only made the students more apprehensive and nervous.

Current experiences

The class I am teaching now is Chem100, an introductory course for nonmajors. I am applying all the lessons I have described above, including the ones I learned from my experiences in Chem127. I am using PowerPoint presentations in all my lessons and making lecture handouts available on the Web before class so that students do not have to worry about writing down every word on the slide. Before I begin every class period, I take a moment to remind myself of their situation as learners and to prepare myself mentally to answer their questions patiently, in class and outside of class, and do whatever it takes to help them learn more effectively. I am setting aside class time for review and discussion of quizzes and exams. Finally, I am using an absolute grading scale, telling the students that the grade cutoffs may go down but they will never go up. Once again, these steps are designed to make the students more comfortable in the course. Any steps that can be taken to make the course predictable, comfortable, and nonthreatening will encourage constructivist learning. As a result of following these steps, the class is much more relaxed and enjoyable. I am certain that the students are learning the material, which is the goal of the whole enterprise.

Conclusions

I have learned several specific lessons as a result of my experiences. First, you should go out of your way to connect with your students (Palmer 1998). In my case this translated to answering e-mails promptly, encouraging questions in and outside of class, being predictable in the class and the lessons that will be taught, and making sure all the class components fit together seamlessly. Second, you should be selective of the examples you follow and the advice you take. There are many, many good teachers out there, and many more places where you can find advice for your class (this book is chock full of it). However, those teachers and that advice came from different situations than you are in. Follow models, certainly, but do not expect to get the same results they did, and be prepared to adapt their techniques to your own unique situation. If I had sought out more on-site mentoring and advice, this adaptation process might have gone more smoothly for me.

Since presenting this talk at the ACS national meeting in 2001, several people have told me and the editors of this book that its primary value is not the specific lessons described in the previous paragraph. Rather, its primary value is showing new teachers that no matter how well prepared they may be (as I was, between BCCE, PFF, a postdoctoral fellowship in chemistry education research, and other activities), there is still no substitute for actual contact with students. Things can go far astray of the most well-laid plans, as they did for me. However, the most important lesson is to not give up, to pick yourself up, to learn what lessons you can, and to move on. The education of today's college students depends on you, your enthusiasm, and your willingness to learn from both what goes well and what does not go well. I wish you the best of luck.

Bibliography

Maslow, A. H. (1954). *Motivation and Personality*. New York: Harper and Brothers.

Herron, J. D. (1996). *The Chemistry Classroom: Formulas for Successful Teaching*. American Chemical Society.

Cole, R., & Todd, J. (2003). Effects of Web-based multimedia homework with immediate rich feedback on student learning in general chemistry. *Journal of Chemical Education*, in press.

Palmer, P. J. (1998). *The Courage to Teach: Exploring the Inner Landscape of a Teacher's Life*. San Francisco, CA: Jossey-Bass Inc.

3

Is Your Teaching Style Compatible with a Diverse Group of Students?

Cinzia M. Muzzi
Department of Chemistry
Truckee Meadows Community College

Abstract

All students have different personalities and learning styles. Learning to accommodate a diverse group of students is one of the greatest challenges every new instructor faces. Understanding student behavior and adjusting one's own teaching style to accommodate a wide range of students is an expedient way to make all students feel comfortable and open to learning the subject of chemistry. This chapter introduces faculty to different learning-style models and provides a personal account of a new instructor's attempt to accommodate diverse learning styles in the classroom.

Biography

I am a full-time faculty member at Truckee Meadows Community College in Reno, NV, and am now in my fourth year of teaching. Before becoming a faculty member at Truckee Meadows Community College, I completed my doctoral work in organic chemistry at the University of California, Davis. While finishing my graduate studies I participated in a yearlong mentored teaching program entitled the *Program in College Teaching* at U.C. Davis. Through this program, I gained experience in everything from using different assessment techniques to accommodating diversity in the classroom while instructing several courses. Currently I am an active member of the Division of Chemical Education of the American Chemical Society, where I co-organized and co-chaired the *Survival 101 for the New College Chemistry Instructor* symposia, leading to the publication of this book.

Why did I personally choose to examine learning-style theory?

Four years ago I taught my first "Chemistry 101" course as a full-time faculty member at Truckee Meadows Community College (TMCC). Since I had taught several courses as a graduate student, I felt confident with both my knowledge of the subject material and with my ability to teach. Despite my earnest preparations in graduate school to become a teacher, my first week of teaching as a full-time community college faculty member was certainly not what I anticipated. In all three of my Chemistry 101 sections my students appeared to be completely apathetic and disinterested. Some even seemed to be fidgety students who continuously disrupted the course. I later discovered that the first week of class was indicative of what the rest of that first semester and later semesters would be like.

As a new instructor I thought I knew exactly what I *should* be doing in the classroom. For example, I already knew that my students should be actively engaged in the course material. I also understood the importance and utility of using key visual aids, hands-on experience, and a peer-led learning environment. Despite knowing these latest theories and strategies, practical implementation was very difficult during the first several semesters.

To improve the classroom environment and to be a more successful instructor, I consciously made an effort to determine *why* my endeavors at implementing new pedagogical approaches had failed. I have been described as an outgoing, friendly, and energetic instructor, so I also wanted to determine why the classroom portion of the course seemed to degenerate into a somewhat hostile and unfriendly environment.

First, I considered my own teaching style. Throughout the semester, I had tried to develop a few small group activities as well as use computer animations during lecture, but I really hadn't integrated these practices into the course to the fullest possible extent. I also didn't attempt anything new and innovative during the first week or two of classes. Upon reflection, I found that throughout the semester I relied heavily on using the standard lecture format. I also felt compelled to stick close to the content of the textbook, and I shied away from doing too many demonstrations or integrating too many practical real-world examples. When all was said and done, I really wasn't as innovative as I thought I was.

I then cast a critical eye toward my students. Who were they? Why were they behaving so differently than the students I had taught previously? As a graduate student I had been a teaching assistant, co-instructor, and then an instructor for students in several two-semester organic chemistry courses. Most of my experience was with sophomore, junior, and senior-level students. I realized that these older students had already learned how to sit through a college lecture. Consequently, these students thought I was an excellent, innovative instructor when I occasionally showed a video animation or included a demonstration. In contrast, most of my Chemistry 101 students at TMCC were freshmen as well as first-time science students with very little science and mathematics background. They also seemed to have fairly poor study habits and very little experience in actually being a student. In addition, my TMCC students were a much more diverse group than the students I had taught in graduate school. The diversity in the class wasn't only in ethnicity but also in age, culture, and family support. Many of my students were the first members of their families to attend college, and a good portion of the students consisted of working mothers and fathers.

Thankfully, not all my training and experience in graduate school was wasted. From the *Program in College Teaching* I knew that one way to accommodate diversity in the classroom was to provide for different learning styles. I was sure that improving my understanding of learning-style theory would improve the learning environment and the students' interest in the course.

This chapter provides an account of my own beginning look into learning styles and how my understanding of students' learning styles has helped improve my teaching and classroom skills. The chapter is by no means a comprehensive survey regarding learning styles, but it is an account of how my search for answers took place.

Learning style: what is it?

The term "learning style" has been around for many years and has many different definitions. One of the most comprehensive definitions comes from Keefe in 1986: "Learning styles are characteristic cognitive, affective, and psychological traits that serve as relatively stable indicators of how learners perceive, interact with and respond to the learning environment."

A learning style is something that encompasses many aspects of an individual's preferences for learning. It is important to point out that a learning style is broader than just a person's cognitive style, affective style, or physiological style singularly. Cognitive style is the way a person processes information. These are distinctive ways in which a person perceives, organizes, and retains information. An affective style s related to a person's "personality traits that have to do with attention, emotion, and valuing," while a physiological style may be regarded as a way a person responds physically in different learning situations (Keefe 1986; McKeachie 1994). Considering only a single one of these facets will provide an incomplete picture of a person's overall set of learning preferences. It is important to consider all three areas simultaneously.

Theorists vary in opinion regarding what factors influence a learning style. Most seem to agree that a learning style is greatly influenced by genetic factors, such as how a person's brain is wired, his/her gender, etc. In addition, most agree that a learning style can, to a lesser extent, be influenced by environment and can change over time. All students have different cultural backgrounds and life experiences that can alter a student's learning preferences as they grow older.

What learning-style models are out there? Which one is the best?

When I first began to search for information on learning-style theory, I was overwhelmed. There are numerous learning-style theories that overlap into educational psychology, personality typing, and other learning-style models. There also doesn't seem to be a systematic nomenclature. This results in a myriad of definitions being used to describe essentially the same or similar aspects of a learning style.

Some of the more popular and widely recognized learning styles or theories include those proposed by 1) A. F. Gregorc and K. A. Butler (Butler 1987), 2) R. R. Sims and S. J. Sims (Sarasin 1999 and references therein), 3) R. Dunn and K. Dunn (Dunn and Griggs 2000), 4) D. A. Kolb (Harb, Durrant and Terry 1993 and references therein), 5) H. Gardner (Gardner 1983) and 6) B. McCarthy (McCarthy and Morris 1996). There are many more popular models as well as personality-type indicators and educational theories that have all been related to learning style in some way or another.

The models or theories each vary in their focus concerning cognitive style, affective style, and psychological style. They also vary in recommending how learning styles should be accommodated in the classroom. As a new instructor, I chose to examine the Myers-Briggs Type Indicator and its relation to learning styles since it seemed to be a very popular choice among the staff at our institution. I also used and implemented the model proposed by Lynn Celli Sarasin because her model was easy to understand and fit in with my own observations and beliefs about student learning. Regardless of which model a new instructor decides to try, examining any of the models or theories will be useful in making a new teacher more sensitive to the differences in student learning.

So what is the Meyers-Briggs Type Indicator anyway?

The Meyers-Briggs Type Indicator (MBTI) is actually a personality-type indicator based on Carl Jung's theory of psychological types. It has been used widely since 1975 to help people understand their own psychological type as well as their interpersonal relationships.

MBTI has 16 possible psychological types based on four dimensions. These dimensions are 1) Extroversion(E)/ Introversion(I), 2) Sensing(S)/Intuition(N), 3) Thinking(T)/Feeling(F), and 4) Judging(J)/Perceiving(P). Many people show tendencies in all or several of the categories, but they will show definite inclinations within a dimension. The sixteen psychological types are based on a person's four main preferences. So a person's type can be an Introversion, Sensing, Thinking, Judgment type (ISTJ), an INFP type, an ESFP type, etc. Based on the type (made up of combinations of the four dimensions), each person will have a characteristic set of learning preferences. For instance, according to Lawrence (Lawrence 1993), a person who is an ISTJ type will be a linear learner with a strong need for order, while a person who is an INFP type may be a global learner who needs help with organization. In the past decade many institutions have had students take the Meyers-Briggs Type Indicator to better understand their own psychological type as a means to becoming a more successful student. It has also been used to help instructors become aware of the needs of their classes.

In 1993 Charles Schroeder (Schroeder 1993) reported a study conducted with 4000 entering college students who were asked to take the MBTI. In his article he focused on two of the four dimensions of the MBTI personality to understand student learning. The dimensions Schroeder emphasizes are Extroversion(E)/Introversion(I) and Sensing(S)/Intuition(N). Students followed the ES pattern (concrete active), the IS pattern (concrete reflective), EN pattern (abstract active), or the IN pattern (abstract reflective). According to Schroeder, ES types are the most frequent learner, making up about 50 percent of the high school population, while IN learners make up about 10 percent of the student population. He also states that 60 percent of the students preferred the sensing (S) mode of learning while 40 percent preferred the intuitive (N) mode of learning. Schroeder then goes on to indicate that faculty have also been surveyed at many institutions across the country. Most faculty prefer the IN (Introversion, Intuitive) pattern to learning, with 75 percent of faculty preferring the intuitive (N) mode of learning, thus showing that the faculty trend to personality type appears to be almost opposite to that of the student population.

Schroeder also reports several interesting statistics obtained from an eight-year study at Saint Louis University. According to this study, first-year academic performance showed that IN student learners made the highest grades, while ES student learners made the lowest grades. He also states that ES learners were the dominant type found in the schools of business, nursing, and allied health, while IN learners were disproportionately represented in arts and sciences and were underrepresented in nursing.

As a new instructor these statistics had a very great impact on how I perceived my students' learning and my own teaching. I realized that the majority of my Chemistry 101 students were nursing and allied health majors. Most of these students were probably ES types, with a few that I could recognize as other types of learners. According to Lawrence (Lawrence 1993), ES learners are those students who prefer group activities, class reports, direct experience, audiovisual aids, and practical tests. In examining my own teaching style, I realized that I probably was not teaching in a manner that accommodated the majority of my students. I decided that I needed to make immediate changes to help my students and improve my classroom instruction.

The MBTI information was helpful in providing an understanding of why some students preferred different learning situations. It also helped inspire me to create different learning situations within the classroom. I did, however, find that attempting to understand all 16 of the psychological types indicated by MBTI was time consuming and difficult to deal with in my hour and 75-minute class time. On the surface the 16 different types looked like they were easy to interpret, but as Lawrence cautions, the types themselves are very complex and easy to misinterpret. I subsequently turned to another learning-style model that offered better practical strategies for accommodating different learners in the classroom.

What is a simple and practical model to use for accommodating learning styles?

The model put forth by Lynne Celli Sarasin (Sarasin 1999) was the starting point for changes to my teaching strategies. She outlines her model in *Learning Style Perspectives*, an easy-to-read book that clearly gives a novice instructor a place to start.

Sarasin uses what is essentially the VAK (Visual, Auditory, and Kinesthetic/Tactile) approach to characterize the different types of learners. A complete description of each type of learner can be found in her book, but a brief outline of the points that I found useful in making changes to my courses are outlined here.

1. Auditory Learner. Sarasin states that teaching strategies for these learners "include lecture, discussion, independent work, objective presentation and practice, questioning techniques or tasks that require exact or specific answers, activities that involve memory, and verbal sorting." Sarasin also points out that these students prefer to learn information piece by piece in a logical sequence. Given this description, I knew that auditory learners were readily accommodated in my class. My course already used a sequential lecture format, and my first quizzes and exams at TMCC were also very traditional. The exams incorporated few conceptual questions and consisted almost entirely of mathematical word problems. Consequently, the exams and quizzes generally required very specific answers or definitions.

    After reading Sarasin's book, I found that I had already created a learning environment perfect for the auditory learner, but I also realized that I probably had few auditory learners in my classes at TMCC. I decided to concentrate my efforts in assisting the visual and tactile learner.

2. Visual Learner. This type of learner proved difficult to accommodate, but the changes made to the course resulted in a more productive and rewarding learning environment for both the students and myself. According to Sarasin, visual learners tend to be students who are holistic learners. They need to see the "big picture" before given detailed information. Many of these students do not do well in highly structured environments but excel in group activities or less formal environments. Suggested strategies for teaching this type of student include the use of visual formats, group activities, models and demonstrations, student presentations, field trips, and computer-aided instruction.

According to Sarasin, visual learners are students who often appear as if they have not studied or as if they do not care about the course. They are also students who may do poorly in a variety of testing situations. Provided with this description of the visual learner, I suspected that I had many of these students in my course. Certainly, some of my students were indifferent students who really didn't put much effort into studying, but the majority of students seemed to be making some effort to understand the material.

I also acknowledged that I did very little in class time to accommodate the visual learner. I had tried to incorporate some group activities and computer animations, but I had not really integrated these strategies into my course to any great extent. It was clear that my teaching style was probably affecting student performance since most of the students lacked the experience to adapt their own visual learning style to my very linear, sequential lecture format. In addition, the traditional assessment techniques I used on exams and in the course would never reveal what these students had actually learned. According to Sarasin, these students benefit from open-ended assessment techniques that assess the process as well as the outcome. Visual learners also excel in group projects or oral presentations as well as on short answer or essay- type questions that require a diagram or picture as part of the explanation. All of these assessment techniques were clearly lacking in my course.

3. Tactile Learner. According to Sarasin, the tactile learner is the student who is the least accommodated at the post-secondary level. These students need to physically interact with their environment in order to understand and learn a topic. Tactile learners are the type of student who function well in the laboratory, but their learning styles are usually neglected in the classroom setting. Tactile learners are students who are "always moving, seemingly disinterested, distracted, and not understanding what is being taught." They may be very reluctant to participate in activities that do not involve some sort of physical interaction with the environment. Teaching strategies for the tactile learner can include any sort of hands-on experience, such as internships and practica, field trips, and demonstrations. These learners also require nontraditional types of assessment, such as explaining using a demonstration, performing a practicum, or creating an exhibit/experiment. All of these nontraditional forms of assessment can be easily accommodated in the sciences but are often not used in freshmen and sophomore-level courses.

What specific changes in teaching chemistry can be made to accommodate different learning styles?

Based on the information provided by the Sarasin model and other material I found in the *Journal of Chemical Education* (*JCE*), I slowly made changes to the lecture portion of the class. Major changes took several semesters to complete, and the process is still ongoing. One basic question I asked myself was "How does this method/technique accommodate all three of the learning styles (auditory, visual, tactile)?" Sometimes a specific technique would only be suitable for one or two of the three types of general learners, but a combination of several different strategies used within the same lecture period assured that all students would have some accommodation. Listed here are several strategies/methods that I found easy to implement and that made significant differences in the classroom environment.

1. An instructor can provide written lecture outlines and written chapter objectives. Providing this material is initially time consuming, but once the lecture outlines and the chapter objectives are complete, they can be easily adapted to other textbooks or even other courses. These two teaching tools assist the auditory learner since they are very detail oriented. Written lecture outlines and course objectives can also accommodate the visual learner if diagrams and pictures typical of a PowerPoint presentation accompany these items.

2. Multimedia software is another useful tool that can assist students with different learning styles. Multimedia packages are now available with almost every textbook. Although I still spend about two thirds of the classroom time using the standard lecture format, I now illustrate the lecture with animations and videos integrated throughout. As a new instructor I had only used an occasional video or diagram to illustrate a point, but currently every lecture contains visual aids that are integrated into the discussion of concepts and into group activities. Students also know this visual imagery is often used on quizzes and exams, and consequently, students learn to pay special attention to the points being made about the imagery.

    When implementing multimedia software into the lecture, I found that timing is everything. Reminders of which animation/diagram to use and when to use it are found throughout my lecture notes. Some initial time must be invested in making certain that the classroom is properly equipped to handle the desired multimedia software, and arriving 10-15 minutes early to check all equipment before every lecture is essential.

    I have found that effectively incorporating visual aids into the lecture portion of the course can help all three types of learners because it facilitates students making connections between the macroscopic world and the microscopic world. It is, however, probably most effective for visual learners who may never be able to understand a concept without some sort of visual representation. Tactile learners can also benefit from the use of multimedia if they can physically interact with the software that is being used or if the visual imagery is used to supplement some other type of activity, such as a demonstration or student presentation.

3. Group activities provide the social interaction and less rigid class structure required by visual learners. They can also provide tactile learners with a chance to physically engage with demonstrations or models during class rather than just during the laboratory. Auditory learners benefit from group activities as well because they are given the opportunity to discuss what they have learned both with other students and the instructor.

    JCE is an excellent resource for finding many different types of group activities that accommodate different learning styles. For instance, two activities that are utilized in my course are concept maps (Regis 1996) and an activity regarding significant figures where students actually have to take measurements of an index card (Pacer 2000). Both of these activities were taken directly from *JCE* and required little modification to fit into lecture.

    Because I feel it is essential for students to make connections between the macroscopic and microscopic scales, many of the group activities that I choose to do involve a demonstration where the students are required to draw a representation of what is occurring at the molecular level to explain the macroscopic observation. For instance, for the "collapsing can trick" (Shakashiri 1985) or "egg in the bottle trick" (Ford 1993), volunteer students are allowed to perform these demos with my assistance in the classroom. Using small groups, the students are then asked to discuss why the can collapsed or the egg pushed into the bottle. Students are also asked to draw a diagram or picture of what is occurring at the molecular level. There are many other safe demonstrations that can be used as group activities in this way, but it is necessary to invest some initial time in finding appropriate ones.

In addition to these demo-based activities, students are asked to use small groups in the solving of multistep problems. Students are required to solve the problem and explain why they performed each mathematical step. Other group activities include the "minute paper" (Cross 1996; Timberlake) and a term paper or oral presentation that can be done as a group project.

Regardless of the specific group activity, I have learned that making these strategies a central part of the course is important. Occasional use of a demo, visual aid, or group activity will not convince the students of the importance of these techniques, and I believe this is why my early attempts at using some of these strategies failed. Regular use of these various methods to accommodate different learning styles immediately shows students the value of these techniques and creates an environment that assists *all* learning styles at least during some portion of the lecture period.

Lastly, it is important to assess students using some of the same techniques used during class time. This assures further "buy-in" on the students' part, and also allows the visual and tactile learners a chance to demonstrate their knowledge, which may not be evident on a traditional chemistry exam. To help different types of students, I now try to dedicate about one third of each exam to "nontraditional" types of questions. For instance, here are two essay questions that I have used on exams.

---

1. The video animation shows the effect of temperature on the pressure of a fixed amount of gas at constant volume. Using kinetic molecular theory, explain why the pressure increases. Be very detailed in your answer.

2. A student examines the following reaction:

$$Co(H_2O)_6^{2+} (aq) \ + \ 4 Cl^- (aq) \ \longrightarrow Co(Cl)_4^{2-} (aq) \ + \ 6 H_2O (l)$$

   Pale Pink   Colorless   Dark Blue   Colorless

   From previous experiments the student knows that the $Co(H_2O)_6^{2+}$ ion is pale pink and the $Co(Cl)_4^{2-}$ ion is dark blue. She is attempting to determine whether the forward reaction is endothermic or exothermic. Describe how she might accomplish this in the laboratory and what she would expect to see. Make sure to explain your reasoning in terms of Le Châtelier's Principle, and draw a picture representing ion concentration to aid your discussion.

Using essay questions that incorporate visual aids or require a student to recall what they have physically done in the laboratory assists in the assessment of students that are visual or tactile learners. To further assist these students, I count a couple of the group activities performed in class as a quiz score or some portion of the course grade.

There are many other activities or strategies as well as assessment techniques that can be used to effectively teach students with different learning styles. The Sarasin model was easy for me to understand and implement. Regardless of which model is chosen, it is essential that a new instructor use the strategies on a regular basis.

Conclusion and a word of caution

This chapter has looked at only a small portion of learning-style and personality-type models. There is much more available to an instructor who is willing to take the time to look. But it is necessary to provide a few words of caution. It is possible to have "too much of a good thing." Trying to accommodate different learning styles can be time consuming. It becomes a balancing act that requires some practice regardless of which model an instructor chooses to try. During the first couple of semesters that I tried to implement new techniques, I fell behind on some of the course topics. I found myself occasionally making up class time during laboratory sessions. It is also important to remember that no student will be a perfect ISTJ or a perfect auditory learner. Students will show abilities in all areas of learning. Using any model or learning strategy can only be treated as a loose set of guidelines for assisting students who show greater ability in one style of learning versus another.

New instructors may also meet some resistance from fellow faculty members. Opinions such as "An employer is never going to adjust their personality type (or their learning style) to fit that of a new employee, so why should students be treated any differently?" or "Students should adjust their learning style to an instructor's teaching style" may be voiced in the department. New instructors probably stand little chance of completely changing the opinions of more seasoned colleagues, but they might gain some small support if they point out that older junior and senior students who have had more experience in the world of academia can probably adjust their learning styles quite readily. By accommodating different learning styles in the classroom at an introductory level, an instructor is just teaching a student one more important skill for the real world. An instructor who accommodates different learning styles is only teaching students how to adapt to different learning environments.

Finally, there is one last word of caution. Understanding and using learning styles theory has been very helpful in my quest to improve my teaching and classroom skills, but it has not been a "cure-all" for every difficulty I have faced as a new instructor. It is important to understand that the benefits gained from using learning-style theory can be intangible. For instance, I cannot say that after implementing some of the strategies mentioned here that I have seen class averages increase by 10 or 20 points. In fact, the class averages over my teaching career have stayed roughly the same. I can say, however, that accommodating different learning styles in the classroom has definitely improved my classroom environment, raised my student evaluations, and made teaching chemistry an even more challenging and rewarding endeavor. The ultimate benefit has been watching my students become actively engaged in their own learning of chemistry and knowing that I helped facilitate their growth.

References

Butler, K. A. (1987). *Learning and Teaching Style in Theory and Practice.* Columbia, CT: The Learner's Dimension.

Cross, K. P. (1996). *Classroom Research: Implementing the Scholarship of Teaching.* San Francisco, CA: Jossey-Bass.

Dunn, R., & Griggs, S. (Eds.) (2000). *Practical Approaches to Using Learning Styles in Higher Education.* Westport, CT: Bergin & Garvey.

Ford, L. A. (1993). *Chemical Magic.* New York, NY: Dover Publications, Inc.

Gardner, H. (1983). *Frames of Mind: The Theory of Multiple Intelligences.* New York, NY: Basic Books.

Keefe, J. W. (1986). *Learning Style Theory and Practice.* Reston, VA: National Association of Secondary School Principles.

Harb, J. H., Durrant S. O., & Terry, R. E. (1993). Use of the Kolb Learning Cycle and the 4MAT system in engineering education. *Journal of Engineering Education*, (April) 70–77.

Lawrence, G. D. (1993). *People Types and Tiger Stripes: A Practicle Guide to Learning Styles.* Gainesville, FL: Center for Application of Psychological Type, Inc.

McCarthy, B., & Morris, S. (1996). *The 4MAT Course Book: Volume 1.* Burrinton, IL: Excel Corp.

McKeachie, W. J. (1994). *Teaching Tips: Strategies, Research, and Theory for College and University Teachers.* Lexington, MA: D. C. Heath and Company.

Pacer, R. A. (2000). How can an instructor best introduce the topic of significant figures to students unfamiliar with the concept? *Journal of Chemical Education, 77,* 1435–1438.

Regis, A., Albertazzi, P. G., & Roletto, E. (1996). Concept maps in chemistry education *Journal of Chemical Education, 73,* 1084–1088.

Sarasin, L. C. (1999). *Learning Style Perspectives: Impact in the Classroom.* Madison, WI: Atwood Publishing.

Schroeder, C. C. (1993). New students—new learning styles. *Change* (September/October) 21–26.

Timberlake, K.
   http://www.karentimberlake.com/student-centered_classoom.htm

Bibliography

Preparing Future Faculty Web site (PFF):
   http://www.preparing-faculty.org/

Preparing future faculty link Teaching Resources Link
   http://www.preparing-faculty.org/PFFWeb.Resources.htm
   http://www.preparing-faculty.org/PFFWeb.Resources.htm#teaching

Dr. Richard Felder's Web site:
   http://www2.ncsu.edu/unity/lockers/users/f/felder/public/

Myer-Briggs Type Indicator
   To order the MBTI: http://www.mbti.com/

Association of Psychological Type
   http://www.aptcentral.org/

Section

II

GETTING STARTED

4

Writing a Syllabus: A Tool and a Contract

Christina (Tina) A. Bailey
Department of Chemistry and Biochemistry
California Polytechnic State University—San Luis Obispo

Abstract

The course syllabus sets the tone of organization and expectations for the entire term. It is also a contract between student and instructor that should outline the conditions for successfully navigating the content of the course and achieving specific levels of competence.

Biography

Currently I am a professor of chemistry and biochemistry at California Polytechnic State University in San Luis Obispo. http://chemWeb.calpoly.edu/chem/bailey

After more than 30 years at Cal Poly, I am still deciding what I want to be when I grow up. In talking with both my younger and more seasoned colleagues, this seems to be a recurrent theme. I have had the privilege of teaching a wide variety of courses on every level of the undergraduate curriculum as well as a graduate course. An instructor plays so many roles—facilitator, advisor, friend, and coach. Each term and each course allows me to reinvent myself in terms of approach, expertise, and relationships with my students.

Why is a syllabus important?

The course syllabus is one of the most important communication links between student and instructor. No matter what form it takes, one could consider it a contract agreed upon at the beginning of the term. The student is informed of the conditions for success, and the instructor is then obliged to deliver the content in such a manner as to promote student success in the course.

A syllabus can be simple or detailed; it can be in hard copy or electronic. The mode of delivery will, at times, determine how much information is imparted with one document. The syllabus will usually be the first impression made upon the student by the instructor. As such, it shows the motivation, organization, and emphasis intended. A well-written syllabus is the "Rosetta Stone" of a course.

What is the minimum information that should be contained in the syllabus?

The two essential parts of a syllabus are **course information** and **topic schedule for the term**.

At a minimum, the information needed by the student to introduce him/her to the course and instructor should include:

- Instructor's name (including nickname if appropriate)

- Office phone

- Office building and number

- (Department office building and number)

- Office hours (sometimes it helps to also have the class hours). Be sure to find out department and university policies on the number and distribution of office hours.

- E-mail address

- Text (author, title and edition)

- Grading policies

Have an outline of work and point distribution. Don't forget the contribution of lab to overall course grade if relevant. Lab may be a separate course in some circumstances. Students, especially freshmen, frequently don't understand the decrease in weighting of homework versus the increase for quizzes and exams in determining the final course grade compared to high school.

Final course grade determinations should be clear. Students deserve to know what the absolute course grade cutoffs will be ahead of time.

Questions that you might want to anticipate and include in the syllabus are:

- Will there be +/- (extra credit or deduction) grading?

- Is there a "curve" to the grade distribution? (Few students understand the meaning of a "curve.")

- Will improvement in grades during the term be considered in the assignment of final grades? I have found that telling the class I reserve the option to lower the cutoffs to reward improvement in the course helps to set a positive tone.

- Is there a specific grade required on the final exam in order to pass the class?

- If laboratory is part of the final course grade, what happens if the student "passes" lab and fails the lecture portion of the course? How about the converse?

- Our department has standards for the averages expected from each lab section. Students who fail the course can apply a lab average of 70 percent or higher to another term's course grade. In addition, if a student earns lower than a 60 percent in lab while passing the lecture portion of the class, she/he receives an F grade for the course. These policies bring their own administrative problems in those courses that have a linked requirement for registration into lecture and laboratory sections. We have created "ghost" lab sections with codes that are accessible only through our department office. So the student has to do some footwork to "activate" the system.

- If a high course grade is maintained throughout the term, can one be excused from taking the final exam?

Check on your department and institution policies for the conditions concerning withdrawals and incompletes. For our university, the student must have established a C grade or higher and have written extenuating circumstances to be given an Incomplete grade. The conditions of course completion have to be specified by the instructor and be fulfilled by the end of the sixth week of the following academic term. Again, you may wish to include this information in your syllabus or give a reference or link to these policies.

My personal philosophy on grading for general chemistry is the more points available and the more varied the graded aspects (quizzes, worksheets, mini-projects, lab reports), the better for the students. This allows students to ease into the community college or university environment and learn how to manage their time and study habits. No one quiz, exam, or assignment should be the mark of doom for the final course grade. For upper-division courses, there are usually fewer grading opportunities, although I have found that students appreciate frequent quizzes with some latitude for dropping a bad score.

A downside to having many graded assignments is the physical act of grading all of this material. If your department has funds for graders, this isn't such a daunting task. If you do all of your own grading, you could develop a grading rubric, which focuses on certain aspects of a lab report or assignment. You can grade written assignments holistically, that is, grade on the overall quality of the work and not on specifics.

Several years ago I attended workshops on "Writing Across the Curriculum" and found one exercise to be invaluable when grading upper-division lab reports. It is called a "Read Around," and the results have been excellent. Early in the quarter I have the students write a short, complete lab report on a simple experiment. They turn in a typed copy with only the cover sheets bearing their names. I code the cover sheet and the rest of the report and tear off the cover sheet, then randomly distribute the reports to the various lab tables. The students are instructed to read the report they have received, not make any marks on the paper, and pass it to the next person at their bench upon a given signal. After everyone at the bench has reviewed all of the initial papers, the students rank which is the best paper in the group with two reasons for its choice. The papers are then picked up and passed on to the next bench for reading and evaluating. When all of the students have evaluated all of the reports, I ask the groups to discuss their best papers using only the codes. The codes are listed on the board along with the rationale for the choices. It is truly amazing to see the coherence in the qualities that constitute a good lab report. Note that this is a positive exercise; no negative comments are allowed. The students have essentially come to an agreement with the instructor as to those aspects of a report that define excellence. The instructor should be prepared to add one or two enhancements, if necessary. The process has greatly improved the quality of reports in my lab sections and made grading easier. Students have participated in "holistic" grading and better understand the instructor's situation of having to grade many reports in a short period of time.

How should I design my schedule of topics?

Use a table format

- Week/Date

- Meeting (1st, 2nd, etc.)

- Topics—General (not too general), more specific

- Text Readings—more detailed for freshmen

- Schedule of Quizzes and Exams

- Important Assignments—reports, papers, homework

- Problems from text—key problems to sections, level, problems with answers/without

- (Labs)

- Date and time for final exam

Goals and Objectives

I believe that it is important for the students to know that a great deal of thought was put into the curriculum, how each course fits into the plan, and that every topic covered in a course is part of a continuum of learning. It sets the context of the material in the larger picture of the educational process. This can be included on the course information page or as a supplement.

Expectations

A reciprocal expectations list can be a place to overview the atmosphere inside and outside of the classroom. It is also an opportunity to reemphasize the amount of time required to study and the overall work ethic required in the university, especially important to freshmen as well as students entering the first course in a yearlong sequence (organic, pchem, biochem).

Some items that may or may not be included in the syllabus:

- Calculator policy—any, none, just scientific calculators

- Lab manual (Lab notebook)—if applicable—especially for integrated courses

- Lab manual—hard copy/online

- Lab notebook—hardback, graph paper, copy, format

- More detail on graded materials—format of quizzes and exams, format of final exam, policy on absences (class, quiz, exam)

- Drop one quiz/exam, no drops, makeups, and valid excuses

- Advice: Don't establish a policy of administering makeup quizzes and exams on a regular basis. You will be inundated with excuses and requests. It's better to consider cases on an individual-need basis with some forethought as to how to handle legitimate absences.

- Course/university withdrawal policy and dates

- Cheating policy is a sensitive issue. Some wish to address it immediately, and others will wait for a more opportune moment.

- Supplementary materials such as student study guides, tutorials, CDs—availability of tutorial services and established supplementary instruction classes

Should I provide a hard copy of the syllabus to every student and/or make it available on the Web?

As you can see, a syllabus can become an extensive and formidable document for the student to navigate. If you were going to provide a hard copy, my advice would be to limit the content to two pages of paper, which can have material on front and back. Anything not addressed could be given out later in the first week or term. The advantage to a hard copy is that it is physically there, and a student cannot say it wasn't available. One disadvantage is the effective length; another is the fact that students lose these items on a regular basis. A third problem arises in the fixed nature of the schedule. An instructor becomes hesitant to make adjustments in some assignments because students are easily confused when given more than one set of due dates. My personal preference is an electronic syllabus. The Web and its universal access are hard to top for flexibility and communication. A student can also print out a hard copy if they prefer that form.

The introductory Web page can be brief, containing links to all-important areas of information. The schedule can have links to more detailed topic outlines, quiz/exam keys, labs, on-line tutorials, other Web sites, and sample report sheets. Web pages and linked documents can be written in MSWord (.doc for PC users), as an Acrobat Reader file (.PDF), or in Web-page format (html). The last can be produced using an interface program such as Dreamweaver®(Macromedia), Go Live®(Adobe), or Front Page®(Microsoft).

Where can I get examples of a syllabus?

Glad that you asked. One of the best sources will be the syllabus of an instructor who is familiar with the course in question, preferably a senior faculty member. This will serve as a template and starting place for the development of your own syllabus. The physical format will differ depending on the mode of delivery. A hard copy should not be more than about two pages, double-sided, in length (about four sides). The longer the document, the less likely a student will read and absorb the information. For an electronic version, you must consider what the eye can assimilate on a monitor screen.

The delivery of an electronic syllabus requires forethought in terms of a hierarchy of importance and organization of design. In general, it is best to have information on one screen with little need to scroll. An introductory course page can have links to other important pages similar to the table of contents of a book, or it can contain fundamental information as well as links. Subsequent course pages should have a link to get back to the first page. This may take the form of a table located to the side or bottom of the screen or a simple Return button. The Web is a rich source of freeware, that is, sites having icons and buttons that can be downloaded without needing a citation.

In the Appendix, you can find some examples of the content of an electronic syllabus. Figures 1 and 2 represent Web pages I use for my general chemistry course. The other figures illusrate the designs of Web pages for general chemistry and an upper-division course in metabolism. I have used Adobe Go Live® and Macromedia Dreamweaver® as my Web page generators and Adobe Photoshop® for the graphics. These Web pages are complemented with a detailed schedule of topics, text references, problems, a study guide, quiz, exam, and lab dates as well as links to the on-line lab manual. Metabolism involves many handouts and illustrations. These are effectively delivered as pdf files or graphics files at a linked site.

You can see other examples of course Web pages linked to my home page at:
> http://chemweb.calpoly.edu/chem/bailey.

There are many advantages to an electronic syllabus.
- It is a 24-7 source of information.
- Once you are proficient with an authoring program, you can easily alter specific content on short notice.
- Answer keys, study guides, extra copies can be posted for instant accessibility.

Disadvantages include possible dead links for ancillary materials.

As with the design of any Web pages, the guiding principle is K.I.S.S. ("Keep It Simple, Stupid"). Unless a graphic has meaning, don't use it. Be careful of animated pictures or backgrounds. They are very distracting. A white background gives you more flexibility with color for fonts and emphasis areas.

Conclusion

Keep in mind that the syllabus can represent what is best and what is worst about a course and its instructor. At its worst, it bears no relevance to the content and organization of the course and leaves the students guessing as to how they will approach and master the material during the term.   At its best, it is an essential guide and invaluable tool to student success. It takes time and experience to develop a syllabus. Be patient and seek advice not only from your colleagues but also from your students.

Bibliography

You can use the Google search engine (www.google.com) to find links to the Teaching and Learning Centers of several universities and community colleges that have posted guides to writing a syllabus. Use the topic "creating a syllabus."

Faculty Development Web site, Honolulu Community College
> http://www.hcc.hawaii.edu/intranet/committees/FacDevCom/index.htm

Davis, B. G. (1993). **Tools for Teaching**. San Francisco: Jossey-Bass Publishers.
> http://teaching.berkeley.edu/bgd/syllabus.html

University of Michigan Center for Teaching and Learning http://www.crlt.umich.edu/D4.html

Appendix

Figure 1. Sample of a course home page

Chemistry 124
General Chemistry for
the Engineering Disciplines

Fall 2002

click on a title to go to that information

Instructor's Home Page   Course Information

Goals & Objectives   Course Materials

Study Checklists   Grading Policies

Figure 2.   General reference information

Chemistry 124
General Chemistry for
the Engineering Disciplines

Instructor: C.A. (Tina) Bailey   *Office: FOE (Faculty Offices East)-129*

Phone: 756-2443   *Email: cbailey@calpoly.edu*

Office Hours Link   *Chem 124 Home Page*

Figure 3. Sample of a grading policies page

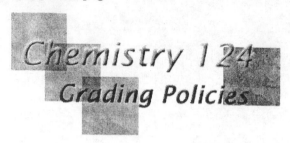

Assignment of Grades

We will be following a traditional grading distribution based upon a 1000-point system. If you earn 90% or more of the available points (>900) you are guaranteed an A in the course; 80-89% will be guaranteed a B grade; 70-79% a C; 60-69% a D; below 60% an F will be assigned. Plus/minus grading may be used. These are the guaranteed grades. I reserve the option to lower the grade cutoffs under special conditions. I will not raise these demarcations. In other words, should you earn 790 points during the quarter, you are guaranteed a C BUT might receive a C^+, a B^-, or a B.

Grading opportunities will be distributed as follows:

Item	Number	Points Per Item	Total Points
In-class quizzes	6 (lowest grade is dropped)	50	250
Diagnostic quiz	1(20 pts)	Scaled to 50	50
In-class exams	3	100	300
Final exam	1	250	250
Reports/Data Sheets (In-class assessments and assignments, attitude, effort, and attendance.)	(both scheduled and unscheduled)	varied	150

Please note: This class is not graded on a curve. The grading policies described above are the guidelines for the course.

Exams - There will be three 60-minute, in-class exams given on the dates specified on the class schedule. No exams will be taken at times other than those listed unless there are certified extenuating circumstances which must be documented in writing before the day of the exam. The format of the exams will include objective (matching, multiple choice, etc.), short answer, calculations, and essay types of questions. Each exam is cumulative. Answers to exam questions will be posted on the Web.

Final Exam - The final exam is a comprehensive test written in the same format as the two class exams. It must be taken at the time scheduled. There are NO exceptions.
Please note that if you are a DRC student, you can make arrangements either with me or through the DRC office for your specific situation.

Quizzes - There will be six scheduled quizzes, about 20 minutes each. The lowest grade will be dropped. Format for these quizzes will be similar to that of the exams. Answers will be posted on the Web.

Report/Data Sheets - This is an integrated course, which means that laboratory is major contributor to the course content. As you do experiments you will be asked to turn in your lab notebook copies and lab reports (electronic versions or hard copy). The reports are given various point values and then, at the end of the quarter, all of these grades plus any other grades you have received for in-class work will be "normalized" to account for 15% of your final grade.

IMPORTANT: You can see your recorded grades at any time using the Blackboard link.

Figure 4. Home page for an upper-division course

Spring 2002
Chemistry 372

METABOLISM

Instructor: Dr. C.A.(Tina)Bailey   *Office: FOE(Bldg. 25) Room 129*   *Phone: 756-2443*

Email Link   *Course Goals & Objectives*   *Syllabus*

Grading Policies   *Handouts in pdf format*   *Your Grades*

To avoid any photo copyright infringement, I usually take my own digital photos and work them into my pages. This one was taken on a trip to the National Zoo in Washington, D.C. The camel's hump consists of lipid, the nutrient providing the most metabolic energy and a source of metabolic water.

Processing of the photos and creation of titles and captions were done using Adobe Photoshop®.

Figure 5 illustrates a set of grading policies for the upper-division metabolism course. I find that having a number of grading experiences is desirable at any level. The students realize that no one exam or assignment will doom his/her course grade. Our university operates on the quarter system, so the testing occurs frequently.

Figure 5. Grading policies for an upper-division course

Spring 2002
Chemistry 372
METABOLISM
Grading Policies

Grading is based on a 1000-point scale. Guaranteed letter grade levels are A 90-100%, B 80-89%, C 70-79%, D 55-69%. I reserve the right to lower these cutoffs based upon improvement. The workload will be distributed as described below.

Item	Points per	Total	% of final grade
Quizzes (4 of 5)	50	200	20
Two Exams	300	300	30
Final Exam	300	300	30
Journal review	100	100	10
OnLine HW	Variable	100	10

Exams: The mid-term exam and final exam will be given on the dates and at the times indicated in the syllabus. Any exceptions to this testing schedule must be appealed in writing with documentation for cause well before the exam date.

The exams will be comprehensive. All exams will have formats with short answers, short discussions, mechanisms, essays, and objective type questions. University-level composition skills are expected. Partial credit will be given wherever appropriate.

In-Class Quizzes: At the times specified in the lecture schedule, five (5) quizzes will be given. The format will follow that mentioned for exams. Only four (4) of the five (5) quizzes will be considered for the final course grade; the lowest score will be dropped. These quizzes will be administered during class time only. Anyone missing a quiz will have that quiz count as the one dropped. Subsequent missed quizzes will count as zero credit.

Journal Review: During the last week of the quarter, on the date specified in the syllabus, each member of the class will be expected to submit an individual review of a journal article related to metabolism. More information is available at the link.

OnLine Homework: There is a special Blackboard account available for each Chem 372 student on the Web. At various times you will be informed that problems will be available for various topics. You will be given information concerning this aspect of the course via the Blackboard LINK.

Figure 6 is an example of an expanded course schedule. This is a flexible page, and it evolves throughout the term.

Figure 6. A week-by-week outline

Topic Outline for Metabolism

Week	Topics	Text & Problems	Links	Testing/Other
1 4/2-4/5	Introduction; Thermodynamics	Ch 3 Ch 18	Handouts Scientific American article on Water & Life	RPI Molecular Biochemistry Site
2 4/8-4/12	Glycolysis: Anaerobic	Ch 19	Go to Handouts	Friday Quiz 1 Answer Key
3 4/15-4/19	Glycolysis: Aerobic (Krebs Cycle); Pentose Phosphate Pathway	Ch 20 Ch 23	PDHase mechanism movie	Friday Quiz 2 Extra Credit Seminar Answer Key
4 4/22-4/26	Electron Transport System & Oxidative Phosphorylation	Ch 21	F_1-F_0-ATPase movie	Friday – Exam 1 Answer Key
5 4/29-5/3	Oxidative Phosphorylation Shuttles	Ch 24	*-Please note that our quiz schedule has been revised because of our guest speaker*	
6 5/6-5/10	Lipid Catabolism: Beta Oxidation and Ketone Bodies	Ch 23		Guest Speaker
7 5/13-5/17	Gluconeogenesis	Ch 25		Friday Quiz 3 Answer Key
8 5/20-5/24	Lipid Biosynthesis; Cholesterol; Urea Cycle	Ch 22	Online Homework #5 is activated	Friday Quiz 4 Answer Key
9 5/27-5/31	Photosynthesis	Ch 22		Friday – Exam 2 Answer Key
10 6/3-6/7	Regulation of Metabolism			Wednesday – Quiz 5 Answer Key
Finals	Monday, June 10, 2002 *4:10-7:00 p.m.*			Journal Review due on Friday, June 7, 2002

Constructing Web pages takes some time and not a little bit of effort. However, it adds to the personality of the course and can be a source of valuable information.

5

A Beginner's Guide to the Selection of Textbooks and Course Materials: It's All That and More

Christina (Tina) A. Bailey
Department of Chemistry and Biochemistry
California Polytechnic State University—San Luis Obispo

Abstract

Selection of a textbook for a course depends upon many factors: audience, content, level, continuity, and resources, to name a few. Consideration of any course materials must be set in the context of the institution and department wherein the course will be taught. My context will be that of a medium-sized state university, with a sizable chemistry faculty, and a large repertoire of courses on the introductory level. We will look at

- fundamental considerations

- audience

- continuity

- classroom environment and pedagogy

- existing resources

- text-selection process

Biography

Currently I am a professor of chemistry and biochemistry at California Polytechnic State University in San Luis Obispo.

I knew that I wanted to be a teacher when I became an undergraduate teaching assistant for organic chem at the College of St. Elizabeth outside of Morristown, NJ. That was in 1963. Since then my experience has evolved as a graduate TA, a high school teacher, a part-time general chemistry and organic instructor, and a tenured faculty member. My husband and I have written six editions of a short-course organic chemistry text—a test on any professional and marital relationship (to say nothing of the effort of raising four children). Our textbook has been translated into Japanese, Spanish, and Korean. Over the past nine years I have been the coordinator for the integrated lecture-laboratory general chemistry course for engineers, for which I designed the facility and revised the curriculum. And to think that in disguise, I am a biochemist! So what follows is one person's perception—as textbook author, textbook advisory board member, and course coordinator—on to how to select a textbook.

Start with the basics: How is the course described?

Even though this may seem obvious, the subject of the course holds an important key to textbook selection. Is it a course in basic chemistry principles, a survey course, the continuation of a series of courses, or an elective course on a special topic or area?

Know what is offered at your institution. In general chemistry, for example, is your course designed for all majors—a one-size-fits-all approach? Or are you teaching in one of several general chemistry courses tailored to the needs of particular majors? At Cal Poly we have five different ways of presenting general chemistry. They are:

- Prep Chem—for those who haven't taken chemistry before or who are very unsure of the quality of their preparation for college-level chemistry.

- Chemistry for General Education—a course relating fundamental chemistry to current issues on a national and global basis.

- General Chemistry for Nontechnical Majors—the first in a yearlong sequence of general, organic, and biochemistry topics.

- General Chemistry for the Engineering Disciplines—one- to two-term course covering concepts essential to engineering programs that must pass accreditation standards.

- General Chemistry for Science Majors—full-year sequence of courses designed to prepare science majors for future required and elective chemistry courses.

These variations could be accommodated with five or more different textbooks. More than five textbooks could be used simply because different instructors may choose the prerogative of personally selecting a text. This happens especially if the course is a "terminal" course (has no subsequent dependent course). In this situation, texts are chosen by individuals and not by a consensus of multiple instructors. Even when teaching organic and biochemistry, it is important to know whether the course is a one-term stand-alone survey course or the first of a series of related courses. The difference is critical in the textbook-selection process. Choosing a textbook that does not correspond to the level and topics you will cover can put the students into a situation for which they have no resource except the notes they take in class. This may be satisfactory for the most able notetakers but not for most of the class.

On a similar note, courses covering topics that seem the same may be quite different in the approach to teaching these topics. General chemistry courses for engineers and science majors frequently have a higher math prerequisite than prep courses. Courses for non-science majors may have different math expectations and no high school course prerequisite. This has a dramatic effect on the choice of a textbook in terms of the level of presentation and the availability and quality of supplementary materials. You would also want to check the pace of the course in terms of the number of topics you wish to cover in the term.

What is the demographic of the student body in the class?

As mentioned above, the math preparation of your students matters. Many studies have shown the direct correlation between success in physical science and level of math experience. A "one-size-fits-all" course may use a text requiring a single year of algebra preparation and offer numerous supplementary materials for those less prepared as well as those who had precollege calculus. Textbook selection is a delicate balance among the needs of your audience.

No less of a challenge is the choice of a textbook for a course with a distinct clientele and proscribed topics such as chemistry courses for engineers. Since higher math skills and preparation are usually required of these students for university entrance, an instructor may start at a more advanced level and desire relevant ancillary materials to address applications to technological fields. For example, in our engineering general chemistry course, we do not cover the fundamentals of atomic structure, mole calculations, gas laws, and stoichiometry. Thermochemistry and introductory thermodynamics are the starting points with considerations of periodic properties as they relate to the structures and physical properties of materials. This is followed by a brief excursion into organic chemistry, including polymers and instrumental analysis.

A factor that can level the field of student success no matter what the student's chemistry and math preparation is a set of good study habits.

General chemistry courses are the usual entry point to organic chemistry for chemistry and biochemistry majors. Therefore, it is important to be aware of the subsequent courses that follow your course and textbook. Check with instructors of the subsequent courses and consider their expectations when selecting your textbook. For instance, a thorough text presentation of acid-base calculations might serve as a good background for those taking biochemistry who need to master the concept of buffers. For chemistry majors, representations of valence bond and molecular orbital theories lay the groundwork for organic hybridization theory as well as for the quantum mechanics used in physical chemistry courses in other parts of the academic program. Likewise, an overview of the properties of the elements can lead to a better understanding of the nutritional needs for trace metals for dietetics majors, and solution concentration calculations may be part of an agriculture course in irrigation or soil science. For that matter, concentration calculations can be essential to environmental engineering courses as well as those in nursing.

What is the mode of instruction in your course?

How would you characterize your course? Is it traditional (lecture and separate laboratory), integrated (lecture and lab together), case study, or inquiry-based? Is technology a part of the course or readily available to the students? Do the students have Web access in their dorm rooms or at home? Do you have large class sizes or small? Will there be teaching assistants covering recitation sections? Are team activities planned for the term? Are full-time faculty members responsible for all lecture and laboratory teaching assignments? All of these factors will contribute to the selection of textbooks and ancillary materials.

With all of this to consider, how do we go about the process of choosing a textbook?

As with any decision, it helps to have more than one choice and more than one person making the choice. Or maybe not.

In this section we consider some aspects of selecting textbooks:

- sources of textbooks
- desk copies
- author's preface
- audience
- table of contents and index
- chapter layout
- chapter problems
- supplementary materials

Where do we go to find out what textbooks are available?

Sometimes this is a short walk to your colleague's office or the campus bookstore. Experienced instructors are deluged with examination copies and other materials. In larger departments there might be a central location where new textbooks are stored for perusal. Once you are established in a faculty position, you will find opportunities to have publishers send you copies of their new textbooks. An excellent source of chemistry text publishers with contact information can be found on-line at the Web site of the *Journal of Chemical Education:* Chemical Education Resource Shelf (Journal of Chemical Education On-line 2002).

By going to the home sites of each publishing company, you can find titles, authors, and detailed text information. You can even test out Web sites and interactive exercises that accompany your text that are designed for students. There are on-line resources, such as that developed at the University of Notre Dame (Smith & Jacobs 2003), that summarize surveys of students and instructors about their textbooks. These sites are easy to navigate and understand.

When you have narrowed your choices to several possibilities and have review copies in hand, proceed to read the author's preface. It should address the issues of the intended audience, pedagogical philosophy, and approach. There should also be a summary of key features that distinguish this text from the others in the same category.

Does the text meet your needs in content, organization, reading level, and depth?

I once heard that most introductory college textbooks are written at a 10th to 12th-grade reading level. Therefore, there shouldn't be a problem with sentence structure and ordinary vocabulary. However, most first-year students are just learning the vocabulary of chemistry, and terms have to be clearly defined and used. Most textbooks have a glossary of terms at the end of the book and list new terms in a summary at the end of a chapter. Be sure to point this out to your students.

Consider the table of contents and the topic coverage as well as the placement of topics and the relative amounts of coverage. Will you be able to assign chapters and sections in an understandable sequence? Are concepts introduced and developed in a way that is sequential, or can some topics be covered out of chapter sequence? Students can become confused if they are required to leapfrog around the textbook in what seems to them to be a haphazard route. There are some textbooks that follow a very specific schedule with little room for deviation; other textbooks are written so that certain topics can stand alone; still others contain summaries interspersed among the chapters to illustrate the coherence of concepts and applications.

Pick out five to 10 topics you know you would cover, and check the index for those topics. Keep in mind that the text becomes a reference book after a short while, and the easier it is for students to find isolated items while studying, the better.

How is each chapter organized and laid out? Is it easy to assign sections?

I find that I rarely, if ever, use every text section, box, and problem in a chapter. At times I like to emphasize one aspect over another, especially if I notice that students seem to be having difficulty grasping a concept. It is much easier to assign text by section heading and subheadings than by page and paragraph. This ease of assignment is a factor that can direct textbook selection.

Where are the figures and tables related to relevant text?

Are figures and tables on the same page as the related explanation, a facing page, or not in the immediate vicinity? In my experience, students, especially freshmen, do not know how to use a textbook, especially the tables, pictures, graphs, and figures. Are the figures and tables relevant or superfluous to the topic on the page? Students can be totally unaware of the learning style that is best for them and ignore the excellent graphics and conceptual figures that could help them enormously in negotiating the material. The figures, graphs, tables, and delineated equations are also a tremendous aid in reviewing for quizzes and exams. However, this has to be pointed out to the students as you go through the concepts.

How are the problems presented?

Are there worked examples? Do they flow with the text? There are usually three general types of end-of-chapter problems: conceptual, drill, and comprehensive. The problems are frequently grouped according to text sections for ease of assignment. In addition, it is now almost traditional to have paired, color-coded problems for which some answers are provided at the end of the book. The comprehensive problems bring together current concepts with topics covered in previous chapters.

What are the degrees of difficulty in the problems? This is especially important for the general chemistry course used for all majors. There should be problems that all of the students can master and those that will offer a greater challenge in terms of combining concepts and extrapolating to new situations.

How much supplementary material in terms of on-line resources, CDs, and student study guides should be required or recommended?

A word of advice: Do not adopt a text because of its supplementary materials alone. It is the textbook that will be the reference for the term or terms of the course. A good textbook, written at student level and strongly correlated to your course materials, should be able to stand alone in terms of pedagogy and presentation. Be careful of on-line services for testing, because existing test banks may be difficult to review and modify for content and are extremely time-consuming when checking for errors, which may be numerous. On-line homework problems are also available through publishers. These programs usually come at a price to the students, although discounts are available if associated with the adoption of a textbook. Be aware that if you decide on such a package, it will have its own ISBN number, which must be relayed to the campus bookstore. Be sure that your students know there is an on-line program available and that the textbook might contain an access code. We have had a recent experience in which our students threw out the access code card because it looked like the advertising that is included in the bookstore shopping bags.

Students also need help in navigating on-line resources. Spend time showing the class where the materials are located on the Web and how they can incorporate the programs into their study plans. What seems self-evident to us is an unnegotiable maze to the inexperienced student.

Many campuses now support course-management programs like Blackboard, WebAssign, and WebCT (Blackboard 2003; WebAssign 2003; WebCT 2003). Check with the campus technology department to find out what is available, who is the person directing implementation and trouble-shooting, and what training is available for efficient use of the program.

Be selective when choosing ancillary materials. Start with the text and add on supplementary materials if you are relatively sure your students will make use of them. And don't be reluctant to change or eliminate these extras if necessary. Also check with your bookstore to see what can be used for resale. Younger students don't always appreciate a supplementary handbook if they haven't been required to read and study from it. Upper-division students usually keep the textbooks required for their major courses, but even then some students have to use the money from resale to fund the textbooks for the next term.

What about resources for instructors?

Overhead transparencies, animations, CD resources, PowerPoint presentations, test banks—there is almost no end to the amount of material offered to aid in instruction. By all means, obtain and use whatever is available. Again, be careful of accuracy and start out simple.

Most of all, teach your students how to use the textbook and incorporate it into a sound study program.

Students may start out with the best of intentions to read and use the textbook during the term. For most students intention gives way to expediency, and they revert to rote memorization rather than understanding. I have frequently talked with students in my office after they have had a low quiz or exam score, and they rationalize that reading the text several times should impart understanding. One way to demonstrate that there is more to studying is to open the textbook to a table, graph, or figure and ask them to tell you what information is being illustrated and where they could find the accompanying text explanation. A student quickly sees that there are indeed a thousand words in a picture.

Conclusion

A textbook is an invaluable resource if chosen carefully and used skillfully. The instructor is the facilitator for both of these activities.

Bibliography:

Journal of Chemical Education On-line: Chemical Education Resource Shelf (2002). http://www.umsl.edu/~chemist/books/index.html

Smith, B. and Jacobs, D. "TextRev: A Window into How General and Organic Chemistry Students Use Textbook Resources," *Journal of Chemical Education 80* (January 2003), 99.

Blackboard (2003). http://www.blackboard.com.

WebAssign (2003). http://Webassign.net.

WebCT (2003). http://www.Webct.com.

6

Integrating Library Research into a Chemistry Course

Mary M. Flekke
Roux Library
Carmen V. Gauthier
Department of Chemistry and Physics
Florida Southern College

Abstract

To effectively teach research in the college environment, a thorough familiarity with the library and its resources is critical. The twentieth century saw an overwhelming trend toward specialization within disciplines, not only in the sciences but in most fields. Therefore, to provide students with the ultimate instruction in research and the tools for doing research, a collaboration between the scientist and the librarian may become necessary. The following article details what that collaboration might involve and the advantages in collaborating.

Biography

Mary M. Flekke and Carmen V. Gauthier are on the faculty of Florida Southern College (FSC), a small Methodist- affiliated four-year college in Lakeland, Florida. Flekke holds a master of science in library science from St. Cloud State University. Since 1982, she has been an Instructional Services Librarian at FSC, primarily responsible for library instruction and database management. Gauthier earned a doctorate in inorganic chemistry from the University of New Hampshire and a bachelor of science degree in chemistry from the Pontifical Catholic University of Peru in Lima. She started her teaching career at Salem State College in Massachusetts and moved to FSC in 1999. She is an associate professor and chair of the Chemistry and Physics Department.

Questions for consideration

1. What is the most effective method to familiarize chemistry students with the research available in the library?

2. What does a chemistry professor do if she/he is unfamiliar with the resources of the local college/university library?

3. What does a librarian/chemistry professor collaboration bring to the students?

> *"Research instruction is often carried out by chemists with little or no library training or by librarians with little or no chemistry training."*
>
> (Huber and Baysinger, 1997)

Introduction

In recent years the *Journal of Chemical Education* has published numerous articles regarding the integration of a library research component into the chemistry curriculum. As Shibley and Milakofsky (2000) point out, this integration is important at all levels of the undergraduate curriculum. At Florida Southern College (FSC), although the library research component has been encouraged at all levels of the chemistry curriculum, it is a key component of the senior seminar capstone course. This chapter briefly discusses the need for and the limitations of integrating library research within the chemistry curriculum. It then describes the collaboration between FSC's instructional services librarian and a new chemistry professor to create a senior seminar capstone course that incorporates library research despite limited availability of resources.

At the undergraduate level, the ability to do library research is important for preparing students for later graduate work and training in their scientific field. Undergraduates often participate in seminars that allow them to practice the skills needed to transmit scientific information to large and small groups. To prepare for these seminars, undergraduates must have access to adequate library resources with articles and books related to their presentation topics. Besides preparing undergraduate students for research within their discipline, in the past two decades many institutions, such as FSC, have been emphasizing "writing across the curriculum" programs. More and more employers and graduate schools are expecting students to graduate from the undergraduate level with more than just adequate writing skills within their fields of study. At FSC writing has become a major component within the senior seminar capstone courses offered by the different majors, including chemistry. To assist in fulfilling this writing requirement, the students come to the library to learn database search techniques so that they may effectively access the research and literature. In the ideal world, libraries would have unlimited budgets and space to hold the wide variety and numerous scientific publications available these days that students need to meet the research and writing components of their coursework.

The reality, however, is that across the country, large and small colleges and universities have limited library resources and funding. These limitations place constraints on the numbers of books and journals that may be physically purchased and housed in the college or university library. In addition, books and journals in the sciences are extremely expensive, which places a major strain on library budgets. For example, major research resources, such as *Chemical Abstracts* and *Journal of the American Chemical Society,* are costly. As a small, private liberal arts college, FSC, like many other institutions, does not have the kind of budget that allows the library to acquire extensive collections of chemistry materials. To overcome this limitation, FSC supplements what it does have with electronic databases that provide either full-text articles from, or indexing to, professional scientific journals. It also purchases the abstract portion of *Chemical Abstracts* and the microfilm copy of the *Journal of the American Chemical Society,* as well as paper copies of several other scientific journals. Between the on-site materials and the databases, FSC undergraduate students are exposed to major references in chemistry literature.

Having adequate library resources, however, does not mean that the undergraduate students get the training they need to find and use these resources. According to Huber and Baysinger (1997), "Research instruction is often carried out by chemists with little or no library training *or* by librarians with little or no chemistry training." Thus, to effectively add the library component to the senior seminar course necessitates a meeting between the professor and the librarian. This collaboration brings all the critical elements to the table. For a new chemistry professor who is prepping classes, working with the librarian can help him or her to quickly become familiar with the library's resources. The librarian gets to know the chemistry professor's needs and can keep the professor abreast of changes in the library collection. The librarian/professor collaboration is a win-win situation for all, especially the student.

Next, this chapter will examine the FSC senior seminar capstone course that illustrates how this collaboration between professor and librarian works.

Senior seminar course description

The senior seminar (SS) course is designed to provide the student with an in-depth exposure to library research. At FSC only limited student-based research at the undergraduate level is done. The main emphasis is on students researching in-depth current chemistry topics and then presenting their findings in seminar fashion at the end of the semester.

At FSC the senior seminar course meets once a week. This concept is relatively new at the college, and many students have no real idea of what a seminar course entails. Prior to the class meeting with the librarian, they learn the concept of a seminar-style class, how it affects their future in their chosen field, the attributes of a good seminar, and how they should organize their presentations and papers. For the chemistry seminar, the students are expected to choose a current research topic in chemistry. A brainstorming session between the professor and the students precedes a visit to the library. During this session, the students discuss what type of scientific research interests them and the feasibility of their selected topics for the required presentation and paper. Several scientific journals are suggested as sources for topic ideas, including journals in the library holdings such as *Science, Nature, Chemical Reviews,* or *Accounts of Chemical Research.* Following the library research, the students write a paper draft, a final paper of 20 to 25 pages and then present the research in an oral presentation to their classmates, professor, other department faculty, and the librarian. Course evaluation is based on class participation (10%), abstract (5%), drafts of research paper (15%), peer review (5%), seminar evaluation (5%), research paper (30%), and oral presentation (30%). Class participation includes in-class discussion of review articles published in *Accounts of Chemical Research* or *Chemistry Reviews,* mandatory class attendance, and attendance at chemistry department–sponsored seminars. The time line of the seminar class is as follows:

Week 1: Why a seminar course?

Week 2: Library skills (meet in library)

Week 3: Seminar topic and discussion of a chemical research paper/article

Week 4: Chemistry department seminar

Week 5: Abstract and short presentation of seminar topic to class

Week 6: Discussion of a research topic; topic to be selected by students

Week 7: 1st draft and peer review

Week 8: Spring break

Week 9: How to give effective oral presentations

Week 10: 2nd draft and faculty-student conference

Week 11: Oral presentations

Week 12: Oral presentations

Week 13: ACS—National Meeting

Week 14: Research paper due and major field test

Library instruction

Prior to choosing a topic, the chemistry professor brings the class to the library for a meeting with the librarian. It seems to be more effective for the class to actually come and see the library rather than for the librarian to go to the class. Sometimes students tend to be shy of libraries, and a class visit helps to reduce anxiety. They soon realize that despite the proliferation of materials in database and Internet formats, some necessary items are still in paper. Prior to the semester in which a course is taught, the professor should also meet with the librarian to check the resources available for the class. While it is possible to get materials via Interlibrary loan in a timely manner, it is frustrating for the student if a professor assumes that library owns a book and the student then discovers that the library does not have that book. If faculty members require a book for the library, then they should order it in a timely manner, a couple months in advance of their class so that the book(s) will be in the library prior to the start of class.

Bringing the students to the library as a class is critical to the success of the literature search the students must do. The faculty attitude in this portion of the class is important. If the professor does not enthusiastically embrace the need for the library, the students will not either. Librarians find it is important to have the professor present during library instruction. Not only does the professor serve as a reminder of the importance of this portion of the seminar, but they can also ask pertinent questions that the students may not think to ask. A general misconception among students is that if they have used a library once, they are library literate. Electronic databases are evolving environments with ever changing formats. It is very helpful for students to be able to meet and feel comfortable with the librarian who will be helping them with their research. The following is an outline of a typical library visit.

Library Tour
(This can be done quickly in an hour if necessary, or expanded for longer periods as needed.)

1. Explain the Online Book Catalog
   a. Describe search options.
   b. Define effective search strategies.
   c. Using a sample topic, do actual search.

2. Explain the Scientific Electronic Journal Databases
   a. Describe search options.
   b. Define effective search strategies and limiting.
   c. Using a sample topic, do actual search.

3. Explain the Interlibrary Loan Process
   a. Demonstrate initiating interlibrary loan, within databases.
   b. Explain initiating interlibrary loan, when not provided within databases.

4. Internet Searching
   a. Demonstrate possible Internet search strategies.
   b. Using a sample topic, do actual search.
   c. Discuss evaluating Internet sites.

Using on-line book catalogs in libraries varies from institution to institution; they do not all follow the same formats. In general, however, on-line catalogs should offer searching by author, title, subject, and usually keyword. For most students searching topics, a keyword search is the most effective. Most college libraries have Web sites where one may gain access to the library's on-line book catalogs as well as a variety of electronic journal databases. Most library catalogs are free to be browsed by outsiders—people in the general public or students from other schools. Electronic databases, on the other hand, are usually password protected for use by the school's students, faculty, and staff. Electronic databases differ from Internet search engines in the fact that the school pays for and obtains licensing ensuring that *only* their own clientele will have access. Internet Web sites are generally free and may be accessed by anyone having connections through an Internet provider, and Internet Web sites have little in the way of supervisory control. Database services are the modern equivalent of the paper index, with more versatility by virtue of being "housed" on the Internet and taking advantage of its "surfing" features. Databases generally provide citation references or full-text journal articles on-line. Database access may be via password or via an IP address set up through the campus server. IP addresses allow databases to be restricted to only computers on the campus system, while passwords allow access via any server as long as the user has the password. While password access allows for flexibility in location, it is more impractical administratively, as it needs to be changed on a regular basis to protect the integrity of the system from non-college personnel.

In addition to discussing the databases, which are of value to the seminar class, the library portion of the class also involves instruction on use of the on-line library catalog, effective search strategies for both books and journals, instructions for searching the Internet, and Internet evaluation. Reminding the students that they now have access to these materials from their dorm rooms or, in most cases, from their homes even if they live off campus is critical. Journal articles and Inter-Library Loan can now be initiated or retrieved without coming to the library.

Budgetary constraints limit the numbers of journals or resources a library can purchase, including the number of databases that are available. Databases range in price from the "pay as you search" systems to several thousands of dollars per year. However, access to even a few databases greatly enhances a collection, providing more professional journals than any one library can afford in paper subscriptions. FSC provides database access to FirstSearch®, an On line Computer Library Center (OCLC) product, which provides access to more than 70 on-line databases, which in turn provides access to over 10 million full-text articles, as well as millions of article citations and an international book catalog. (www.oclc.org/firstsearch) BasicBiosis, General Science, and other databases within FirstSearch® cover the sciences. FirstSearch® at FSC is set up on a cost-per-search basis, the cost of which is absorbed by the library. Science Direct is a new collection of databases that provides 23 scientific databases, each of which has a separate subscription fee. DIALOG® is a collection of over 300 databases that offer fee-based searching. The fees are based on time spent in the database and the per-record cost of each database. Each of the databases within the DIALOG® collection has its own independent fee structure, and the library picks up the costs of the search if the students have faculty permission to utilize these databases. STNEasy is another similar collection of databases that also operates on a fee-per-search basis. DIALOG® offers BIOSIS and Chemical Abstracts (CA) Search. STNEasy also offers access to Chemical Abstracts among other databases. The advantage of STNEasy over DIALOG® is that STNEasy provides the actual CA abstracts, while DIALOG® only provides the citations. Other databases, such as EBSCOhost, are set up in licensing agreements that allow all students direct access for a flat subscription cost. EBSCOhost, a product of EBSCO Publishing, offers a varied array of databases on a variety of topics designed to meet library needs. These databases offer both full-text and citation-only searching, depending on licensing agreements with participating journal companies. (www.epnet.com)

Database descriptions

FirstSearch® provides access to over 70 databases through its subscription service. It has access to other databases for an additional fee. For the sciences the main databases are generally BasicBIOSIS, *Biological and Agricultural Index, Applied Science and Technology Abstracts,* and *General Science Abstracts.* The first is an abbreviated version of the BIOSIS database, covering the latest three to four years of such titles as *Biochemical and Biophysical Research Communications, Biochemical Journal, Biochemistry, Biochemistry and Cell Biology, Environment (Washington, D.C.), Environmental Science & Technology,* and other natural science titles. The remaining three are on-line versions of the H. W. Wilson indexes of the same titles. Coverage on these three databases go back to about 1983 and include access to a selection of full-text articles. *Biological and Agricultural Index* covers journals in the fields of environment and other natural sciences, including *Agricultural and Biological Chemistry, Archives of Environmental Contamination and Toxicology, Bulletin of Environmental Contamination and Toxicology, Environmental Science & Technology, Biochemistry,* and *Journal of Natural Products (Lloydia). Applied Sciences and Technology Abstracts* provides coverage in the areas of management, careers, financial and technological trends in the sciences, and such titles as *Analytical Chemistry, Biotechnology and Applied Chemistry, Chemical & Engineering News, Chemical Engineering, Chemical Reviews, Chemistry & Industry,* and *Chemtech. General Science Abstracts* includes indexing from 160 scientific journals from the United States and Great Britain, including *Analytical Chemistry, Annual Review of Physical Chemistry, Biochemistry, Canadian Journal of Chemistry, Chemical Reviews, Inorganic Chemistry,* among others.

Science Direct has subscription access to 23 databases, including such topics as agricultural and biological sciences; biochemistry, genetics, and molecular biology; chemical engineering; computer sciences; chemistry, medicine, and many other subsets, each available for a separate subscription fee.

DIALOG® provides access to approximately 600 databases (this number changes as databases come and go.) A number of these cover various aspects of the scientific community. The two used the most at FSC are BIOSIS and *CA—Chemical Abstracts*. DIALOG® commonly bills on a per-use basis, with the prices varying depending on each database and the type of record accessed. To use DIALOG® at FSC, the students pick up an application form in the library, present it for their professor's signature, and then set up an appointment with the librarian. The student must be present for consultation while the librarian runs the search to ensure accurate and efficient search results. The student also must select a search topic prior to running the search; this is done to control costs.

DIALOG® does have some very nice features to work with. These features include (1) available on the Web, or via the "classic" telnet searching; (2) an easy and flexible guided search mode utilizing free-text or keyword searching; (3) use of DIALINDEX if the user is not sure which of its databases to use; (4) Alerts that can be set up to let the user know when more information on the topic is available; and (5) search results can be saved or printed in HTML, plain-text formats or e-mailed, faxed, or received via postal service.

One of FSC's newest databases is STN*Easy,* which provides affordable access to *Chemical Abstracts* after 5 p.m. STN*Easy* also has about 85 other databases available in its collection, but the most important database in this collection for FSC students is the *Chemical Abstracts* database because this is the simplest and cheapest means of providing the abstracts and citations on-line. The start-up charges for this database were minimal, $119 at the time FSC began, which included a copy of the Online Express Software, user instructions, and an instructor package. Billing is done on a per-search basis, and these charges are reflected on the screen throughout the search. When FSC subscribed, the company recommended that the librarians hold the passwords for billing control. At FSC the students and faculty who wish to utilize this database come to the library after 5 p.m., and one of the librarians enters the password/login into the computer and assists if necessary with the searching. STN*Easy* allows for simple searching of keywords, advanced boolean searching, or searching by CAS number. If the user is connected to services such as EBSCOhost or a patents database, the user may be able to access articles full-text if the articles the search pulls up are covered by EBSCOhost indexing.

EBSCOhost is one of the easiest databases to learn. The FSC librarian uses this one to teach search strategies as it is available on a yearly flat subscription rate. It includes some science journals in its general academic database and also has 57 other subject matter databases, including *Biological Abstracts* and BasicBIOSIS, available from the company to which an institution may subscribe. One can do simple or advanced searches combining keywords using boolean logic. Searches may be of titles, keywords, authors, subjects, abstracts, or a simple default choice that will search the entire record.

All of the databases discussed are hosted on the Internet, which makes the facilitation of the search much easier than using the book indexes. However, many databases go back to only certain dates, not retrospectively converting old records to machine-readable materials. Therefore, at times, going back to paper indexes may be necessary. Using the Internet as a platform allows hotlinking of search terms and the combination of terms by boolean search strategies that cannot be done in paper indexes.

Other advantages of the Internet include the ease of searching for other topically oriented databases or Web sites. Some of the Web sites recommended to FSC chemistry seminar students that they can search free include ChemWeb Databases @ www.chemweb.com/databases. This Web site contains the Beilstein and Medline abstracts. It also has a chemical dictionary, and students can download free software to draw chemical structures. The Chemical Database Section of the WWW Virtual Library @ www.liv.ac.uk/Chemistry/Links/refdatabases.html contains links to other chemical Web sites offered throughout the world, both free and fee-based. Environmental Protection Agency @ www.epa.gov provides excellent coverage of environmental resources. **TOXNET** @ Toxnet.nlm.nih.gov is a toxicology resource giving information about LD_{50}'s, carcinogenicity, other details about the health-risk assessment of substances, as well as providing links to other toxicological Web sites. Ingenta @ www.ingenta.com

provides chemical article citations but charges for full-text access. There are also many other Web sites available on the Internet. Some of the other Web sites found on the Internet are also free; however, some ask the user to set up a login and password for access, and others may ask the user to subscribe using a credit card.

Topic selection process

Following the library instruction, the students select topics for their paper with the assistance of the professor. In selecting a topic, students are encouraged to follow these steps:

1. Read or review some of the scientific literature to find a general topic that interests them. Choose a topic that has a significant relationship to chemistry and will be understood by an audience with a background similar to the student's.

2. Avoid topics that are too broad or too specialized.

3. Select topics in which several articles are available. A seminar based on a single paper in a review journal is unacceptable.

Topic examples include the synthesis of Efavirenz, the identification of aroma-active compounds in Bulgarian rose oil utilizing gas-chromatography-olfactometry, and the effects of Methoxychlor on the female rodent reproductive system. Some of the databases used for these topics included Chemical Abstracts from STNEasy, *General Science Abstracts, Biological and Agricultural Index,* and BasicBIOSIS, as well as some of the scientific Web sites mentioned earlier. After the professor has approved the student's topic, the student gathers research and writes the paper using the ACS format.

Papers and presentations

After the initial review of resources and preliminary research, the students submit a one-page abstract to the professor. If the professor approves the abstract, the next step is to do the in-depth research and write the first draft. The first draft of each paper is reviewed by the professor and by one of the student's classmates (peer review). This peer review asks the students to critique the papers as follows:

Peer Review

Please review your classmate's research paper. Answer the following questions thoroughly in the space provided. If you need extra space, you can write on the back. You are not editing the paper; you are reviewing for content.

1. List the areas you found most interesting.

2. List the areas where you would like more information.

3. Specify the sections of the draft that were not clear to you.

4. Include suggestions to improve the paper.

Following the peer critiquing, the students again meet with the professor to discuss the peer and professor's critiques. Reviewing these critiques makes the students aware of areas in their papers that need more research and clarity. The second draft is then prepared. In addition, the students prepare a PowerPoint presentation as part of the oral presentation to the class, professor, assisting librarian, and other departmental faculty. The audience has the opportunity to both question the presenter and complete a paper evaluation of the presentation. The evaluation of the student presentations covers these issues:Senior Seminar Evaluation

Name of Speaker: _____

Your Name:_____

Please evaluate the following aspects:

1. What was the level of presentation of the seminar?
2. Was the speaker prepared?
3. Did the speaker show any distracting mannerisms?
4. How did the speaker handle questions?
5. Please comment on the quality of the visual aids.
6. What did you learn from the seminar?
7. Other comments

The final paper for the senior seminar is expected to follow the *ACS (*American Chemical Society) *Style Guide* and be 20 to 25 pages in length. It is read by the seminar professor and sometimes by other faculty colleagues, especially if the student works on a project that is a specialty of someone in the department. The advising librarian is also invited to read and critique the papers. Finally, the students are asked to evaluate their peers' oral presentations. This helps students pay attention to and learn from their peers' presentations.

The quality of the research papers generated from this process of peer and professorial evaluations prepares the students for what they can expect to find in the real world of a research chemist. Academic collaboration between the chemistry professor and the librarian enhances the quality of the student research and presentations. The professor has the advantage of gaining a better understanding of the library resources, which are continually evolving and changing, and the librarian is afforded a chemistry contact who is able to provide verification of the quality of the literature search done by the student with the librarian's assistance. The collaboration provides the students with knowledgeable mentors in all areas of their work. In addition, these collaborations provide the means to integrate research into the chemistry curriculum in institutions with limited budgets and resources.

Bibliography

Anthes, S. H., & Crow, L. (1991). The Collaborative Course: Innovative Teaching and Learning. *Community/Junior College Quarterly of Research and Practice, 15*, 369–79.

Drum, C. A. (1997). Partnerships in Undergraduate Chemistry Education. *Science & Technology Libraries, 16*, 89–97.

Huber, C. F., & Baysinger, G. (1997). Training the Trainers: Creating a Workshop on Teaching Chemical Information. *Issues in Science and Technology Librarianship, 16*. Retrieved October 11, 2002, from http://www.library.ucsb.edu/istl/97-fall/article1.html.

Lee, W. M., & Gary Wiggins. (1997). Alternative Methods for Teaching Chemical Information to Undergraduates. *Science & Technology Libraries, 16*, 31–43.

Penhale, S. J. (1997). Cooperative Learning Using Chemical Literature. *Science & Technology Libraries, 16*, 69–87.

Porter, K. R., & Woerner, T. (1997). On the Way to the Virtual Laboratory: Integrating Chemical Information into the Undergraduate Physical Chemistry Laboratory Program. *Science & Technology Libraries, 16*, 99–114.

Ricker, A. S. (1997). Chemistry Information for the Undergraduate in a One-Credit Course: Faculty/Librarian Team Teaching. *Science & Technology Libraries, 16*, 45–67.

Rossi, F. M. (1997). Writing in an Advanced Undergraduate Chemistry Course: An Assignment Exploring the Development of Scientific Ideas. *Journal of Chemical Education, 74*, 395–6.

Shibley Jr., I. A., & Milakofsky, L. M. (2001). Incorporating a Substantial Writing Assignment into Organic Chemistry: Library Research, Peer Review and Assessment. *Journal of Chemical Education, 78*, 50–53.

Somerville, A. N., & Carr, C. (1997). Chemistry Librarians as Teachers: New Partnerships for a New Environment. *Science & Technology Libraries, 16*, 31–30.

Section

PEDAGOGY AND CLASSROOM INSTRUCTION

Interpreting and Addressing Student Apprehension

Diane M. Bunce
Chemistry Department
The Catholic University of America

Abstract

Students often respond to the difficulty they are having learning chemistry by covering up their frustration. Instead of being able to analyze the problems they are experiencing and the help they need to be successful, they sometimes lash out at the instructor/course or complain that the course is too hard, unfair, or the like. Students may be quick to point out how hard they are trying and how poor their test results are. Rather than responding to the actual words the student is using to express the frustration, the instructor should look beyond the actual words and emotion to the basic problems in the learning process that spark this frustration. This chapter will attempt to explain some possible causes of student frustration that result in classic complaints about chemistry and offer different approaches to teaching and/or course organization that could be used to address such student concerns.

Biography

I love chemistry. I love its logic and the ability it offers to explain phenonmenon. Matter of fact, I am so excited about chemistry that I want everyone to share its excitement with me. So I find myself engaging people I meet in the discussion of chemistry behind everyday occurrences. Unfortunately, many people don't intially share my love of the subject. I even had an oral surgeon (who was about to remove my impacted wisdom tooth) admit that he started out as a chemistry major but lost interest and switched to oral surgery. How did I get to this love of chemistry? Well, it wasn't easy. I was an undergraduate chemistry major who couldn't picture myself spending the rest of my life in a lab, so I became a high school chemistry teacher instead. I enjoyed teaching high school but soon realized that students were experiencing the same problems with the same chemistry topics year after year. This led me to leave high school teaching and return to graduate school for a degree in chemical education. Chemical education offered me the best of both worlds—a chance to spend my time sharing my love of chemistry with others and doing research on why chemistry seemed so hard to learn. Chemical education research has now become my focus. I serve as editor of the chemical education research feature of the *Journal of Chemical Education*. I am also past chair of the Division of Chemical Education (DivChed), a member of the chemical education research committee of DivChed, and a presenter of chemical education workshops and professional papers. But when it comes right down to it, I love chemistry and people, and I am never content until those who want to understand chemistry can.

Introduction

Sometimes teaching chemistry to undergraduates, especially freshmen, can seem like a thankless job or even an impossible one. As teachers, we select a topic, break it down into its components, search for examples and problems that epitomize what we are talking about, do sample problems in class, assign other problems for homework, urge students to study, and still they don't seem to get it. And to make matters worse, there are some students who believe it is our fault they are having trouble learning chemistry!

If you talk to students or if they come to see you during office hours, you may hear comments such as the following:

- "I studied for hours, and I still can't do well on *your* tests."

- "There is *so* much to learn—I can't possibly remember it all."

- "I've *never* been good at science (or the math involved in science)."

- "I can understand the problems when the teacher does them in class, but I can't do them on my own when I am home."

- "Lab is a waste of time and doesn't relate to anything we are learning."

- "Why do we have to learn this?"

These typical comments reflect student frustrations and also give us an insight into the disconnect between our teaching and their learning. By starting with the students' own comments, we can explore what is actually causing their frustrations and search for or develop different teaching approaches that can address these concerns. We will thus use the students' own words to guide our search for understanding in this chapter.

"I studied for hours, and I still can't do well on *your* tests."

The most important thing to do when a student says something like this is to acknowledge that they *have* studied for hours. The next step is to help them look at the effectiveness of the way they studied. Many students read or reread the textbook in preparation for a test. Highlighting the textbook in one, two, or even three different colors does not necessarily mean they are learning the material in the book. Highlighting the text may have been a viable study strategy for the student in previous chemistry courses but will probably not work in college-level chemistry courses. Helping the student realize that this approach is inadequate can be a tough sell. The same type of problem may arise in terms of studying notes. The student may believe that memorizing the notes word for word means that he/she has learned chemistry. The common message here is that memorizing without understanding does not necessarily equate to learning. College-level chemistry courses usually put more emphasis on understanding a topic rather than simply memorizing definitions or relationships. Getting the students to realize that memorizing does not necessarily mean that they understand a topic can also be a tough sell. There are, however, some things you can do to help bring home this idea.

Compare and contrast. We tend to teach in a linear fashion following the outline of chemistry topics presented in a textbook or syllabus. When we finish one series of concepts or chapters, we give a test and proceed onto the next. In the process, we may inadvertently convey the idea that the concepts in different chapters or parts of chapters are unrelated to each other. It takes a small change in the way we present chemistry to dispel this myth. Try posing questions in class, on homework, in recitation, or on tests and quizzes that encourage students to compare and contrast concepts both within a chapter and across chapters. For instance, we usually teach weak/strong acids and bases and concentrated/dilute solutions in two different chapters. After you have taught each of these concepts, ask students to draw a particulate level picture of the molecules/ions of a **concentrated, weak acid** or a **dilute, strong base**. If you have students work in groups on this question and walk around to survey their discussions, you will see them actually learn chemistry as they put these two concepts together.

Another question you can ask your students is to explain bonding without using electron configuration. When they run into a problem doing this, ask them to explain why they need electron configuration to fully explain bonding.

Concept maps. Concept maps are a device that encourages the learning of individual concepts and examples as an integrated whole (Zeilik, www.flaguide.org/cat/minutepapers/conmap1.htm). The idea behind Concept maps is to arrange the components of a concept in hierarchical order from general to specific and link and crosslink these concepts with each other, specifying the interconnections between them. A Concept map is constructed by writing the concepts in a topic in individual boxes and connecting these boxes with lines on which are written verbs that explain the connection. An example of a concept map for alcohol is given in Figure 1.

Figure 1. Concept map of alcohol

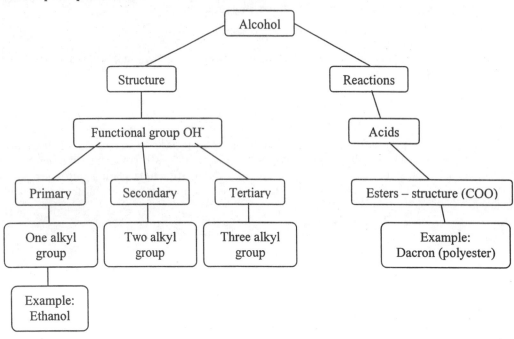

Concept maps can be used effectively in a couple of different ways. Once students have been shown how to construct concept maps, they can be encouraged to construct them as part of their preparation for tests. Concept maps can also be constructed within classes or recitations as group work to prepare for tests or in lecture to sum up a topic before proceeding to the next topic.

Particulated diagrams. As chemists, we tend to understand chemistry on a particulate (molecular/atomic/ionic) level (Nurrenbern & Pickering 1987; Johnstone 1983). When we use equations such as $pH = -\log [H_3O^+]$, we understand that the numerical value of pH is actually based upon the number of H_3O^+ ions. In class, we might try to help students understand pH by demonstrating the effect of an acid with a specific indicator. What is often not done for students is to show them a representation of our particulate understanding of the concept. We, as experts, move back and forth among three different representations of pH (symbolic—equation, particulate—ions and macroscopic—demonstration) without much effort. The same is not necessarily true for students. They might not see that all three of these—equation, particulate, and demonstration—as different manifestations of the same concept of acids. They also might not understand that all three manifestations are based upon the action of the H_3O^+ ions. It is our job to help students understand the connection. If we can help students visualize chemistry concepts on the particulate level of molecules/atoms/ions in addition to the symbolic and macroscopic, we will help them truly understand concepts rather than just memorize facts or algorithms. There is also some evidence that males and females benefit differentialy from the use of the particulate level of matter. Although teaching the particulate level of matter did not seem to increase the achievement of males in one study, females' achievement in chemistry increased significantly when the particulate level was taught (Bunce and Gabel 2002).

Teaching using the particulate level can involve the use of animations that show how molecules/atoms/ions interact with each other. It can also involve the use of particulate diagrams found in many popular textbooks. Even without these formal artistic representations, students can still be asked to explain a chemical concept by drawing their own particulate diagrams. This is much easier if the students are familiar with particulate diagrams from class. Figure 2 includes a simple particulate diagram that demonstrates graphically to students the difference between subscripts and coefficients in a balanced equation.

Figure 2. Particulate diagram of subscripts vs. coefficients

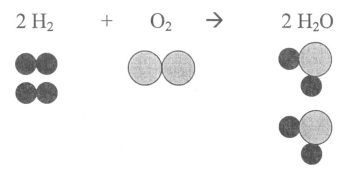

Directed paraphrase. There are ways for students to practice whether or not they truly understand a chemistry topic. One of these is the use of the *directed paraphrase* procedure. In directed paraphrase, the student is asked to explain a chemical concept to someone not in the class, like a family member or friend. This is most effective when the directed paraphrase activities include written explanations. I sometimes use this device on tests for open-ended questions, an example of which can be found in Figure 3.

Figure 3. Directed paraphrase example

Your younger brother is microwaving soup in a plastic bowl. He heats the soup on high for three minutes. Explain to him why you would not expect the outside of the plastic container to be hot. Use the chemistry you learned in this course to support your explanation.

There are several reasons why the directed paraphrase device works. One reason is that in order to explain a chemical concept to someone not in the class, a student must synthesize an answer that is not dependent on parroting back chemical terms that he/she might not understand. It is a natural response to explain chemistry to someone not in the class in everyday language. In order to move from rote memorization of chemical definitions to an understanding of these chemical concepts, the student must think about what the definitions mean. This process promotes true understanding.

There are more examples of teaching techniques to promote understanding found in the book *Classroom Assessment Techniques: A Handbook for College Teachers* (Angelo and Cross 1993).

"There is *so* much to learn—I can't possibly remember it all."

A statement like this from students is a pretty good indication that they are trying to learn everything as a series of isolated facts. The students are correct when they say there is too much to learn! If they are trying to learn everything as a series of unrelated facts, then there is TOO much to learn.

This becomes especially important in organic chemistry. Most organic chemistry teachers present students with a general template for a particular type of reaction followed by specific examples. More than likely, the assigned homework from the textbook will include other examples of reactions that the students must categorize and complete according to the templates they have learned. Presented in this fashion, the memory load that these reactions require is kept to a minimum, and the student is able to demonstrate understanding by categorizing a new reaction according to one of several templates and then applying the template to work out the products or mechanism of the reaction. If the student does not see the presentation of material in class as that of template and specific examples, then the student may see each problem as a brand-new reaction that needs to be memorized. Little learning from one example is carried over to the next in this scenario, and the memory load of chemistry is astronomical. One way to help the student cope with the organization of the material is to point out the use of templates and help the student practice categorizing each new reaction and then completing it according to the prescribed template. It would also help to explicitly mention to the students that large sections of chemistry that are being handled by blind memorization are probably areas where the student has missed the unifying concept. These are good areas to discuss with the student during office hours.

"I've never been good at science (or the math involved in science)."

Many students believe that their inability to do mathematical chemistry word problems is due to a weak math background. When it comes right down to it, 90 percent of the math in most general chemistry courses is addition, subtraction, multiplication, and division. If asked, most chemistry students would agree that they can add, subtract, multiply, and divide, even if they use a calculator to assist them. The real problem is not the mathematical manipulations but rather knowing *which numbers* to add, subtract, multiply, and divide. That's not math. It's logic. Logic is the basic underpinning for all scientific thought, so it is not unreasonable to believe that chemistry should be taught according to the principles of logic. Herein lies the problem. Unless teachers realize that the lack of logic is the problem, they wind up blaming poor chemistry grades on poor math skills. Even students who do well in math often lack the logic needed to solve chemistry word problems. Logic has to be explicitly taught, and problem solving is a good way to start.

There is research that shows that students do not need to understand chemistry topics to be successful at solving chemistry word problems, nor do they need to be able to successfully solve chemistry word problems in order to understand chemistry concepts (Bunce, Gabel, et al. 1991). If, then, we are to teach logic through the solving of chemistry word problems, it is necessary to be explicit on what and why each part of the solution is necessary. Not all students in the class need such explicit instruction, but most good students will not object to the use of an explicit problem-solving approach in lecture as long as they are not required to duplicate it in their own work. Weaker students, on the other hand, can really benefit from seeing and using an explicit approach to problem solving.

One way to approach problem solving in an explicit fashion is to break the analysis, categorization and rule rearrangement, plan, math manipulation, and review into separate parts of the process. The Explicit Method of problem solving (Bunce and Gabel 1991) does this by including a written analysis of each problem using the sections: **Given, Asked For, Recall, Plan, Math** and **Review** sections. The Given and Asked For sections represent the original analysis of the problem while the Recall section incorporates the categorization and rule rearrangement steps (See Figure 4). To be most effective, these explicit problem-solving categories should be written out each time a problem is solved in class. This may seem like overkill, but to convince yourself that it is really needed, take a look at your students' notebooks. It is not uncommon for students to have recorded a solution to a chemistry word problem by writing a string of crossed-out numbers set equal to an answer. Ask individual students to use their notebooks to explain a problem solution to you for a problem you did two weeks ago in class. Many will have trouble explaining the solution based upon their own written record. This doesn't mean that they didn't understand it when you did it in class, only that their notes on the solution are inadequate. To remedy this, try writing out the sections of the Explicit Method for a couple of weeks and then repeat the test to see if students have a better understanding of the solution in their notes two weeks later.

A typical general chemistry word problem and its solution using the Explicit Method are included in Figure 4.

Figure 4. Chemistry problem solution using the Explicit Method

Burning coal to fuel electrical power plants results in the formation of the pollutant sulfur dioxide SO_2. Through a series of reactions, this SO_2 can react with the O_2 and H_2O in the air to produce sulfuric acid (H_2SO_4) according to the following equation:

$$2 H_2O \text{ (l)} + O_2 \text{ (g)} + 2 SO_2 \text{ (g)} \rightarrow 2 H_2SO_4 \text{ (aq)}$$

If 0.500 g of sulfur dioxide react with the water and oxygen in the atmosphere, how many grams of sulfuric acid will be formed?

Given: 0.500g SO_2

Asked For: g of H_2SO_4

Recall: Mass-mass stoichiometry problem

From Balanced Equation: 2 moles SO_2/2 moles H_2SO_4

From Periodic Table: 1 mole SO_2 = 64.064 g
1 mole H_2SO_4 = 98.078 g

Plan:
g of SO_2 $\rightarrow$ moles of SO_2 $\rightarrow$ moles of H_2SO_4 $\rightarrow$ g of H_2SO_4

Math:

$$0.500 \text{ g } SO_2 \times \frac{1 \text{ mole of } SO_2}{64.064 \text{ g } SO_2} \times \frac{2 \text{ moles } H_2SO_4}{2 \text{ moles } SO_2} \times \frac{98.078 \text{ g } H_2SO_4}{1 \text{ mole } H_2SO_4} = 0.760 \text{ g } H_2SO_4$$

Review: Read over the original problem and the first four sections of the Explicit Method solution (Given, Asked For, Recall and Plan) to emphasize *how* the problem was categorized and solved.

"Lab is a waste of time and doesn't relate to anything we are learning."

Many students fail to see how lab fits into the topics they are covering in lecture, and sometimes they are right to be lost. Coordinating lecture and lab in many colleges and universities is difficult, and as a result, the lab component exists as an independent course. This makes it especially difficult for students to understand how the lab experiences "fit in" with lecture. Even if this is not the situation, the change of books from lecture to lab may introduce slightly different ways of referring to or explaining concepts or calculations. This alone can cause students some distress. Let's concentrate on the difficulties students have in lab even without these two situations.

When a student comes to lab, there is learning to take place on several different levels. First, the student must learn a new procedure or instrument to take a measurement or test for a result. This learning is a combination of tactile and cognitive skills. This is more than enough to exceed the student's short-term memory. Add to this the idea that not only must a student learn this procedure or instrument but that the student is being judged on the accuracy of his/her execution of the new procedure or instrument. To make matters worse, the student will probably have to complete some mathematical equations to calculate the answer of interest and then explain the connection between the concept being measured and the calculated answer. The student must do this in one afternoon with or without the skilled guidance of a well-trained and dedicated guide in the form of a teacher or teaching assistant. Chances are that you will find students asking if they got the right result or checking with others in the class on how to do the calculations or what the answers mean. As instructors, we are of little help to students if we spend the prelab stressing the mechanics of the procedure or instrument at the expense of helping the student see how all the measurements in lab relate to different parts of the concept in question. Student behavior or attitude toward lab may actually be an artifact of how we have structured the experience. There are several things we can do to help students in this situation.

- Make sure that the concepts covered in lab have been previously taught or experienced in the lecture portion of the course. If not, then present a short prelab introduction to the concept.

- To help students understand how what they do in lab is related to the chemical concept in question, help the students construct a Gowin's Vee diagram (Novak and Gowin 1986). A Gowen's Vee diagram lists the concepts to be covered in lab on the left side and the procedures used in lab to observe/measure these concepts on the right. The two are separated by the sides of a large V. In the middle of the V are the focus questions that help students see the relationship between the concepts and the measurements. An example of a Gowin's Vee diagram for density is given in Figure 5.

Figure 5. Gowin's Vee for density

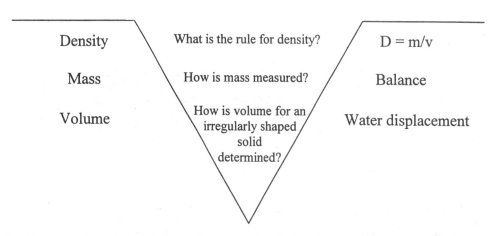

By listing the concepts that the lab will address and then listing the procedures or instruments that will be used in lab, the student can develop an overview of the lab experience. Gowin's Vee diagrams can be constructed individually by students either before prelab as a means for understanding what will take place in lab that day or in groups/whole class during prelab. The use of Gowin's Vee does not interfere with the general approach of the lab, whether it is traditional or guided inquiry. In a guided inquiry approach, the Gowin's Vee can be developed as part of the experimental procedure discussion. The purpose of the Gowin's Vee is to help students relate chemical concepts with experimental procedures used in lab. It should work regardless of the specific lab design.

"Why do we have to learn this?"

Students sometimes use another more direct phrasing of this question, such as "Is this going to be on the test?" In general, these questions mean that the students don't see how the current topic fits into a larger scheme. If we as teachers are not able to place the new information within a larger context, the student will attempt to satisfy us or pass the test by memorizing the seemingly "unconnected data." Such memorized information is quickly forgotten and does little to help the student apply the basic principles of chemistry to new situations.

The context in which you help the student place the new information may be different depending on the particular general chemistry course you teach. For science majors, it may be necessary to explain how the current acid-base equilibrium, for example, is a specific application of the general equilibrium concept that was covered in a previous chapter. The construction of a concept map may be helpful in this situation. For non-science majors, it might be more beneficial to relate the concept to a question from the real world. For instance, to teach frequency and wavelength for the electromagnetic radiation concept, it might be helpful to explain how the ozone hole, global warming, and microwave ovens are all related by the fact that electromagnetic radiation of varying energies is responsible for each phenomenon. For example:

- UV radiation (short wavelength, high frequency, high energy) breaks the ozone molecule apart, thereby contributing to the ozone hole.

- IR radiation from the Earth (longer wavelength, lower frequency, lower energy) causes carbon dioxide molecules to stretch and bend (without breaking bonds) and eventually is returned to warm the Earth.

- Microwaves (longer wavelength, lower frequency and lowest energy of the three) causes water molecules in food to rotate (not break or stretch bonds), thereby causing friction between the rotating molecules that heat the food.

The American Chemical Society's curricula for non-science majors *Chemistry in Context* (2003) presents all the chemistry topics of the course embedded within social and personal issues, such as global warming, acid rain, nuclear power, nutrition, over-the-counter drugs, etc. The basic philosophy of this curriculum project is to teach chemistry on a "need to know" basis. This means that the teacher or curricula materials must first create a "need to know" within the student by engaging them in the political, social, or scientific issues of the day. This is a fairly effective approach for liberal arts students, many of whom come into the course believing that they are not particularly interested in chemistry.

Conclusion

Sometimes at the end of the day it is very easy to blame the student for being lazy or unmotivated when it comes to learning chemistry, but in reality this might not be the case at all. What may appear as student laziness or apathy may be a cover for student frustration. It is sometimes easier for students not to try to succeed than to try and fail. One way to differentiate between the two is to talk with students informally. Talks with all sorts of students, not just the ones whom you think are the most approachable. Convey to students your own deep commitment to their success. Tell them the things you have incorporated into the course to help them learn, and periodically ask them to tell you what is working or not working. Ask for suggestions on what *they* think they need to succeed. This discussion can take place informally before or after lecture, in recitation or lab, but it probably won't work unless it is one-on-one and takes place regularly. Some people with large classes structure this discussion by having the class elect a Board of Directors who meet with the instructor once a week or once every two weeks to discuss issues of course management and student concerns. Others ask students to write out what is working or not working on a sheet of paper at the end of class periodically during the course. These student responses should be anonymous to help ensure an impartial assessment by students. Even if you do all of this, you will have students who complain bitterly that the course is too hard and you expect too much of them, etc. Don't ignore these complaints out of hand. Search the whole set of student responses to see if this is a common theme, even if some students express it more delicately than others. Just because the students say your course is too hard, it doesn't mean you have to lower your standards. What it does mean is that you should examine the kind of support system you provide for students who want to learn but need more intermediate opportunities between your lectures and tests to work with the material. Although it might seem like a waste of time to regularly ask students how they are doing in your course, it does reflect a concern on your part to help students learn. After all, chemistry should be understandable by all who are willing to put in the effort. Our job is to make that possible. Chemistry was invented by humans to help understand their world. It should be understandable by the students who want to learn it. As Mary Budd Rowe said, "Let's take chemistry off the killer list" (Rowe 1983)!

References

Angelo, T. A., & Cross, K. P. (1993). Classroom Assessment Techniques. A Handbook for College Teachers. 2nd Ed. San Francisco: Jossey-Bass Publ.

Bunce, D. M., & Gabel, D. (2002). Differential Effects on the Achievement of Males and Females of Teaching the Particulate Nature of Chemistry. *Journal of Research in Science Teaching, 39*(10), 911–927.

Bunce, D. M., Gabel, D. L., & Samuel, K. B. (1991). Enhancing Chemistry Problem-solving Achievement Using Problem Categorization. *Journal of Research in Science Teaching, 28* (6), 505–521.

Johnstone, A. H. (1983). Chemical Education Research: Facts, Findings, and Consequences. *Journal of Chemical Education, 60* (11), 968–971.

Novak , J. D., & Gowin, D. B. (1986). *Learning How to Learn* (pp. 55--75). New York: Cambridge University Press.

Nurrenbern, S. C., & Pickering, M. (1987). Concept Learning versus Problem Solving: Is There a Difference? *Journal of Chemical Education, 64* (6), 508–510.

Rowe, M. B. (1983). Getting Chemistry Off the Killer Course List. *Journal of Chemical Education, 60* (11), 954–956.

Stanitski, C. L., Eubanks, L. P., Middlecamp, C. H., & Pienta, N. J. (2003). Chemistry in Context: Applying Chemistry to Society. 4th Ed., New York: McGraw-Hill Publ.

8

Teaching Your Students HOW to Learn Chemistry

Saundra Yancy McGuire
Center for Academic Success
Department of Chemistry
Louisiana State University

Abstract

Learning chemistry requires more than good instruction, a positive attitude, and expenditure of effort. It requires that students use appropriate learning strategies to master the material. Because most students enter college without having learned how to learn or how to study, it is important for chemistry instructors to teach them how to learn in general, and how to learn chemistry in particular. This chapter presents several learning strategies, based on cognitive science research, that can be taught to students enrolled in introductory-level chemistry courses. The strategies are easy to implement and result in rapid improvement in chemistry performance when applied consistently. When students see positive results after implementing the strategies, their motivation increases, and students who appear to be doomed to failure in chemistry begin to excel and enjoy the course.

Biography

I am director of the Center for Academic Success and adjunct professor of chemistry at Louisiana State University. Prior to joining LSU in August 1999, I served as director of the Learning Strategies Center and senior lecturer in chemistry at Cornell University in Ithaca, New York, where I received the Clark Distinguished Teaching Award. I have been teaching first-year chemistry courses for over 30 years and wrote the *Student Study Guide, Instructor's Teaching Guide,* and the *Problem Solving Guide and Workbook* for *Introductory Chemistry* by Steve Russo and Mike Silver. I have a passion for helping students understand that learning chemistry can be fun and have been rewarded for my efforts in this area. Most recently I was named the winner of the 2002 Dr. Henry C. McBay Outstanding Teacher Award presented by the National Organization for the Professional Advancement of Black Chemists and Chemical Engineers (NOBCChE). My greatest joy in teaching has been to witness the transformation that occurs when students realize that when they learn *how* to learn, learning chemistry is not hard at all!

Why Are They Failing the Exam?

The students in Dr. Ruth Green's Chem 101 class seemed to be making good progress during the first few weeks of class. They were completing all of the homework assignments, and did well on the short weekly quizzes. Dr. Green was shocked when the average on the first test was 62%. By all reasonable standards, the test was fairly straightforward, even though several problems required students to combine more than one simple concept. It appeared that although Dr. Green thought that the students were learning the concepts (the students thought so too!), the performance on the first test indicated otherwise. Many students protested that the test was unfair, and they seemed discouraged by the results. It was clear that Dr. Green had to get to the root of the problem and teach the students how to learn chemistry. She considered the following questions in her search for answers.

Why do introductory chemistry students have trouble mastering chemistry?

The answer to this question is usually found in the students' prior experience with chemistry, or with other science courses they may have taken in high school. Interviews with students about their experience in these courses often reveal that the emphasis was on memorization of definitions and formulas, and the examinations were comprised of "plug and chug" problems in which students substituted numbers into the formulas to calculate a result that had little meaning. Furthermore, the day before the test most of their teachers would conduct a review of the test material, and this review consisted of going over the types of problems that would appear on the test. If the students paid close attention to the review, doing no additional studying, they found it fairly easy to make an A or B on the test. When these same students take Introductory Chemistry, they are convinced that they can begin studying one or two nights before the test (the equivalent of the high school review the day before the test) and do well on the exam. They receive a rude awakening when this is not the case. What can the instructor do about this?

How can students be taught that memorizing and learning are different?

One of the major barriers that students face in trying to learn chemistry is their misconception that memorizing facts and formulas is equivalent to learning. Cognitive psychologists make a distinction between rote learning and meaningful learning (Ausubel, Novak, and Hanesian 1978). Rote learning is verbatim memorization, and is not necessarily accompanied by any understanding of the terms. Students are unable to explain information that is learned by rote, and they are not able to paraphrase the information in their own words. For example, they may be able to state the definitions of Arrhenius and Bronsted-Lowry acids and bases, but they will not be able to classify individual acids and bases as Arrhenius, Bronsted-Lowry, or both. Meaningful learning, on the other hand, is learning that is tied to previous knowledge, and it is understood well enough to be manipulated, paraphrased, and applied to novel situations. Most learning is neither completely rote nor entirely meaningful, and can be placed on a rote-meaningful learning continuum (Ausubel 1968).

Although most students enter college not knowing the difference between rote learning and meaningful learning, when they are taught this distinction, they are able to implement strategies that promote meaningful learning. When they fully understand the difference between memorizing facts and formulas for a test, and working to understand the course concepts and how they relate to each other, their greater conceptual understanding and their success on problem-solving tasks and examinations increases substantially.

Emphasizing meaningful learning as opposed to rote memorization, however, does not mean that memorization is unimportant. In fact, content knowledge of facts and formulas is a major determinant of success in problem solving (Fisher, Wandersee, and Moody 2000). The ability to apply concepts and solve problems requires that students have a well-developed knowledge base in which individual bits of information reside within a conceptual framework. Knowing only specific bits of information represents learning at a very different level than developing a conceptual framework that contains bits of information that are interconnected.

One particularly effective way to present the different levels of learning is through a discussion of the hierarchy of learning levels, shown here, similar to Bloom's taxonomy (Bloom 1956).

Figure 1. Bloom's Taxonomy

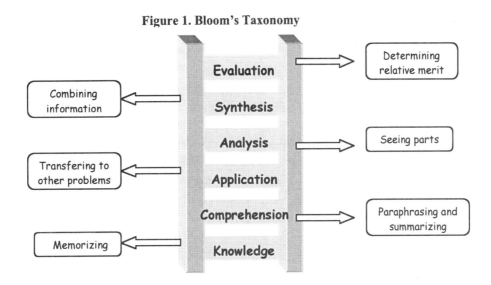

Although faculty generally assume that students know that memorizing information is not the same as learning, this assumption is unwarranted. Formally introducing them to differences in the levels of learning is crucial to developing the understanding of this distinction in today's students. The differences in the levels of learning can be introduced at the beginning of the course and referred to throughout. One effective way to do this is to give periodic quizzes that require learning at different levels to achieve mastery. Students can easily see that memorizing will not produce superior performance, and they will be motivated to move themselves to higher levels of learning by spending more time thinking about the material, working problems, and developing their own conceptual frameworks.

Learning chemistry at different levels is illustrated by the following example:

Many students view the unit on gases as relatively easy because they think they can just memorize the formulas and plug in the numbers. They tend to generalize that if the conditions of the gas are changing, they should use $P_1V_1/T_1 = P_2V_2/T_2$. And if conditions are constant, they should use $PV = nRT$. This is learning at the lowest level—knowledge. If students can explain *why* $P_1V_1/T_1 = P_2V_2/T_2$, and under which conditions the relationship is not true, their learning is at the comprehension level. At this level they should also be able to explain why pressure and volume are inversely related, why volume and temperature are directly related, etc. Learning is at the application level if students can use the ideal gas law to determine the molar mass of a gas from its density at a given temperature and pressure. However, if students have been given the form of the ideal gas law from which molar mass can be calculated directly, molar mass = mass of gas x RT/PV, they can solve this problem by plugging values into the rotely learned formula. Finally, if students can devise an experiment to determine the relative densities of two or more gases, they are operating at the synthesis level of learning.

What learning strategies can I teach students to use?

The Center for Academic Success at Louisiana State University has had great success teaching students to use The Study Cycle with Intense Study Sessions. This is a system that we developed at LSU to provide students with concrete steps they can take to improve their learning. The Study Cycle is easy to learn and implement, and students see an immediate result when they start to use it. Cognitive science provides the theoretical basis for the success of each step in the cycle. The four-step process is described here.

THE STUDY CYCLE

Step 1: Preview or pre-read the information that will be covered in class before class. Previewing chapter material (concentrating on the boldface print, italicized writing, figures, graphs, diagrams, etc.) prepares the mind to receive and comprehend the material that will be discussed in lecture. The previewing provides background knowledge for what will be covered in the lecture. Cognitive scientists have empirically demonstrated the importance of background knowledge to understanding and acquiring new information (Bransford, Brown, and Cocking 2000). When students have some familiarity with the material that will be discussed, the level of comprehension during lecture increases, and students indicate that they become more interested in the class. Pre-reading also makes notetaking easier during lecture. Step 1 of the Study Cycle need take only 10–15 minutes, and many students report that they do this step on the bus on the way to class, or arrive early in the classroom to do it before class.

Step 2: Go to class and actively participate in lecture. Although this step should not need to be explicitly stated, the absenteeism in large introductory science classes is often extremely high (approaching 50 percent after mid-semester). Therefore, students must be instructed to attend lecture (unannounced lecture quizzes are a great incentive), and told how to make lecture a learning experience. Active cognitive engagement (engaging the mind during lecture instead of allowing the material to pass from the board or screen onto the notebook pages without passing through the mind of the learner) begins the process of forming and manipulating mental representations of the material. This type of engagement has been termed "mindful learning" (Fisher, Wandersee, and Moody 2000). Active questioning (posing questions to the lecturer or the student's posing questions to her/himself) allows the student to monitor her/his understanding of the material being discussed. This monitoring of understanding is an important component of metacognition (thinking about and monitoring one's thinking) (Bransford, Brown, and Cocking 2000). One of the easiest ways for students to practice metacognition during lecture is to ask themselves "why" questions. If they find that they do not understand why the lecture information is correct, they can make a quick notation in their lecture notes. They should investigate the answers to these questions as soon after the lecture as possible.

Step 3: Review and process class notes as soon after class as possible. The rationale behind this step is based on how the human memory system works. When information is first learned, it goes into short-term memory where it stays for a relatively brief period of time. Information that is reviewed within hours of being heard is moved from short-term memory into long-term memory, where it can be used at a later time for problem solving and other tasks. Reviewing and reworking lecture notes shortly after the lecture provides the mechanism for the information to be stored in long-term memory. Spending 10–15 minutes reviewing the notes soon after lecture can substantially improve retention. Additionally, material that is unclear will be immediately discovered, and the student can ask for clarification in a timely manner.

Step 4: Use Intense Study Sessions. Intense Study Sessions are concentrated study sessions of approximately 60 minutes duration. During this short, but focused, study time, a considerable amount of learning can be accomplished. The Intense Study Session consists of four segments, each of which is important for the session to have the maximum effect on learning. The four segments are:

1.	2—5 minutes	Set goals for the next 40 minutes.
2.	35–38 minutes	Work to accomplish the goals that were set. *For example: The goals might include working three problems, pre-reading for two classes, reviewing lecture notes, etc.*
3.	10 minutes	Review what was studied
4.	10 minutes	Take a break

Three or more Intense Study Sessions should be done each day, if possible, with two during daylight hours and one during the evening. Study hours during the day, when the mind is fresher, are usually more efficient than hours spent studying at night. Most students find that The Intense Study Sessions are real "procrastination busters"—providing a means for targeted study sessions that are efficient and "doable." Short, focused sessions are more effective than three- to four-hour study marathons during which there is little meaningful learning accomplished.

Why is it that many students who do well on the homework assignments do poorly on the tests?

The answer to this question lies in *how* these students do their homework assignments. The first question to ask a student in this situation is, "When you do your homework, do you read the problem, flip back through the pages to find an example similar to the problem, and then do the problem based on the example?" Invariably, these students read the homework problem *before* reviewing the information related to the problem, look for an example, and then "work" the homework problem using the example as the model. It is my experience that this one behavior is the reason that a large number students think they have "done the homework problems" but that instead the examples in the book have done the homework problems. Students, however, usually see nothing wrong with this method of doing the homework problems, especially because this is the way they always did their homework in high school, and they did well in their courses there.

A simple strategy that has proved quite effective in extinguishing this habit is found in the following bit of advice that can be given to students:

- When you start the homework, study the information relevant to the problems as if you will be quizzed on it. Treat the examples in the text and in the notes as homework problems.

- Read the problem statement in the example, but do not look at the answer. Work the example problem by using information learned from studying the concepts.

- When you arrive at the answer, compare your answer to the answer that is provided in the example. If your answer is the same as the answer in the example, you have probably done the problem correctly.

- Next look at how the problem was solved in the example to see if your method of solving it was identical to the method used in the example. If it is not, and you find it easier to work the problem *your* way continue to use your method to solve problems of that type. If you prefer the method used in the example, you can begin to use that method in the future. If you find that you have gotten a different answer than the answer that appears in the example, study the example to find the source of your error(s), and correct them.

- Continue to work on the example until you can do the problems without making errors.

- After having worked the examples this way, solve the homework problems without looking at any examples. In fact, it is quite useful to pretend that you are doing these problems for a test or a quiz.

- When finished with all of the problems that will be completed at that time, check all of the answers. Any problems that were not solved correctly should be noted and returned to at a later date after reviewing the relevant material. (Be sure to reread the text and your class notes on this topic; do not look only at example problems.) Some problems may require several attempts before they can be done correctly without consulting any examples.

The process described should be repeated until all problems have been solved correctly without looking back at any examples in the text or in the class notes. When and only when all problems can be solved in this way can students be confident that they can solve any problem that is given. With an appropriate explanation students easily understand the difference in the skill being tested on an exam and the skill they are developing by using the examples to solve the homework problems. The skill being tested is *not* solving a problem by using an example, but rather solving the problem using only the student's effort. However, when they do problems only by consulting examples, the skill they are perfecting is the skill of solving a problem by using an example as a guide. The knowledge of the difference results in students changing the way they approach their homework assignments, and they see fairly immediate increases in their understanding of concepts, problem solving skills, and test performance. Whereas, it would never occur to most students on their own that looking at an example to do their homework is counterproductive to performing well in the course, they are quite receptive to trying this new way of doing the homework because they understand why it works.

What different learning behaviors are needed for success in the laboratory vs. the lecture?

Getting students to abandon rote learning in favor of meaningful learning is sometimes more of a challenge in the laboratory part of the course than in lecture. This is particularly true when the laboratory experiment must be undertaken before the relevant concepts are discussed in lecture. If students have not been exposed to the relevant background knowledge to relate the lab exercise to theoretical concepts, rote learning is the only option. It is therefore quite important that students learn the theoretical basis for experiments before the experiment is undertaken. If this is impossible due to time or scheduling constraints, students should be prepped for the lab by participating in as extensive a discussion of the relevant concepts as possible before they undertake the experiment. As is the case generally, lab quizzes that test meaningful learning of concepts employed in the laboratory setting provide extra incentives for students to take their learning tasks seriously.

What do I do if a student indicates he/she has test anxiety?

Many students who think they suffer from test anxiety are anxious because they do not understand the material well. A few questions to the student to ascertain whether they fully grasp the concepts will help to determine whether anxiety prevented the student from doing well on the exam or whether their lack of conceptual knowledge is at the root of the problem. If lack of understanding is at the root of the problem, utilizing the study strategies mentioned above will most probably solve the problem. If anxiety is causing the poor performance, relaxation techniques, such as deep breathing, can be suggested. In cases of severe anxiety, students should be encouraged to speak with a counselor. When anxiety is extreme, a visit to the university health center is advisable.

How do I get my students to change their behavior if they are not using new study strategies after they've learned them?

Students often need incentives to implement the study strategies. Periodic pop quizzes will promote using the Study Cycle and working the homework problems in a way that facilitates "crutch free" problem solving. You should be aware, however, that paradigm shifts (large changes in beliefs, attitudes and/or actions) do not come easily to students. If they have always earned A's in high school by memorizing information and regurgitating the information for tests and quizzes, they may find it quite difficult to divest themselves of the notion that this is the way to excel in chemistry. Tests that require application of concepts should be given early in the course to demonstrate to students that they must learn the information in a different way than the way in which they are accustomed. It is very important to contrast the results they got when using the old study methods (poor performance on tests), with the results they are now getting (or will start getting) with the new method (improved performance on tests and deeper understanding of the material).

It is also important for instructors to use different teaching strategies that are designed to engage students and help them meaningfully learn material. Group activities embedded in the lecture, and additional techniques discussed in other chapters of this book, are designed to keep students actively engaged with the material.

Administering an informal chemistry study strategies inventory, with predicted course grades based on the results, may motivate some students to use the strategies. The inventory I have used, with significant success, appears in Appendix A. When students see that their final grades are predicated on improving their study skills, they are likely to commit to trying them. Administering the inventory after students have had their first quiz can be very effective in helping them determine the changes they must make in their study habits in order to earn an A in the course. The inventory can be given after the first examination if the exam comes within the first three weeks of class. It is important that students learn the study behavior changes necessary for improvement very early in the course in order to derive the maximum benefit.

How can I get my students to make more effective use of the resources available?

Most colleges and universities have tutoring centers, learning centers, faculty and teaching-assistant office hours, and other resources to help students who need assistance in learning the material. However, most students are reluctant to use the resources because they think they don't need them. They will simply learn the material the night before the test. Many students who do use the resources think that these resources are available to show them how to work problems and/or to re-teach them material that was taught in class. Of course, neither of these is true. The resources exist to help students *think*, not to provide the answers for them. Students need to be taught how to make maximum use of resources. Two important rules for students are:

1. Always attempt to answer your question before you seek help. Explain to the instructor or tutor what you know about the problem, and have her/him comment on your method.

2. After hearing an explanation of a concept or problem, explain the information to the instructor or tutor. That way they can identify any misconceptions you may have about the problem and help you correct them.

How can I get them to change their attitudes about chemistry?

There is no question that attitude plays a large role in achieving success in introductory chemistry. Self-talk, whether positive or negative, has a significant impact on student performance. Many students are unaware of the negative thoughts that go through their minds when they think of chemistry concepts or attempt to solve chemistry problems. Instructors should encourage students to monitor their thoughts and immediately squelch negative ideas as soon as they enter their consciousness. It is very important that students understand that *effort* exerted in studying chemistry (of which the student has control) and not *innate ability* (generally viewed as fixed from birth) will determine how successful a student is in introductory chemistry. When students use the strategies discussed in this chapter and they see improved performance results, a more positive attitude will soon follow.

References

Ausubel, D. P. (1968). *Educational Psychology: A Cognitive View*. New York, NY: Holt, Reinhart and Winston.

Ausubel, D. P., Novak, J., & Hanesian, H. (1978). *Psychology: A Cognitive View*. New York, NY: Holt, Rinehart, and Winston.

Bloom, B. S. (Ed.), Taxonomy of educational objectives. The classification of educational goals. (1956). *Handbook I: Cognitive domain*. New York, NY: David McKay.

Bransford, J. D., Brown, A. L., & Cocking, R. R. (Eds.). *How People Learn: Brain, Mind, Experience, and School*. Washington, DC: National Academy Press.

Bruer, J. T. (2000). *Schools for Thought: A Science of Learning in the Classroom*. Cambridge, MA: MIT Press.

Fisher, K. M., Wandersee, J. H., & Moody, D. E. (2000). *Mapping Biology Knowledge*. Norwell, MA: Kluwer Academic Publishers.

Kean, E., & Middlecamp, C. (1994*). How to Survive (and even Excel in) General Chemsitry*. Columbus, OH: McGraw-Hill.

Robinson, Adam (1993). *What Smart Students Know*. New York, NY: Three Rivers Press.

Web site for the Center for Academic Success at Louisiana State University. www.cas.lsu.edu

Appendix A

Chemistry Study Strategies Inventory

The inventory below lists behaviors that you should exhibit in order to excel in chemistry. Write true or false beside each of the following statements describing the way you study. Use the scoring scale at the end to predict the course grade likely to result from your current study habits.

1.   I always read the lecture material before I go to lecture.

2.   I go over my lecture notes as soon as possible after lecture to rework them and mark problem areas.

3.   I try to work the homework problems without looking at the example problems or my notes from class.

4.   I go to office hours or tutoring regularly to discuss problems on the homework.

5.   I rework all of the homework problems before the test or quiz.

6.   I spend some time studying chemistry at least five days per week (outside of class time).

7.   I make mnemonics for myself to help me remember facts and equations.

8.   I make diagrams or draw mental pictures of the concepts discussed in class.

9.   I participate in a study group where we do homework and quiz ourselves on the material.

10.   I rework all of the quiz and test items I have missed *before* the next class session.

11.   I realize that I can still do well in this class even if I have done poorly on the quizzes and tests up to this point.

The predicted grade for your performance in chemistry is provided below:

Number of True Responses	Predicted Grade
9 or more	A
6 – 8	B
4 – 5	C
2 – 3	D
less than 2	F

Note that you can change your predicted grade at any point by changing your behavior such that more of the statements are true.

What Works and What Doesn't in General Chemistry

John C. Kotz
Chemistry Department
State University of New York—Oneonta

Abstract

This paper outlines current practice in my general chemistry course. Lectures and lecture materials, the operation of recitations, open-book examinations, and the use of an on-line homework system are described. Student surveys show that students most highly value recitations and instructor-provided notes in helping them prepare for examinations. Finally, the surveys reveal the anxieties students feel in coping with the workload in general chemistry and with the quantitative aspects of chemistry.

Biography

Currently I am a University Distinguished Teaching Professor at the State University of New York, College at Oneonta, and the coauthor of *Chemistry & Chemical Reactivity*, a textbook for general chemistry, now published by Thomson/Brooks/Cole in its fifth edition. As well, I am the coauthor of the *General Chemistry Interactive CD-ROM* (now in its third edition) from Thomson/Brooks/Cole. I have been teaching general chemistry and inorganic chemistry at the college level for 37 years. In addition, I have been involved in a leadership role for educational technology at the College at Oneonta for the past 10 years.

After 37 years of teaching general chemistry and writing over 10 books for general and inorganic chemistry, I should know exactly what to do. What is the proper sequence of topics? What is an appropriate level for the material and for students? What is the right mix of conceptual and quantitative material? The questions are clear, but after all of these years, the answers are not always obvious.

Teaching chemistry is like shooting at a moving target. Over the past 37 years the relative balance of topics in general chemistry has changed—thankfully we no longer spend weeks on the gas laws—and new topics such as VSEPR have entered the curriculum. Beginning with the classic general chemistry book by Michael Sienko and Robert Plane in the 1960s, there has been an expanded emphasis on physicochemical aspects, such as quantum chemistry, kinetics, and thermodynamics. In the 1980s there was renewed interest in descriptive chemistry (a trend that has died away), and there is now a desire to have more environmental chemistry, materials chemistry, and biochemistry. And not least of all, the nature of our students has changed. They bring different skills and attitudes now than they did 30 years ago. In general, students seem more passive and less questioning and seem less inclined to read textbooks. However, they often have good, basic computer skills.

The observations about changes in students were confirmed by a study by Levine and Cureton (1998). They state that "higher education is not as central to the lives of today's undergraduates as it was in previous generations." They also contend that "students are behaving like consumers," that "they want convenience," and that students "want high-quality education but are eager for low costs." And finally, on a point relevant to this paper, Levine and Cureton argue that "there is a growing gap between how students learn best and how faculty teach."

Yet another recent article describes changes that have occurred in student study habits over the last decade (Young 2002). This article, in *The Chronicle of Higher Education*, cites a great deal of evidence that students are paying less attention to homework. Young notes that "nineteen percent of full-time freshmen say they spend only 1 to 5 hours per week preparing for classes." The idea that students look on college as a full-time job and that they spend two or three hours outside of class for every hour in class is now an old-fashioned concept.

So, if you are new to teaching general chemistry at a college or university, where do you begin? A best guess is that you will adopt an approach of a favorite instructor from your own college experience. That will likely be effective for some students because your college instructor may be the reason you became interested in chemistry and wanted to become a college professor. But we all must remember that our objective is not to produce clones of ourselves and that, as Levine and Cureton have noted, students have changed.

When you join a college or university chemistry department it is likely that a particular general chemistry book has been used in that program for some time. As a textbook author, I do not examine the books written by my competitors. I am certain they have wonderful ideas in their books, and I do not want to adopt them as my own. Nonetheless, I believe all of the major general chemistry books now in use in the United States are fine books and would serve your students well. However, one book or another may fit your style, and may suit the level of your students, better than another.

Given the background outlined above, this paper will describe current practice in the author's general chemistry course and summarize student feedback. Examples will be drawn from a commercially produced textbook, CD-ROM, and on-line, Web-based homework system (Kotz & Treichel 2003; Vining, Kotz & Harman 2002; On-line Web-Based Learning System 2002).

General chemistry at the College at Oneonta

Because it is important to put current practice in the context of the situation at the College at Oneonta, we begin with a description of that course. The course has a total enrollment of approximately 150 in the first term and 100 in the second term. It is divided into two lecture sections, and the author of this paper teaches one of those sections with an enrollment of about 75 in the first term and 40–50 in the second term. There are three 50-minute lectures per week and one three-hour laboratory. Each laboratory section has a 50-minute recitation meeting. The grading system changes slightly from year to year. For the fall semester of 2002, grades were based on examinations (65%), laboratory and homework (13% each), and class participation (work in lecture and recitation, 9%). It is important to note that attendance in lecture and recitation is not mandatory, but failure in the laboratory (owing to lack of attendance or to not submitting reports) is grounds for failure in the course, regardless of the record in other areas of the course.

Student characteristics. As a background to the data presented below, we obtained the following information from our students in September 2002 (86% reporting).

Table 1. Student demographics

- 39% freshmen, 25% sophomores, 21% juniors, and 15% seniors
- 95% are 23 years old or younger
- 52% women
- Virtually all are residential students
- 7% had no previous exposure to chemistry

This demographic information is evidence for the considerable changes that have occurred in the past 30 years. Whereas the course used to be almost exclusively first-year students, we now have students at all stages in their college career. Another interesting and important aspect of our enrollment is the gender balance. Whereas the course was largely male in years past, we now have a slight predominance of women. This reflects the changing gender balance in our college, in which 60 percent of the students are women. This is true in many universities and colleges in the United States and is a trend that will surely change the nature of our society, economy, and government in the years to come.

The data in tables 2 through 7 come from a voluntary survey completed by 43 percent of the students in the lecture section in the first month of the course in the fall of 2002. (The survey is part of the on-line homework system.) It seems likely that the same survey in another public, four-year, residential college would give roughly the same results.

Table 2. Student career plans

- About 55% planned majors in the biological sciences or were aiming for a career in the health professions.

- About 25% of the students were in geology, engineering, and physics.

- The remainder were in a broad range of curricula, including science education, environmental studies, and nutrition.

- Very few students began our program as chemistry majors.

The predominance of students in the biological sciences is clearly a national trend. It was recently reported that graduate enrollment in the biological sciences increased by 13.3 percent over the decade of the 1990s, whereas it has declined in chemistry (–4.9%) and in physics (–21.6%) (*Chemical & Engineering News* 2002).

Another question indicated that our students—who are generally majoring in biology, geology, human ecology, and pre-engineering—were interested in chemistry. Nonetheless, they are quite concerned about workload and understanding the material.

Table 3. Self-reported level of interest in chemistry

Very high	2%
High	49%
Medium	40%
Low	9%
Very low	0%

Table 4. Students level of concern regarding performance

Area of concern	Hi	Med	Low
Balancing workload	67%	30%	3%
Understanding concepts	63	28	8
Understanding lectures	47	40	13
Doing quantitative work	55	33	12
Staying motivated	35	44	11
Performing on exams	3	79	18

The lecture. Professor G. Farrington, a chemist and now president of Lehigh University, recently published an article on educational technology in undergraduate education (1999). Among the many interesting statements in the article, he said that "the lecture may actually be mostly a waste of everyone's time, but it is a ritual that is followed out of habit (the faculty) or out of fear of missing something that might be on the exam (the students)." In spite of this, many chemistry instructors put considerable effort into presenting what they hope will be effective lectures, and this has certainly been the case in our department.

We have developed computer-based materials and methods, and some are described below.[1] This has been done in part in the belief that it can lead to more effective learning. A study just published by the National Research Council states that "we envision a future, enabled by information technology and driven by learner-demand, in which two of the major (and taken-for-granted) ways of organizing undergraduate learning will recede in importance: the 55-minute classroom lecture and the common reading list. That digital future will challenge faculty to design technology-based experiences based primarily on interactive, collaborative learning. ... They may be far more effective, particularly when provided through a media-rich environment." (*Preparing for the Revolution* 2002).

Using PowerPoint. For the past 10 years the general chemistry lectures at Oneonta have been done using Microsoft PowerPoint. (The best student in the class recently asked how professors taught before the days of PowerPoint.) Over 1200 slides have been prepared and revised many times during this period. A digital library of visual materials has been accumulated, and the animations and videos from the CD-ROM in use (Vining et al. 2002) are imbedded in the slides.

In a typical lecture a topic is introduced using one or more PowerPoint slides containing relevant images, often with a live demonstration as well. The topic is usually further developed on the chalkboard. The lecture emphatically does not consist simply of students viewing a sequence of slides and taking notes from the slides.

One general theme of the lectures, and of the slides, is the triangular matrix of concepts (Gabel 1999; Johnstone 1991). This is the interrelation of macroscopic observations, the symbolic notation chemists use to describe these observations (element symbols, chemical equations), and the view, typical of chemists, of concepts at the atomic and molecular level (Figure 1). James Birk says that chemistry courses typically emphasize the interplay between the macroscopic and symbolic (personal communication). The rapid development of computer technology, and advances in chemistry in recent decades, however, allows us to display what we believe occurs at the atomic and molecular level. Birk states that while the "comfort zone" for students is the macroscopic level, and they sometimes struggle to translate that to symbols, chemists work on all three levels. It is this difference in viewpoint that can make communication between student and instructor difficult. Nonetheless, a full understanding requires a synthesis of these viewpoints, and so this is the emphasis of our lectures at Oneonta.

Figure 1. The triangular matrix of concepts (Kotz & Treichel 2003).

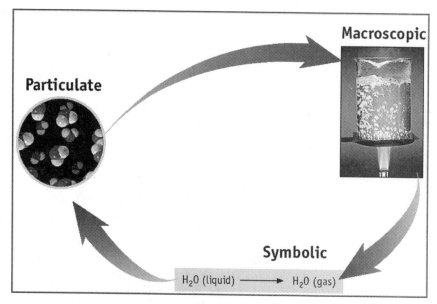

For technology to be effective, lecture rooms need to be properly equipped. Our lecture room for chemistry has two computers (a PC and a Macintosh), a VCR, a laser disc player, and an excellent sound system. There are two LCD projectors—one for the computer output and another to show videotapes or video discs.

There is an overhead projector, and blackboards cover the front of the room. Finally, and most important, the lighting in the room is placed so that the LCD projector images are bright and yet there is enough light for students to take notes.

Supporting materials for lectures. Students in our course are encouraged to come to lecture to absorb the concepts introduced and to rely on the textbook for details. Nonetheless, students want to take notes. To accommodate this desire, and to ensure that they have accurate notes, we provide printed copies of the key PowerPoint slides at the beginning of each major topic. For each lecture the peripheral or introductory slides are removed from a copy of the file. Then, on the key slides, important pieces of information are removed. What remains are the most important slides, these slides containing data for problem solving (but not the problem solution), molecular structures that we wish students to see, important definitions, and other key points. During the lecture students can then concentrate on the most important points rather than writing down all of the points on a slide.

Anyone who has given lectures in universities will know that student attention begins to wane after 30 minutes or so. Thus, we often perform demonstrations at about this point (see below), or we have a worksheet prepared. The worksheets, which have a problem to be solved or statements to be completed, are handed out, and students are asked to work with their neighbors on the solution. These worksheets, which generally take about 5 minutes of lecture time, are collected after the lecture. Students receive a few points in their "class participation" grade (9% of the course grade).[2] These worksheets serve to keep students on task during lecture, give them some immediate practice, and are a way of taking attendance.

Demonstrations. Demonstrations of chemical reactions and phenomena in lecture are extremely important to illustrate chemical principles, and we try to do at least one in each lecture. Loretta Jones has commented that "images and sounds are how we first learn about the world. They are powerful ways of communicating information" (1993). Demonstrations, as well as the laboratory, convey the sights and sounds of chemistry. Students from previous years often comment on their favorite demonstrations.

The demonstrations we do are not elaborate, take only a few minutes, and are usually targeted to illustrate a single concept. As our college does not have a person to set up demonstrations, we keep supplies and solutions on a shelf in the stock room. Only 5–10 minutes are needed to pull together the necesssary chemicals and apparatus.[3]

Appropriate demonstrations can often be found in the instructor's manual that accompanies general chemistry textbooks. In addition, there are several series of books that have detailed directions (Shakhashiri 1992).

If local conditions do not allow for live demonstrations, the *Journal of Chemical Education: Software* has videotapes, CD-ROMs, and laser discs of demonstrations that would be unsafe to perform in a lecture setting or that require extensive setups (http://jchemed.chem.wisc.edu).

Weekly recitation. Student feedback strongly suggests that the weekly recitation is a valuable part of the course. Our laboratory sections are generally capped at 20 students, although we occasionally allow up to 24 students. Each section meets for one additional hour each week to practice the material from the previous week's lecture.

For a number of years the practice was to assign homework and then to expect students to ask questions about that homework in recitation. As the years went by, students seemed less diligent about homework, and recitation attendance declined (Young 2002). When asked, the students said they did not come to recitation because they had not done the work and would be embarrassed when asked about it.

To rectify this situation, we now hold recitations in the department computer laboratory. The students are given a worksheet consisting of questions and problems. Each set of questions or problems has a reference to a screen on the CD-ROM in use (Vining et al. 2002). There they can see a solved problem, do a tutorial or exercise, simulate an experiment, or read background information. We explicitly ask students to work together in groups of 2 or 3. The instructor then works individually with students or with small groups.

Periodically the entire class discusses answers. The advantage of this approach is that students who are too reluctant to ask questions in an open forum will readily ask for help from their fellow students or from the instructor. The instructor can also see when a student is struggling. And finally, students practice the material on a regular basis.

The students earn credit toward their "participation" grade by handing in the worksheet at the end of class.[2] The sheets are not graded, but the answers are posted and the sheets are returned to the students for their use in studying for exams.

This approach requires a facility with 10–12 computers and seating and work space for 20 students or so. Although the author of this paper instructs all of his recitations each week (four of them), this approach can work with multiple instructors in an institution of any size. It should be especially suited to situations involving graduate teaching assistants.

Our experience with this approach to recitation has been positive. It is almost always the case that the students have to be reminded to leave when the class hour is over. Furthermore, attendance at recitation now exceeds 90 percent.

Homework. Homework has traditionally been assigned because students must practice the material. In our course students are asked to work on 10–15 textbook questions/problems per week, and a few of these are used verbatim on examinations. Also in our case, the homework is not graded because of the time required to do so.

We believe there is now a better way to handle homework. We use a commercially available, on-line, Web-based homework (On-line Web-Based Learning System 2002). This system, which was developed over a number of years at the University of Massachusetts–Amherst, consists of units of questions, along with tutorial modules, covering virtually all of the topics in general chemistry. Many of the questions are numerical, but there are conceptual questions, questions asking the student to write net ionic equations, and questions to be answered after observing the simulation of an experiment. (Many of the simulations and tutorials use the same materials developed for the CD-ROM.)

Each homework unit consists of one to six questions on a topic. Each question is generated from a database of questions and data. For example, a student may be asked to calculate the amount of substance in 15 g of iron(III) oxide. The quantity of material (15 g) and the compound [iron(III) oxide] are generated for the question, and each student will see a different set of information. Regardless of whether the student answers the question correctly or not, extensive feedback is provided outlining the answer. Students can try the question a pre-set number of times, but each time the quantity and compound will be different.

The on-line homework system allows one to set up a homework assignment to become available at a particular date and time, and to turn off at a time and date. (This can be overridden for individual students in case they cannot complete the assignment on time for some reason.) The instructor can also see each student's progress, the answers they have submitted, and the time they have spent. A built-in e-mail system enables students to communicate quickly with the instructor.

As outlined in the student feedback section below, the on-line homework system has been successful in our course. Although students find it a great deal of work—as they should for homework—they generally agree it is worthwhile. And, not surprisingly, there is a good correlation between their progress in the on-line homework system and their examination grades. (See the Student Feedback section below.)

The fact that the on-line homework system provides feedback on graded work and is a secure system means that we can use it as a significant portion of the course grade (13%).

Other course materials. Computer technology has added a valuable dimension to teaching and learning (*Preparing for the Revolution* 2002),[1] but it has also added considerable work for faculty. Our course has a website that contains all of the lecture and laboratory schedules, policy statements, weekly announcements, and laboratory experiments, as well as pdf files of all of the PowerPoint lecture notes, previous examinations, and a test bank of review questions.

Our college uses CourseInfo's Blackboard™. Much of our course information is also contained within this shell, and, as it is password protected, we can also list student grades as well as homework answers and other proprietary materials that we do not want on the open World Wide Web.

Examinations. There are three preliminary examinations (100 points each) and a comprehensive final examination (150 points) each semester. (Often in the fall semester there has been a brief, introductory examination worth many fewer points. This test helps freshmen in particular get a foretaste of the types of examinations given in the course.) Examinations account for 65 percent of the final grade.

The examinations consist of many types of questions: multiple choice, true-false, fill-in's, essays, and problems to be worked out. On occasion, there have been "visual" questions. Students are asked to watch a live or taped demonstration and are then asked a series of questions. Examinations are given in the evening and students have up to two hours to complete the exam. (This allows us to give more thorough examinations, and it has eliminated undue text anxiety.)

I believe that students have not been trained to use books as learning tools, and some do not value books as a primary learning resource. They have been trained to take notes in class and then to use those notes to prepare for examinations. Some ignore textbooks, which, in general chemistry, are generally excellent resources. (See the Student Feedback section below.) Because class notes represent only an outline of the material (and can be inaccurate), students replying on class notes may have only a superficial understanding at best.

To counter this trend, and to emphasize the importance of the textbook in their learning, *all examinations except for the first one of the year, are open-book.* This enables the instructor to ask more searching questions, and it also requires that students know where to find information in the book. The usual constants and similar information are not supplied on the examination because they are found in the textbook. Thus, students treat the book as many professional chemists use books, as an information source.

Anecdotal information from students indicates that they understand that the trade-off for open book examinations is that the exams are more difficult. (This is in fact explained to them before the first open-book examination.) They also know that an open-book exam does not mean that they do not have to study. The best students often do not open the book except to find a constant. For the weaker students, it has further reduced test anxiety. Finally, we believe it has achieved our goal: students begin to understand the value of their textbook.

Laboratory. The laboratory program in our college is typical of many. We have attempted to develop new experiments that use modern instrumentation, but this is a work in progress. The laboratory is worth 13 percent of the final grade in our course.

Student feedback. The on-line homework system provides two surveys. Our students in General Chemistry I (43 out of 75) voluntarily completed one of these surveys during the first month of the fall 2002 semester. The end-of-year survey was completed by the General Chemistry II class in May 2002 (after having had one full year of general chemistry). We report below some of the information from these surveys.

Surveys at the beginning of the course and at mid-semester

Table 5: Beginning of the course. Based on their experience in other science courses, students were asked what method or approach they find most effective in learning a new concept.

Method/Approach	Not effective	Moderately effective	Very effective
Visual representations	0%	50%	50%
Problem solving	4	44	51
Oral descriptions	7	56	37
Computer-based tools	12	53	35
Hands-on experience	0	28	72
Working 1:1 with instructor	2	19	80
Reading the textbook or other written material	23	67	9

These data confirm our sense that students at our public university do not rely on books as primary learning tools. There may be several reasons for this. First, their experience in secondary schools with books was not positive, perhaps owing to the fact that public high schools have a difficult time acquiring the latest textbooks. Second, there are great demands on our students' time, both real and imagined. Studying from notes is perceived to be more efficient.

Another part of these data that should give us pause is the report of the great effectiveness of problem solving. This is likely a reflection of the belief that there is an emphasis in general chemistry on quantitative work with a smaller emphasis on conceptual learning.

Table 6: Beginning of the course. Report on the extent to which students rely on various learning resources in similar courses. (Where the total is not 100%, the answer was "not relevant.")

Method/Approach	Not at all	Moderate extent	Great extent
In-class lectures	5%	42%	53%
In-class problem solving	7	56	37
In-class interactive discussions	7	65	28
CD/Web site accompanying text	26	60	11
Course Web site	26	56	14
Instructor-provided notes	0	36	65
On-line homework	19	94	30
Written homework	16	56	21
Recitation sections	9	70	19
Study groups with peers	23	47	23
Extra help from instructor	30	21	40
Textbook	21	65	14

Again we note the lower value placed on textbooks in other, similar courses.

Table 7: Beginning of the course. Report on their perceived confidence to carry out the learning activities in the course. (Where the total is not 100%, the answer was "not relevant.")

Task	Not confident	Somewhat confident	Very confident
Calculate answers to problems	16%	49%	35%
Understand underlying concepts	7	60	33
Understand chemical terminology	7	67	26

These data show that they are not too confident in their ability to solve problems, which parallels their report that in-class problem solving is important to them.

Other information collected in the initial survey included their expected grades. A grade of A was expected by 44%, and 49% expected a B. This is of course very far from the grade distribution at the end of the course. The grade distribution in the fall of 2002 is not unusual: 12.6% A and A-; 35.2% B+, B, and B-; 29.6% C+, C, and C-; 14.1% D+, D, and D-; and 6% E. (In each of the grade ranges, there were more grades in the minus category than in the plus category. This distribution also reflects our grading system in which students can do rather poorly on exams but at least pass the course with a C or D.)

The students also reported that they expected to spend an average of 7.7 hours per week on the course (with a range of 2 to 30 hours!). A survey at the end of the course indicates that this is somewhat greater than the time actually spent.

After considering the data in Tables 5 and 6, we decided to survey the students on their opinions just after mid-semester. This survey was done in class, and 61 of 71 students participated. The survey reflects their opinions after more experience in the course.[4, 5]

Table 8: Mid-semester. Students were asked to rate the relative value of various resources for learning chemistry.

Resource	Not Valuable	Some Value	Valuable	Very Valuable	Extremely Valuable
Lecture	2%	16%	41%	38%	3%
Recitation	0	11	26	44	19
Laboratory	0	31	39	27	3
Textbook	5	33	38	15	7
CD-ROM	18	22	47	10	3
On-line homework	6	25	31	23	15
Review exams	0	2	22	35	42

Recitations and review exams were clearly the most valued of the resources available. (The review exams are generally the exams from the previous year, with some added questions. Students find it helps them focus their studying. Nonetheless, they invariably comment that "last year's exam was much easier than this year's exam!"). In all other categories the largest percentage of students indicated the resource was "valuable." The textbook and CD-ROM were slightly skewed to the less valuable side, whereas the lecture was skewed to the more valuable side (which may be due to the availability of PowerPoint note outlines). Opinions about the value of the on-line homework system was more evenly distributed.[5]

Surveys at the end of the course. At the end of the course in the spring of 2002, one question on the voluntary survey asked students if they felt they had met their goal in terms of a grade for the course. Of 25 students (42 enrolled), nine students said they had, seven had not, and nine did not yet know. What, they were asked, was the most important barrier to meeting their goal?

Table 9: Barriers to achievement. (Numbers below are numbers of replies out of 25 total replies.)

7	Balancing the workload for the course with other class-related work
4	Balancing workload for the course with commitments outside of class work
4	Performing well on exams
3	Understanding the concepts presented in the course
3	Understanding the materials presented in lectures
3	Staying motivated
1	Had no significant problems in the class

(Students were also asked for the second and third most important barrier to meeting their goals. Performance on exams grew in importance.)

With regard to questions of the barrier type, and to the questions that follow, another question asked about their attendance at lectures. Of the 25 students responding, 12 said they always attended, and 11 said they frequently attended. One each stated they sometimes or rarely attended lectures. From observing the attendance over the year, this is an accurate assessment.

A number of questions probed the usefulness of the on-line homework system. The answers were important to us, as we needed to decide if we were to continue the use of the system for the 2002–2003 academic year.[5]

Table 10: Usefulness/effectiveness of on-line homework system. (The numbers below are number of replies out of the 25 students who completed the survey.)

Question	Strongly disagree	Moderately disagree	Neutral	Moderately agree	Strongly agree
Useful learning tool	1	4	5	6	9
Helped to learn from mistakes	1	2	4	12	6
Useful to prepare for exams	2	3	2	8	10

Another indication of the effectiveness of on-line system—which is really an indication of the effectiveness of doing homework—is the correlation between examination grades and homework grades.

Table 11: Correlation between average examination grade (after two exams) and on-line homework scores in fall 2001.

Exam Grade	% of Group with > 55% of homework points completed	% of Group with <55% of homework points completed
A	63	37
B	72	28
C	60	40
D	43	57
D–	38	62

As an instructor, these results are not a surprise. They are, however, a valuable result to show to students.

Perhaps the most interesting question in the end-of-year survey was the activity on which students reported they relied most in learning chemistry.

Table 12: Importance of various activities.

Activity	% Response
Lecture	39
Reading textbook	15
On-line homework	15
Notes provided by instructor	11
Discussion sections	8
Extra help from instructor	8
Written homework	4
Study groups	4

The survey also asked students to estimate the time spent on the on-line homework and on reading the textbook and how much total study time they allocated.

Table 13: Time for on-line homework and the textbook and total study time per week. (The numbers that follow are number of replies. 26 students out of 42 responded.)

Time	Homework	Textbook	Total time studying
More than 6 hours	0	0	2
4–6 hours	3	2	7
2–4 hours	10	4	10
1–2 hours	9	8	4
Less than 1 hour	0	11	2

One question in the survey asked if they felt comfortable applying what they learned in general chemistry in future courses. Six students (of 24) strongly agreed, 14 moderately agreed, 3 were neutral on the question, and 1 moderately disagreed. The majority of the students leave the course believing they have learned useful concepts that they can carry over to future work.

Finally, in another survey, students were asked (on the usual five-point scale) for their degree of agreement on some of the practices in the course.

Table 14: Degree of agreement on various practices in the course.

Subject/Activity	% who agree or strongly agree
Continue open-book exams	94%
Have more recitations, fewer lectures	71%
Molecular models in the textbook are useful	61%
Molecular models in PowerPoint lecture notes are useful	74%
Animations/videos in PowerPoint lecture notes are useful	94%
The outlines of the PowerPoint notes are useful	77%

In a survey completed at the end of the academic year several years ago, a student made the comment that "the use of multimedia clarifies ideas that seem to be very abstract. My retention of material is at a much higher level than in other classes." The most interesting aspect of this comment is that the student perceived that our approach led to a greater "retention of material." This may only be a perception (and if so, may give the student confidence to perform well in subsequent courses). Or, it may be true and so represents a valuable outcome of our approach. In any event, this is an outcome that may be testable by a person skilled in educational research.

Summary and conclusions

The pedagogical practice in our general chemistry course is not too different from that followed in many U.S. universities. Based on student surveys, we can state the following general conclusions with some confidence:

Textbooks. Students at our college do not regard textbooks as the primary learning resource. Better textbook design and better correlation with other learning resources (CD-ROMs and on-line homework and tutorial systems) may enhance the value of the book in the eyes of students.[5]

Lectures and recitations. Students are still attuned to learning material in the long-standing tradition of lectures. They now expect, however, that these lectures be accompanied by PowerPoint lecture notes (which include animations, videos, molecular models). They find instructor-provided notes to be especially useful as a learning resource. Students are also much in favor of recitations to support the lectures, especially when these involve group work and interactive computer resources.[6]

On-line homework system. While students find it time-consuming, there is general agreement that the on-line homework system we use is valuable. Students value experiences for which they get credit. Thus, as they get a significant portion of the course credit for doing homework through the on-line system, they use the system and find it helps them perform better on examinations. [5]

Open-book examinations. Our survey shows a high degree of acceptance of open-book exams even though students are aware that these exams may be more difficult than the traditional closed-book exams.

In all the years the author has taught general chemistry, the course has never been the same. Each year we try to answer the same questions. How do we keep students interested and even get them excited? How do we help students with a variety of learning styles, backgrounds, interests, and abilities? How do we get them to learn more effectively and have more than a superficial understanding of chemistry? The methods outlined here seem effective to a degree. Student-centered, constructive approaches are clearly the answer, but they must be implemented within the time and resouces we have available, must be accepted by the students, and the instructor must be comfortable using them. It is likely there is no one approach effective for all students or for all instructors. We can only make progress toward our goal, shifting our methods to best suit the needs of our students.

References

Birk, J. Arizona State University, private communication.

Chemical & Engineering News (2002 October 28), p. 48.

Farrington, G. (1999). The new technologies and the future of residential undergraduate education. In *Dancing with the Devil—Information Technology and the New Competition in Higher Education*. San Francisco: Jossey-Bass Publishers.

Gabel, D. J. (1999). Improving teaching and learning through chemistry education research: A look to the future. *Journal of Chemical Education, 76*, 548–554.

Johnstone, A. H. (1991). *Journal of Computer Assisted Learning, 7*, 75.

Jones, L. L. (1993) *Campus Tech,* Spring, p. 27.

Kotz, J. C., & Treichel, P. M. (2003). *Chemistry and Chemical Reactivity* (5th edition). Belmont, CA: Thomson/Brooks/Cole.

Levine, A., & Cureton, J. S. (1998). Collegiate Life—An Obituary. *Change*, May/June, 13ff.

Owl, an On-line Web-based Learning System. (2002). Belmont, CA: Thomson/Brooks/Cole.

Preparing for the Revolution—Information Technology and the Future of the Research University. (2002). National Research Council of the National Academies, National Academies Press, www.nap.edu.

Shakhashiri, B. Z. (1992). *Chemical Demonstrations: a Handbook for Teachers of Chemistry* (Volume 4). Madison, WI: University of Wisconsin Press.

Vining, W. J., Kotz, J. C., & Harman, P. (2002). *General Chemistry Interactive CD-ROM* (Version 3.0). Belmont, CA: Thomson/Brooks/Cole.

Young, J. R. (2002). Homework? What homework? *The Chronicle of Higher Education*, December 6, A35.

Footnotes

1. Many of the features of this course are also discussed in the following article: Kotz, J. C. (1999) "Computer-Enhanced Chemistry," published in *Chem NZ*, a New Zealand Institute of Chemistry publication, Number 76, August, pp. 31–36.

2. Students receive 3 points for submitting a worksheet done in recitation or lecture. They can earn up to 65 points for this work as a "participation grade" in a total of 750 for the course. (More than 65 points worth of work is given, but 65 is the maximum that can be earned.)

3. Our lecture room has neither running water nor gas. Water is not a major problem, and a butane camping stove serves well as a burner. Many demonstrations of reactions can be done in shallow glass dishes on an overhead projector. Finally, many campuses have video cameras that can be used to project images of demonstrations through an LCD projector.

4. A very similar survey was done at the University of Wisconsin–Madison by Paul M. Treichel where the same textbook is used. In that course (235 responses for 335 students), 60 percent rated the textbook as "very" or "extremely valuable." The Wisconsin survey had similar results to ours for the lecture, whereas our students rated the recitation and laboratory somewhat more valuable than the Wisconsin students.

5. This paper was ready for press at the end of the 2002–2003 academic year. A survey identical to Table 8 was repeated at the end of the year. There was a significant shift of opinion to "extremely valuable" for the recitation. Also, 85 percent now rated the textbook as valuable, very valuable, or extremely valuable. Finally, the on-line homework system was rated by 70 percent as valuable, very valuable, or extremely valuable.

6. In the spring term, 2003, we added "personal response devices" to the lecture. This was successful and will definitely be continued in the 2003–2004 academic year. (As an example of such devices, see http://www.educue.com/.)

10

Innovations in Lecture: Some Cases of Student and Faculty Response

Norbert Pienta
Department of Chemistry
University of Iowa

Abstract

Innovations or changes in the content or delivery of introductory courses can take many forms. These can range from the introduction of demonstrations or group activities in a classroom to the revision of a curriculum. New faculty members may have enthusiasm and a desire to have an impact by introducing some feature that they believe will improve student learning. This chapter outlines several cases of change or innovation in lecture classes and some outcomes from the students and faculty colleagues. Specific examples include the use of outside readings on the Internet, homework quizzes using a course-management system such as WebCT, electronic homework, and course redesign (i.e. curricular changes) at two institutions. For example, students in a course for non-science majors were very positive about WebCT-based quizzes covering course readings; these assessments provided a contribution to students' grades that were an alternative to multiple choice exams. The students completed an average of 10.7 out of 12 quizzes and did so with an average score of 78 percent. However, students in a general chemistry course were not enthusiastic about "electronic" homework, apparently because they were confronted by their shortcomings in a direct manner (by an "inanimate" object, the computer), were required to make a serious time commitment, and often considered this homework as more of an assessment than a skill-building activity. Over a five-semester span, students completed 50 to 65 percent of the required homework assignments for the semester. They reported spending an average of 4.0 hours per week on the homework (out of a total of 5.6 hours per week on outside class activities) but gave this aspect of the course low marks among all the course components that they felt helped them learn. Besides the intended change in content or pedagogy, an instructor often will need to "support" the innovation with additional effort. For example, the use of technology often involves questions about how to use it that extend beyond the printed instructions or availability of IT on campus. A manifestation of this is the number of e-mails to which an instructor must respond. In the courses that implemented some of these new methodologies, the average number of e-mails per student was 50 to 100 percent higher than in comparable ones without these changes; in courses with enrollments of 400 students, the additional e-mails can be a substantial time investment. A course redesign that reintegrated the laboratories with the lecture/discussion portions and made some pedagogical changes to increase student participation has been widely accepted by students and faculty; another redesign in which traditional lectures were replaced by a case-study approach to the organization of the content met student resistance. Some of the factors that led to the different outcomes are discussed.

Biography

I have been an associate professor and director of undergraduate studies at the University of Iowa since 1999. My scholarship is in chemical education, and I have recently implemented major changes in the general chemistry curriculum, including the reintegration of the laboratory with lectures that include a more active student role and discussions conducted in a cooperative learning environment. I started my academic career in 1980 at the University of Arkansas, Fayetteville, teaching organic chemistry and conducting research in photochemistry and other physical organic topics. In 1989 I moved to my Ph.D. alma mater, the University of North Carolina at Chapel Hill, where I was director of laboratories. In that role I developed new experiments and curricula for all the chemistry laboratory courses. I have been actively involved in the production and use of interactive multimedia materials, including tutorials, study guides, and self-assessment materials. I have been changing things (or trying to fix them) all of my academic career.

What is an 'innovation' in a lecture class?

If you attend Division of Chemical Education technical sessions at American Chemical Society meetings or read the *Journal of Chemical Education* or the *Chemical Educator* on a regular basis, you are bound to get inspired to try something new in a lecture course. It is beyond the scope of this chapter to list them all, but some categories and examples include:

- presentation technology: chalk or whiteboard, overheads, PowerPoint; personal response devices, PDAs, and laptop computers

- course-management: WebCT, Blackboard, local, or publisher-generated management systems

- cooperative learning: study groups, ConcepTests (Mazur 1997; ConcepTest 2002)

- demonstrations: real (Shakhashiri 1983, 1985, 1989, 1992; Summerlin & Ealy 1988; Summerlin, Borgford & Ealy 1988; Borgford & Summerlin 1988) or virtual (Computer Programs 2002)

- self-assessment and skill-building: PHGradeAssist, Mastering Chemistry, OWL, ChemSkillBuilder, CAPA, WebAssign

- writing assignments in large classes (Calibrated Peer Review 2002)

- interactive multimedia: textbook CD-ROM, Web sites, tutorials; for an Internet-based math tutorial, see Pienta (2001)

Students generally enroll in a course only once, and they are not likely to recognize a pedagogical or content change in the course. The "grapevine" (i.e. student-student interchange) represents a form of communication among those who completed a course and students who are about to begin the class. It also may be a very active form of interaction among students enrolled in the class. As a result, students in your class may or may not know about expectations or changes relative to the past or those compared with your colleagues who teach the same course. If you want students to know something about your expectations or course design, then tell them. The course syllabus is a very effective mechanism by which expectations can be communicated.

A change or innovation is more likely to be recognized by one's faculty colleagues. You might wonder then if you should seek the advice of a teaching mentor who may have tried a variety of approaches and can help predict some of the potential outcomes. Alternatively, one can be faced with a colleague who has confused longevity with excellence; doing something for 30 years may not be the best practice. It is likely that new faculty will encounter a set of colleagues who represent a wide range of teaching experiences. The next issues to consider are what scope of innovation is appropriate and what kind of effort it will take to support these changes in your classes.

What types of changes are appropriate for a new faculty member?

Chemists find themselves in academic settings that define a wide range in expectations, from a research university to a community college. A person in either of these settings will be very busy and must consider how to wisely use the time dedicated to teaching. According to some polls, a faculty member is likely to spend more than 55 hours per week on all activities. A typical new faculty member is likely to arrive without any prepared course content and with very little experience in teaching. Even the basics will take time to prepare. The best general advice about innovations is to start conservatively and build or add items to the course during a semester. A complete collection of demonstrations, weekly quizzes using WebCT, and a "molecule of the week" will quickly become overwhelming if you don't even have lecture notes. Designing or implementing a course that is new to a curriculum is not appropriate for the first several years unless you really have an idea about what you are getting yourself into.

Independent of the extent to which individual colleagues are innovative or never change, all of them can give you valuable information about what teaching a course entails at your institution, how long those activities take in and out of class, and what resources are available at your school. The subsequent sections present some actual cases involving change and the results that they elicited from students and colleagues.

What kinds of behaviors and outcomes should I expect from students?

Changes in courses, particularly large enrollment courses described in subsequent sections, were made to enhance student participation, to provide a modern context for the content, to more accurately assess student learning, or to change the content delivery and pedagogy in order to optimize student learning. These changes appear in three courses, two of which the author taught and a third from another university. The first is a one-semester course for non-science majors in which Internet-based readings supplemented the text and weekly homework quizzes on all course reading assignments utilized the course-management system: WebCT. The second examples come from a traditional two-semester general chemistry sequence in which Web-based self-assessment assignments were used as graded homework and in which a major curriculum redesign has been implemented. The latter involves reintegration of the laboratories and a refocus of activities to be student oriented (i.e. cooperative learning in discussion sections and guided inquiry in the lab experiments). The last case summarizes an attempt to dramatically shift a general chemistry course at Duke University from traditional lectures to case studies based on state-of-the-art scientific content taught by a team of six instructors. Subsequent sections describe a change or innovation and provide student outcomes and opinions.

A course for non-science majors

The course for non-science majors, "Technology and Society," is popular and suffers from an enrollment of 400 students per semester, which is the capacity of the lecture room. About 65 percent of the class were entering students in the fall of 2000 and 2001. The course has used a textbook that focuses on learning chemistry in the context of societal issues (Stanitski, Eubanks, Middlecamp & Pienta 2003). In the past, the assessment had been limited to hour exams and the content in the textbook. The course does not convene discussion sections, although teaching assistants are available for grading. Virtually all of the students in the class had completed a high school chemistry course before taking this one but professed a lack of interest (or worse) in mathematics and performing calculations.

Internet-based readings to supplement a textbook. One of the goals in the course was to get students to be able to read critically about science and chemistry. They should learn enough introductory chemistry to understand the principles and applications and have some comfort with numbers, measurements, and simple calculations. For each chapter, three short readings from the national press were assigned. This was limited to Internet-based sites (e.g., CNN, *The New York Times*, *Los Angeles Times*). As a result, reading assignments are easily implemented, provide up-to-date examples, and are not time intensive.

Of the approximately 30 citations, only one URL changed over the course of the semester. (That is not likely to be true if one uses the same sites over a several year period.) All of the news service or newpaper Web sites have archives, so an article may remain available even though its URL citation may change. Furthermore, the variety of potential Web sites makes it possible to give examples of many aspects. For example, an article about "detoxifying" air in one's living space using plants was cited in the *National Enquirer*. Given the reputation of this tabloid, students were forced to think about the credibility of the reporting. (That article sounded credible, but it required a quick calculation. To accomplish effective detoxification of the air, one must have more than 50 large plants in a small apartment!) To encourage the reading of these articles and the textbook chapters, weekly homework quizzes were assigned using WebCT. The first homework quiz is ALWAYS about the course syllabus and Web site; this is an effective practice and is suggested to all new instructors.

Homework on the Internet using WebCT. The course-management system, WebCT, contains a quiz or survey feature. The students' weekly assignment was to complete a four- or five-question quiz using WebCT. The total credit for the homework over the semester was equal to the value of an hour exam. The WebCT system will randomly select a question out of a defined set so every week four- or five- question sets comprised of two to four questions each were generated for WebCT delivery. The format of most of these was matching or multiple choice. The management system also supports calculation problems with algorithmic generation of variables in which one can define a formula and the range of the variables. WebCT allows the instructor to assign a starting and finishing time. Students had at least one week to complete the assignment. The system also allows multiple attempts and has numerous grading options (e.g., highest score, average score, score on first attempt). Students in this course each were given two attempts at the quiz, and the higher score was recorded.

Several weeks into the semester an attempt was made to "wean" the students off the two tries for each quiz. It was clear that the students found security in having the two tries. (A poll in class indicated that > 85 percent wanted them.) It was possible to detect that some students used the first try to determine the nature of the questions, a preview. One of the pieces of information that the course-management system provides for each quiz is the duration of the students' attempts. Thus, a quiz that was completed in one–two minutes was clearly not a serious effort especially since it was often followed immediately by the second try, which took 10–20 minutes. Early in the semester, several students expressed dismay that the second attempt at a quiz didn't have questions identical to the first. Even with 400 students and only two to four questions per set, most students thought that the question test bank was very large.

In fall 2000 the average number of quizzes taken by the class was 10.7 out of 12. All quizzes were taken by 62 percent of the class, while only 6 percent took five or fewer. The average quiz score was 78 percent. The purpose of the quizzes was not to test conceptual understanding but mostly to keep students on task with the reading in the course. Comments on the instructor evaluation and anecdotal feedback both suggested that the quizzes were a popular assessment alternative to hour exams.

The author was the course instructor for two consecutive fall semesters. Some changes were made to the Internet-based readings and to some of the related homework questions. Based on those two offerings, the course currently contains 151 questions in 50 question sets (4 calculation, 17 matching, and 29 multiple choice) for 12 homework quizzes. For the entire test bank, the time investment is about 10–15 minutes per question (including entering it into the management database). That amounts to approximately one to two hours per week, or 30–45 hours total over both semesters. The management system provides instantaneous grading, statistics, and a gradebook. The time investment seems appropriate under the circumstances.

Summary for the "Technology and Society" course interventions. In addition to the time invested in implementing any innovations (e.g., content material, readings, homework quiz preparation), these changes often require additional mechanisms and time to answer student questions and provide help. For the fall of 2000 and 2001 offerings of this course, the instructor answered over 1000 and 800 e-mails, respectively. Even though explicit (i.e. step-by-step) instructions are provided for accessing the course-management system and taking quizzes on it, the high population of first-semester students generates a huge amount of e-mail. Indeed, a large proportion of the e-mail in the first two weeks dealt entirely with the procedures and protocols in the course. To facilitate this process, a word-processing document of common responses is maintained. That text can be used directly or with minor modification. It is interesting to note that the presence of frequently asked questions (FAQ) on the Web site seems to have little effect on the number of e-mail received. The rate of e-mail is an average of about 2 to 2.5 e-mails per student over the course of the semester. An informal poll of colleagues who have taught the same courses recently but without the changes or use of technology suggest that they receive an average of 1 to 1.5 e-mails per student over a semester.

In order to evaluate the impact of innovations in the offering of a course, one may wish to get feedback from the students. Although a complete study may be interesting, it will likely be time consuming, and simpler options are available. Most colleges use a questionnaire to assess teachers, and most of these forms allow the instructor to add her/his own questions. Another method is a focus group or informal meeting of a small group from the class to address some single issue. Some instructors assemble a class advisory board or "board of directors" with whom they meet several times during a semester about such issues. Anticipating problems is always easier than dealing with student anguish.

Two-semester courses for science and engineering students

The two-semester general chemistry sequence is likely to have students enrolled who are more competitive than the non-science majors. As a result, the responses or reactions from this group are likely to be more passionate and vocal. On the other hand, because this group is often large and has a substantial range of skills and expectations, appropriate interventions can have a tremendous impact.

At Iowa virtually all students taking such a course, "Principles in Chemistry," have had at least one chemistry course in high school. However, that course could have been taken any time from the sophomore through senior year in high school, and the rigor and expectations of the courses reported by our students are quite variable. A "prep chem" course is taught in the department, and part of the group enrolled in this course are those students whose high school mathematics or chemistry preparation was not deemed adequate to handle the rigor of the departmental "Principles" course. A new chemistry placement exam has been developed, pilot-tested, and implemented in the department (Pienta 2002). Thus, students in the first semester of the "Principles" course are a better prepared group (i.e. a narrower range of abilities and expectations) than those students enrolled at other institutions where no "prep chem" is taught. The following two sections present two cases from the "Principles" course at Iowa: the use of electronic homework and some course redesign elements. Both include the student outcomes and opinions that were collected. The third part summarizes the results of a major change from traditional lectures attempted in a general chemistry course at Duke (Zurer 2002).

Homework on the Internet using on-line software. The perceived value of getting students to practice problem-solving and increase time on task encourages instructors to assign homework problems. The maximum benefit from such work is likely to be realized under circumstances where timely feedback is provided to the student. The first dilemma arises from the scale of such an effort. A section of our course is comprised of 400 students; an assignment of 15 questions every week generates some 90,000 questions in a semester. At one minute per question, a teaching assistant could ascertain very little more than whether it was completed. It would take five TAs working full-time all semester to accommodate that one section. The students would get little or no feedback beyond whether they completed each question.

We began the systematic use of homework software, particularly packages that were implemented on the Internet, in the spring of 2000. The first on-line homework OLH utilized was one produced via the NSF systemic reform (Wegner 2000). The OLH is administered from a server and is accessible via any browser using the Authorware Web Player plugin. Students can access it anywhere and anytime they have an Internet connection. OLH consists of a series of units, each covering a "chunk" of chemistry content. The units are generally quite focused so the match between the content of a unit in OLH and a chapter in any number of popular textbooks is generally satisfactory. (However, students are often very intolerant of different word usage or context that does not perfectly match their book or instructor.) In turn, each unit consists of two to six modules, each of which poses eight to 12 questions. Those modules represent the practice mode for OLH; if one incorrectly answers a question, information about the question and the answer are provided. Each unit also contains a post-test and these were used by us as graded homework. The post-test takes eight to 12 questions randomly from the modules that comprise it. In the post-test a score is recorded but no feedback or answers are provided. All of the questions in OLH are generated by algorithms that vary the numbers or images in the question. The format of the questions vary, but a large majority of them are fill-in-the-blank and virtually none are multiple choice.

The data in Table 1 outline the number of required and recommended units, the scoring system for each unit, and the total value of these exercises in the course. The scoring warrants further explanation. In the first two semesters the OLH homework represented about 11 percent of the course grade, while in the subsequent semesters it was worth about half of that. (The impact of this reward system is discussed with the results of student usage.) The percentage score on the post-test for each unit was used to generate the number of points. For example, in spring 2000 a student who achieved at a level above 70 percent on the post-test earned the maximum number of points (i.e. three). Lower performance also earned points since a goal was to encourage participation. For all five semesters summarized in Table 1, a student could take the post-test repeatedly and amass points based on the highest score achieved. In other words, taking a unit's post-test could be repeated as many times as a student wished, with no penalty.

Table 1. On-Line Software Used as Graded Homework

semester	units required	units recommended	unit scoring	total value in course
Spring 2000 Fall 2000	25	0	3 pts (>70%) 2 pts (>60%) 1 pt (>50%)	11%
Spring 2001 Fall 2001 Spring 2002	13	16	10 pts (>75%) 6 pts (>50%) 5 pts (>75%) 3 pts (>50%)	5%

Figure 1 shows a plot of the points earned via OLH versus the total number of points that could be earned from all components of the course for the entire semester of spring 2000. The maximum score for the OLH homework was 75 points out of a total of 650 points for the entire course. The data come from 490 students for whom a final grade was recorded. Note that some of the values plotted may be superimposed over others.

Figure 1. A Plot of Total Points vs. On-Line Homework Points for Spring 2000

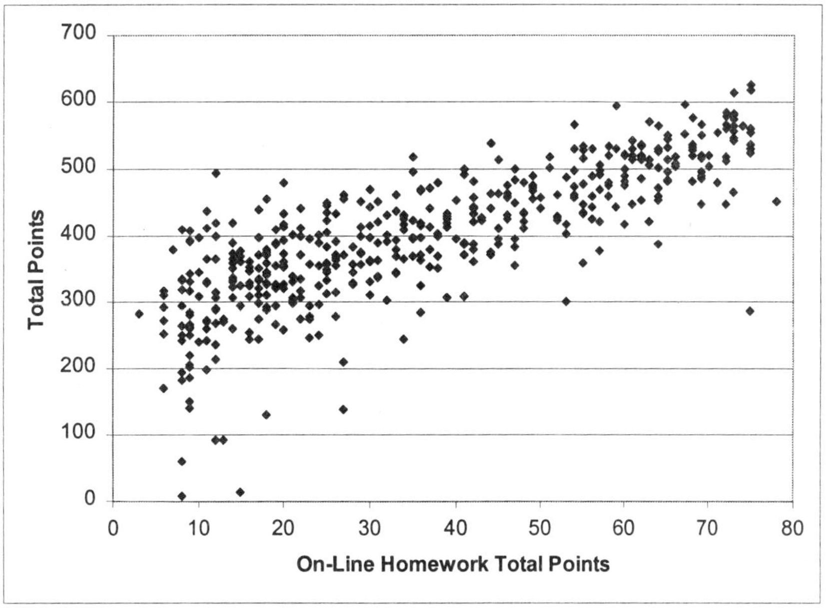

The correlation observed in this first semester encouraged us to continue the use of OLH, and several interesting questions were raised. For example, one can calculate correlations between student scores on hour exams and scores on the homework units that correspond to the content in the hour exam. Correlations as high as $r^2 = 0.65$ have been observed. A preliminary observation is that the early units in OLH correlate with all hour exams and the final. This confirms that the material in the course is hierarchal and builds on early fundamentals. A systematic analysis of outcomes is being conducted, but its discussion is beyond the scope of this chapter. At this stage it is appropriate to examine data about student use and attitude toward this intervention.

The data in Figure 1 suggest that in spite of the opportunity to repeat the post-tests and earn more points, students earned less than 50 percent of the homework points in spring 2000. Since the absolute number of points and the conditions of homework use changed over the five semesters (see Table 1), data about total homework scores is reported as a percentage in Figure 2. Thus, two sets of bars represent the mean ("Avg Pts, %" in front) and median ("Med Pts, %" in back) percentage of the maximum points for homework for each semester. The rise in percent after fall 2001 is most likely due to two factors, the reduction in the number of required units and the persistance of our use of OLH as homework. Even with a drop from 25 to 13 required units, only a marginal increase in completion rate was observed. That might not be surprising since the percentage of the course grade from homework was also cut in half.

We sought reasons for the underutilization of this resource via focus groups and interviews. As might be expected, a wide range of opinions were expressed. In general, students viewed OLH as assessment or self-assessment more than a skill-building experience. Most of the negative reasons could be categorized as minor: frustrations with the format for entering some of the answers, a mismatch between some of the language and examples in the text and OLH, and the lack of feedback and answers on the post-test compared with the practice modules. In order to test whether the limits in student participation was related specifically to OLH, a new Internet-based software package was used in fall 2002. The extent to which students participate will be monitored for several semesters.

Figure 2. Percentage of Homework Points Earned Each Semester

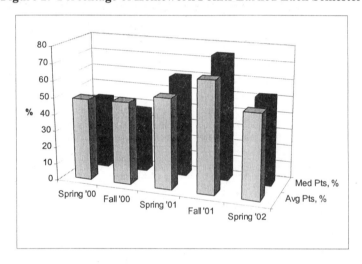

The instructor support for the use of Web-based homework has several components. Aspects of providing "technical support" can be time consuming. About 75 percent of our entering students come with their own computer, and most would like to use it for their homework. Explicit directions for registering and logging into OLH were provided on the course Web site. This included downloading and installing the Authorware Web Player plugin and some fonts. Having a computer only guarantees that a student knows how to turn it on and perform the simplest tasks! E-mail is the conduit by which these issues get addressed, and a vast majority of early e-mails dealt with support for these aspects of the course. For 500 students in spring 2000, 600 e-mails were answered by mid-semester; in fall 2002, for 800 students that number of e-mails was nearly 900 at the end of the semester. The spring '00 implementation of OLH was more problematic, and the average rate of e-mail was about 2 per student per semester. In fall '02 the electronic homework was another software package, a commercial one for which there have been fewer difficulties with student access and use.

Additional technical support came from the Information Technology Centers (i.e. computer labs) on campus. Getting fonts and a plugin loaded on all computers on campus takes a certain amount of lead time even if the IT administration is very cooperative. One has to be vigilant since new hardware and software installed in the campus computer labs during the summer required testing prior to the start of classes. In addition, the release of a new version of a browser (in the case of Internet Explorer 6.0) or proprietary browsers (like AOL) may cause problems and are not always 100 percent compatible with a release of software that is already running. If student frustration builds because of a series of factors that you do not control, you may find yourself annoyed, together with your students. Despite the fact that OLH use as homework did not reach high levels, the students recognized it for what it was and did not hold the instructors responsible for the glitches when they provided feedback in course evaluations.

Table 2 contains student assessment of the value of certain course components. Students enrolled in the second- semester course were asked to evaluate their experience in the first-semester course. The averages are listed and cover the range from least, 1, to most effective, 10. The standard deviation given for textbooks is typical. The values in parentheses are the percentage of responses that rated a factor. In other words, all students who filled out the survey provided a score rating the value of texts, while only 18 percent evaluated paid tutors. In fall 1999 traditional homework was assigned and collected; a version of skill-building software was an optional ancillary for the course. In fall 2000, several homework grading schemes were allowed, although OLH was the only one for which credit was granted. More students rated electronic homework in fall 2000, but few appreciated its value. The scores are not significantly different. Textbooks and solutions manuals are quite popular. The perceived effectiveness of study groups and friends suggests that they should be more highly utilized. However, one should note that second-semester students may not be the best informed about how they actually learn chemistry. Their perception of the value of an item to their learning and the reality of what helped them learn may not completely match.

Table 2. Student Evaluation of Course Components (*1=least effective, 10=most effective)

	*Fall 1999** *N = 261*	*Fall 2000** *N = 228*	*T Value*	*DF*	*P Value*
textbook	7.7 ± 2.0 (100%)	8.1 ± 1.7 (100%)	-2.57	486	0.0104**
solns manual/study guide	6.8 (79%)	7.4 (90%)	-2.55	409	0.011**
CD-ROM	4.0 (68%)	2.5 (56%)	5.16	303	0.0001**
lecture content	5.6 (99%)	6.5 (99%)	-3.66	486	0.0003**
written homework	6.6 (98%)	5.4 (72%)	5.00	420	0.0001**
electronic homework	4.1 (42%)	3.6 (76%)	1.39	287	0.1659
discussion section	5.9 (97%)	4.3 (87%)	5.97	448	0.0001**
TA office hours	4.1 (51%)	3.4 (52%)	1.83	248	0.0685
study group	5.9 (49%)	4.3 (46%)	4.03	232	0.0001**
paid tutor	3.5 (18%)	2.4 (26%)	1.89	106	0.0621
friends	6.8 (83%)	6.3 (73%)	1.95	381	0.0515

* *significant difference between years

About the third week of each semester, the author typically would receive a set of 20–30 e-mails that pointed out that the sender had not been able to do all of the problems. It was stated in language that represented two very different perspectives: (1) "I don't know how to do these problems and never had this difficulty in high school. Where can I get help?" and (2) "I don't have X hours per week to waste on this X#!?$%#!" In the first instance, one could point them to discussion sections, instructor office hours, TA office hours, supplemental instruction sessions, and other resources. It was pointed out that it is better to find this out a week before the hour exam than the day of it. One assumes that most of them got some help or tried to. The second group represented students who were also confronted by their limitations and were very unhappy. One can speculate that they remained that way during the course and eventually quit doing the homework.

Several students in the second group who said that they didn't have one or two hours per week to spend on homework caused alarm. A poll was conducted in spring 2001 about student use of their time in the fall 2000 "Principles" class. They reported spending 5.6 ± 4.1 hours per week outside of class working on the chemistry course. Furthermore, they claimed 4.0 ± 4.2 hours per week spent on OLH homework. Table 3 outlines data from the same survey about how they think they spend time. The chemistry course represents about a third of the time they spend working outside of class, but the overall time may be very disappointing to most instructors. The old "rule of thumb" that prescribes two to three hours out of class for each one in class is not being met. The ratio is barely 1.2:1. For many students the sum of all of their hours was short and often far short of the 168 hours in a week. It is likely that many students don't have a good idea of how they spend their time.

Table 3. Student Use of Time

Weekly Schedule (avg # hrs)	hrs
in class (all courses)	16 ± 4
studying out of class (all courses)	19 ± 11
working at a job [35% of sample]	14 ± 7
entertainment	14 ± 10
"living"	77 ± 30

A new curriculum, and how to fit in as a new faculty member

For many years the "Principles of Chemistry" course sequence had been comprised of two three-credit hour lecture courses and a separate two-credit hour laboratory course that was taken concurrently with the second lecture (or even after it). To promote a better pedagogical approach and alleviate some administrative issues, the laboratory component was reintegrated into the lecture portion starting in fall 2002. The new courses are now four credit hours each and are comprised of three hours of lecture/presentation, an hourlong TA-led discussion section, and lab activities that consist of alternating weeks of a case-study session and the lab experiments. The experiments are all guided inquiry and based on some practical problem or issue. The case-study sessions combine a presentation or demonstration portion and group work on an activity that bridges the lecture content with the practical issues needed in the experiment.

The historical precedent in the "Principles" course is that (in the old and new courses) the multiple sections are team taught. A single instructor is responsible for the lectures in all sections on a particular topic. This assures homogeneity in the coverage of topics and common assessment during communal evening exams. Each lecturer is only responsible for the presentations in half of the course, although both attend each others' lectures, administer the course, and prepare exams. The advantage to a new faculty member is that there is a mentor available, and potential disasters can be averted in some situations. On the other hand, both individuals need to agree to virtually all aspects of the course, including innovations. The more senior member should be made aware of the implications of major changes both in time commitment to a new faculty member and the resulting student opinions expressed in course evaluations. In the process of course or curricular redesign, the opinions of new faculty should be part of the process. They represent the future of those courses. It is probably not a good use of time for a new faculty member to direct the changes; membership on the committee should be sufficient. A series of "brown-bag lunches" has served as a low-stakes way to collect ideas and introduce a group of faculty to some of the potential possibilities and the consequences of implementation of those possibilities.

A traditional general chemistry course replaced by case-studies taught by multiple instructors

A report in *Chemical and Engineering News* in August 2002 documented student displeasure with a dramatic change in how one semester of general chemistry was taught (Zurer 2002; Letters 2002). A traditional first-semester course at Duke was part of some "experimental" changes. In fall 2001 one section was taught by a single instructor in the traditional manner. The second section was comprised of case studies that represented state-of-the-art chemical issues (e.g., the Kyoto protocol on greenhouse gases, combustion, the Antarctic ozone hole) into which principles like stoichiometry, periodic trends, quantum mechanics, and the gas laws were woven. The latter course involved six instructors. It was reported that students in the new course felt that they worked harder and had some concerns that they were the unwilling participants of an experiment. They apparently had difficulty adjusting to instructors' teaching styles and probably with the different ways in which those individuals asked questions on exams. The case-study approach has been used successfully for many years at other institutions (Case Studies 2002).

The report was followed by several letters from the chemical education community (Letters 2002). The Duke "experiment" is only a single point, and many successful implementations of materials and methodologies have been reported, particularly following the multiyear National Science Foundation systemic curricular reform. For example, modular material-use at Berkeley triggered negative student response, but a variety of assessments, including very traditional ACS standardized exams, showed that the modular students outperformed the traditional ones. The lessons learned are that effective changes must be accompanied with communication among all stakeholders (i.e. students, teaching assistants, and instructors), a feedback mechanism involving all groups should be implemented during the process to allow midcourse corrections, and that a test for effectiveness may require multiple iterations once the original glitches have been worked out.

A colleague at Iowa who read the report in *Chemical and Engineering News* asked whether the apparent failure of case studies at Duke meant that our use of them in the integrated labs was destined to fail. He was reassured that our use of case studies was motivated by the same desire to show students modern and relevant context but did not represent as dramatic a change in the entire course structure as Duke's did. Just like the students at Duke who had a "fear of the unknown," one's colleagues can have the same kinds of concerns. As a new instructor, you should take the time to make sure your colleagues know what you are doing and that their understanding is not limited to some simple description like case studies.

Making changes and having students and colleagues appreciate it!

Innovations can take many forms and have a wide range of outcomes. A new approach can provide the instructor with an enthusiasm that transfers to the students. It can also provide additional challenges to both the instructor and students. You have to start with some good information on the how and the why of the innovation, but if you are convinced of the value of an innovation and support it, you are likely to see your students learning more. Go ahead. Try something new. Just go into it with your eyes open.

References

Borgford, C. L. & Summerlin, L. (1988). *Chemical Activities: Teacher Edition*. Washington: American Chemical Society.

Calibrated Peer Review (2002) Web site: http://cpr.molsci.ucla.edu/

Case Studies (2002). Successful use of case studies at a private institution, with many pre-professional students, can be found at: http://chemed.rice.edu/CaseStudies/

Computer programs (2002) and video on CD-ROM are available from J. Chem. Ed. Software at http://jchemed.chem.wisc.edu/JCESoft/

ConcepTests (2002). These questions are posed during lecture and enable a small group of students in the audience to have a short discussion. A Web site that contains a large group of examples in virtually all subdisciplines in chemistry can be found at http://www.chem.wisc.edu/~concept/mainpage.html

Letters (2002). *Chemical and Engineering News, 80*, pp 6–9.

Mazur, E. (1997). *Peer Instruction: A User's Manual.* Upper Saddle River, NJ: Prentice-Hall.

Pienta, N. J., Thorp, H. H., Panoff, R. M., Gotwals, R. R. & Hirst, H. P. (2001). A Web-Based, Calculator Skills Tutorial and Self-Test for General Chemistry Students. *Chemical Educator, 6*, pp 365–9.

Pienta, N. J. (2002). On-Line Chemistry Placement Exam and Mathematics Tutorial Web site for General Chemistry. *J. Chem. Educ.*, in press. This 30-question, hourlong exam is administered via WebCT and is comprised of 15 sets of questions that pair a conceptual one with a calculational one.

Shakhashiri, B. Z. (1983). *Chemical Demonstration: A Handbook for Teachers of Chemistry.* Vol. 1. Madison, WI: University of Wisonsin Press.

Ibid., Vol. 2.

Ibid., Vol. 3.

Ibid., Vol. 4.

Stanitski, C. L., Eubanks, L. P., Middlecamp, C. H., & Pienta, N. J. (2003). *Chemistry in Context: Applying Chemistry to Society. 4th ed.* McGraw-Hill and American Chemical Society.

Summerlin, L., & Ealy Jr., J. L. (1988). *Chemical Demonstrations: A Sourcebook for Teachers.* Vol. 1. Washington: American Chemical Society.

Summerlin, L., Borgford, C. L. & Ealy, J. B. (1988). *Chemical Demonstrations: A Sourcebook for Teachers.* Vol. 2. Washington: American Chemical Society.

Wegner, P. Mastering Chemistry (2000): http://titanium.fullerton.edu.

Zurer, P. S. (2002). An Educational Experience. *Chemical and Engineering News*, *80*, pp 31–32.

Small Groups Are Worth the Effort

Julianne Smist
Department of Biology and Chemistry
Springfield College

Abstract

Within this chapter, I have tried to discuss why small-group learning strategies are a good tool to employ in teaching chemistry. I have addressed some reasons why instructors tend to shy away from small groups in favor of the lecture format. You will find information on creating small groups, using them in all types of classroom settings, at all levels of instruction, and how to use them effectively. I have also given examples of small-group tasks and advice on how to grade small-group activities.

Biography

I received a B.A., majoring in chemistry, from Elms College in 1972, a M.S., emphasizing physical chemistry, from Boston College in 1974, and a Ph.D. in educational psychology, concentrating in measurement and evaluation, from the University of Connecticut in 1996. After graduating from Boston College, I taught high school chemistry for two years and then moved into college-level teaching, serving as a sabbatical replacement, visiting lecturer, and laboratory instructor at several colleges in western Massachusetts. I landed at Springfield College in 1981 and stayed. In 1989 I began work on my Ph. D., on a part-time basis, at the University of Connecticut. It was there that I was introduced to the concepts of collaborative and cooperative learning groups. The concepts were new to me, having come from a traditional "hard science" background of competition and working independently. I found it strange and difficult at first because I did not like relinquishing control to others. I began using small groups in my classes in 1993 after attending a Chautauqua Short Course on "Revitalizing the General Chemistry Course" at the University of Arizona, Tucson. I now use small groups in every class I teach.

What is a small group?

A small group is three or more students working together within a class to achieve a common goal. The goal is to better understand chemistry. In this chapter the term small group is used for both cooperative learning groups and collaborative learning groups. More in-depth discussions of cooperative and collaborative learning strategies can be found elsewhere (Matthews, Cooper, Davidson, and Hawkes 1995; Goodsell, Maher and Tinto 1992).

Why use small groups?

Small-group learning has been shown to promote greater achievement and more favorable learning attitudes (Springer, Stanne and Donovan 1997). The National Science Foundation (NSF) recommends faculty who teach courses in science, mathematics, engineering and technology (SME&T) "recognize that different students may learn in different ways" (NSF 96-139, p.65). In this report (NSF 96-139), NSF also encourages SME&T faculty to create pedagogy to foster communication, teamwork, and critical-thinking skills.

In order to make our teaching "student-centered," we need to employ different pedagogies to try to incorporate the students' various learning styles. We may have some students before us who are passive and prefer the lecture format. They learn best from a dynamic lecturer and exciting demonstrations. We may have other students who have more active learning styles and work well with others. They learn best in a small-group format. We may also have independent learners who like to read the information and process it on their own. They do best utilizing individual self-paced learning programs. So to reach all these different learning styles, we need to incorporate several different techniques. Many teachers who are advocates of small groups still lecture (Cooper, MacGregor, Smith, and Robinson 2000). I also don't recommend focusing on only one technique.

Why doesn't everyone use small groups?

Chemistry college faculty (and probably most science faculty) have not had a lot of exposure to small-group learning in their backgrounds, at least not in science classes. They think that the concept of "get together in a circle and discuss" belongs in the "touchy feely" realm of the social sciences. You can't have feelings or opinions about the atom. Understanding and doing science requires factual-based knowledge, and the best way to deliver that knowledge is through "information dissemination." The most efficient way to disseminate information is through lecture.

Some reasons why people avoid small groups are: First, small groups take time away from lecture. Yes, you have less time to spend lecturing if you give class time to small groups. This is one of the critical points addressed in higher-education circles: Isn't it better to approach the "teaching/learning process" from the student perspective of what they have gained rather than from the teacher perspective of what they have "covered"? (Barr and Tagg 1995). There is research evidence showing positive effects on both achievement and attitudes when students participate in small-group learning (Springer, Donovan and Stanne 1999).

A second reason some faculty give for not using small groups is that there is so much information to be delivered, and if you don't cover all the topics in the freshmen general chemistry text, then the students will not be prepared for the subsequent chemistry courses. I would ask the question, Are all those topics equally important? One approach that was used when an introductory biology class wanted to incorporate small groups is that the biology faculty met and created a list of "essential knowledge" that a student needed to master in the introductory course. The curriculum for this course was then built around this list, incorporating both lecture and small groups (Cooper, MacGregor, Smith, and Robinson 2000).

A third point that is a problem for some faculty is that freshmen don't know enough to discuss a complex topic. Yes, that is true; so don't start out by giving a complex topic. Choose a group activity for which they have the requisite knowledge and understanding to complete.

Chemists (I will use myself as an example of an analytical chemist) tend to be control freaks. We know what information needs to be covered; we know what is important for the students to learn so that they can go on to the next level; we believe we know what is in the best interests of our students. You are in complete control in lecture; you decide what you will say and how you will present it ("teacher-centered"). With the small-group learning format, you give up control to the students ("student-centered learning"). Remember just because you said it in lecture does not mean that the students have "learned" it. In reviewing the effectiveness of lectures, McKeachie (as cited in Cooper and Robinson 2000) found the format to be effective in fostering memorization of factual material but less effective in long-term retention and knowledge transfer. For students to incorporate new information, they need more than just hearing you say it and/or reading it, they need to act on it and "teach" it to others.

Can a small group be used in any classroom setting?

Yes, you can make any setting work. I have used small groups predominantly in "traditional" classroom settings (student desks in rows and columns). If the student desks (or chairs) are moveable, you can have the group make a circle. I have also had small groups in a classroom setting where the student desks are bolted to the floor and in an auditorium made for the performing arts. When you can't move the chairs, you need to have the small groups orient themselves in squares or rectangles rather than circles.

You need to give students a little direction on how to do this the first time you have a group activity. A group of four or six people sitting in a row can't have a meaningful discussion. The people sitting on the ends are either left out of the discussion or they have to talk over the people sitting in the middle. You can suggest the group either make a square (four people) or a rectangle (six people) by dividing the group in half: Two (or three) people sit in one row, and the other two (or three) sit directly in front of them. The front-row people can turn around in their seats to speak with the back-row people.

You can also let the students be creative in setting up their discussion groups: They can sit in the aisles, on the floor, on the desks, whatever works for them. I find it is good to let them move around to get into their groups, especially when you have a longer 75-minute class period as I do. Don't let the physical setting deter you from using small groups. A word of caution: Sometimes the discussions can get lively (loud). Be sure that you are not disturbing classes that are meeting in adjacent rooms.

There are several examples of faculty using small groups, both informally (Cooper and Robinson 2000) and formally in large classes (Smith 2000). Lyman's (as cited in Cooper and Robinson 2000) "think-pair-share" is a popular informal strategy, which is easy to incorporate into a large class. Basically students are presented material for a short time (lecture), the professor poses a question or a problem of some sort; students individually consider the problem (think), discuss it with a partner (pair), and then present their ideas for an answer with the class (share).

Can small groups be used at any level?

Yes, from freshmen through graduate students. You are probably more familiar with the small-group setting in a graduate-level seminar course, but the format also works with freshmen. It does take more planning and work to do it in a freshmen course because of the students' lower maturity levels, lack of knowledge, and greater numbers. You can't throw out a topic (e.g. global warming, acid rain, human cloning), sit back, and expect freshmen to have an erudite discussion.

In a freshmen chemistry class (general chemistry for majors; a service chemistry course for biology or health science majors; a chemistry course for non-science majors), you need to choose your group tasks carefully. The students must have the requisite background knowledge to be able to perform the task, or the group will not function well. In upper-level courses (organic, analytical, physical) the tasks can be more challenging and can require that the students do extensive background work on their own.

How is a small group created?

The small group itself can be created in one of two ways: The instructor assigns the students to groups using a set of criteria for group membership, or the students self select into a group. There are advantages and disadvantages to both methods. I personally use both methods in different situations.

When you assign the members of the group, you are in control of the group's parameters. The students get to know each other and have to learn to work with people other than their friends. One disadvantage to assigning students to groups is a group dynamics problem. The students may not get along with each other. A group that is always in conflict will not be productive. Because you don't know the students well, you can't predict how well they will work together. The strongly motivated student could take over and not let the weaker students contribute. The less motivated students could "ride the coattails" of more motivated students and get by with no real effort

Another problem may arise if you have students from different cultural backgrounds and/or students who are non-native English speakers. For example, Asian immigrant students may tend to be more quiet and subdued in a group setting fearing that their English is not good enough to banter with American students. In turn, the American students perceive the Asian students to be uncooperative (Hodne 1997). To prevent a communication breakdown in the group, you need to remind all students that because communication styles are different, they can be misinterpreted. Scarcella (as cited in Hodne 1997) suggests that you need to give some guidance on cooperation, perhaps asking the more vocal students to hold back while encouraging the more quiet students to speak up. When practitioners were asked (Cooper, MacGregor, Smith, and Robinson 2000) about this problem, most thought small groups were beneficial to those students who were less inclined to participate in other settings. Research is currently ongoing to look at the impact of small-group work on building tolerance between different groups (Cooper, MacGregor, Smith, and Robinson 2000).

If you are going to create groups, you first have to decide on the number of people you want in the group. The ideal number for a good discussion group is four to six members. Three tends to be too small, and if one or two are absent, it can prove to be a problem. When the group gets bigger than six, it is too unwieldy and difficult to manage.

If you are going to assign the members to the group, you need to have some sort of criteria for membership. Some instructors use cognitive ability as a criterion to make the groups diverse (i.e. higher, middle, and lower ability students should all be represented in each group). Because I assign my students into groups after the first class meeting, I do not have knowledge of their abilities, so I do not use ability as a criterion.

I use gender, age, and major as my criteria. I strive to have gender equality in every group. If the class has equal number of males and females, I will assign an equal number of males and females to the groups (I usually have six people in a group). If the proportions are not equal, I will create some single-sex groups if necessary. It is not a good idea to have only one person of the opposite sex in a group. One male with four or five females or one female with four or five males leads to a bad group dynamic. Either the lone man or woman will take control or totally withdraw and not speak up. There is safety in numbers. When you have at least a pair of students of the same sex in a group, no one feels isolated.

I teach a chemistry course for health-related majors (e.g. athletic training, applied exercise science, emergency medicine) that also satisfies the science general-education requirement, so I have several different majors represented among my freshmen. I try to group like or similar majors together so that the students have a common interest to help focus their discussions. This course is primarily freshmen, but there are also upperclassmen present so I try to have at least one or two upperclassmen in a group if possible. They help to keep the freshmen on task. I also teach an organic survey course to the physician assistant majors. The students in that course tend to be 50 percent mature adults mixed in with the traditional sophomores, so I try to have the groups in that course representative of the class age mix.

The other method of creating small groups is to have the students self select. The advantage is that it requires no preparation on the instructor's part. You just tell the class to arrange themselves groups of four to six. One disadvantage to this method is that students will tend to choose to be with their friends, so they will not get to know the other students in the class. If friendships change over the course of the semester, you can get a bad group dynamic, especially if the "friendships" were sexual. Another problem is that students will also want to "cover" for their friends who are not actively participating. Lastly, you could be faced with the problem of what to do about the student that no one chooses.

How long do the groups stay together?

If you assign the groups, I would advise that you have them stay together as a group for the entire semester. If you have students self select, I would advise that you have them regroup periodically. In order to get a good working relationship within the group, it is not a good idea to have the groups only stay together for one task.

In my classes, I have assigned groups that do certain tasks and smaller self-selected groups. I call the self-selected groups "buddy groups." These buddy groups consist of two or three people. I use the "buddy groups" primarily for problem solving and peer review of homework.

Should the groups meet outside of class?

I would not advise that you require the groups to meet outside of class. If they choose to, that is fine. Often the members of the group create such a good working relationship that they want to work on homework problems and study together for the exams. However, it is usually difficult for students to coordinate their outside-of-class schedules. If you have commuting or nontraditional students, it may be a hardship for them to come back to campus in the evenings or on weekends. You should allow a sufficient amount of class time for the group to complete its task.

How does the group work?

Each group has a facilitator whose role it is to lead the group in the discussion. He/she makes sure that everyone gets a chance to speak on the topic and keeps the group on task. The facilitator also must see to it that no one dominates the group. Another important role is that of group reporter. The reporter takes the minutes of the group meeting. The reporter is also responsible for the group report, which is how I grade the group. Both roles rotate though the group so that everyone has a chance to serve as facilitator and reporter. When I initially set up the groups, I assign these two roles. After the first group task is complete, the members of the group decide how they will rotate the jobs. The only direction I give is that each group member must serve both roles at least twice before the end of the semester.

How is a small group graded?

In my freshmen class, the group-work grade counts for 20 percent of the final grade (equal to an exam). Every time the group meets, the reporter is required to hand in a written report. I grade each group report on a 10-point scale. Every member of the group gets the same grade unless he/she was absent from the group discussion. For some group discussions, a "pre-group" individual assignment is completed. If a group member does not complete this outside group assignment, he/she will receive a lower grade than the rest of the group for that assignment.

Additionally on each exam, I include a question that deals with a topic covered only in group work. I do this because students often believe something is important only if they have to know it for the exam. I also have each group do a group oral presentation for the whole class, which the class critiques.

Where do you get ideas for small-group tasks?

The answer to this is anywhere you can. You can adapt problems from your textbook. Get ideas from other people about what worked or did not work for them. Ask the students what they would like to discuss or know about. Choose something seasonal (e.g. the National Chemistry Week theme) or an article in the local newspaper. Get to know the students and what interests them, and let this guide your selection.

Here are some group tasks that I have used successfully. My first group meeting is always an "introduce yourselves" activity. Since I mainly teach freshmen, many people don't know each other the first day of class. After they do the usual thing–say who they are and where they are from–I give them a couple of specific questions to discuss. I ask them to share with the members of their group the sport at which they excel (Springfield College has a rich history of physical education) or the sport that they always wished they could play or their favorite food or rock band--anything to stimulate discussion. In terms of the report, each member of the group has to share something they want the group and me to know about them; usually they will share their anxieties about the course, which again stimulates a good discussion.

The second group meeting can be either a series of critical-thinking exercises or risk/benefit analyses to give the students experience working with a group of people with diverse opinions. The group has to discuss a given issue following a set of clear parameters and then come to a consensus. If they cannot achieve consensus, the group is allowed to submit a "minority" report with the "majority" report.

Next I introduce the idea of outside individual "research" prior to the group meeting. I assign each student a different chemical element. They have to find out all they can about their element. They have a week to gather the information. Then when the group meets in class, they aggregate their information around a set of guided questions, such as which elements were named after people, places, things, who discovered it, what it is used for, etc.

Toward the end of the semester, when they have some knowledge, the group assignments get a little more complex. Students do individual library research and group activities on diet fads, drugs athletes use, polymers, waste management, recycling, pollution, etc. You have to get to know each group of students and where their interests lie, and then selection of appropriate activities will follow. A word of caution here: Remember, it is the interests of your students not *your* interests that should be pursued.

How much time and effort will it really involve?

Before the groups ever meet, you will need to devote a great deal of time for preparation, especially in a freshmen course. Preparing for small-group discussions takes more time and thought than preparing for a lecture. In planning for small groups, you have to get the idea and develop it into a small-group task. You need to have enough for the students to work on the task without overwhelming or frustrating them. You also need to keep students on task, so that the entire time is not just socializing. Successful practitioners agree that students need structure, they need to be made accountable, and they need the challenge of producing a product as a result of their group work (Cooper, MacGregor, Smith, and Robinson 2000).

During the group meeting, you need to monitor the groups without joining the group. If you "join in," your presence may cut off discussion, as the students may not want to say anything "stupid" in your presence and may look to you for the "right answer." You also need to keep an eye out for groups that don't appear to be functioning well. If you see one, then you need to be able to offer some suggestions on how to help the group function more effectively. If that can't be accomplished, then you might have to consider re-forming your groups.

After the group completes it report, you need to grade the group reports and give immediate feedback (i.e. by the next group meeting). This is actually easier than grading homework or exams because you have less papers to actually read. If a group has really missed the point of the exercise, I always give them a chance to open up the discussion and hand in an amended report for a better grade.

Why is the effort worth it?

If you choose to use small groups, you will get to know your students as people, not just exam grades. You will see some of them shine, as they never could through a multiple choice test or mathematical problem. You will have the satisfaction of knowing that you have planted a seed that will continue to grow. When people learn to work with each other, it is a lesson they will remember long after the factual chemical information has been forgotten. In addition to the references cited earlier in the chapter claiming that working in small groups increases performance and attitudes, there is also research evidence that small-group work may be especially effective for minority students and women (Johnson and Johnson 1989), so what have you got to lose?

Final thoughts

Don't be afraid to try small groups. Don't be discouraged if it doesn't go perfectly the first time. Many professors using small groups continually face the ongoing challenge of developing group tasks and finding the right balance of lecture/demonstration presentations and group discussions (Cooper, MacGregor, Smith, and Robinson 2000). Start small. Try two or three group activities in the first semester. Don't worry about making mistakes, just learn from them. Teaching is a learning experience. Ask the students what they think about small groups and how the experience could be better for them. Remember, experience is a great teacher, but each class of students is different. What worked well with one group may not work well in another setting. You have to be flexible. Finally, relax. It can be a fun experience, and you will learn a great deal from your students.

References

Barr, R. B. & Tagg, J. (1995). From teaching to learning: A new paradigm for undergraduate education. *Change, 27*, 13–25.

Cooper, J. L., MacGregor, J., Smith, K. A. & Robinson, P. (2000). Implementing small-group instruction: Insights from successful practitioners. *New Directions for Teaching and Learning, 81*, 63–76.

Cooper, J. L & Robinson, P. (2000). The argument for making large classes seem small. *New Directions for Teaching and Learning, 81*, 5–16.

Cooper, J. L & Robinson, P. (2000). Getting started: Informal Small-group strategies in large classes. *New Directions for Teaching and Learning, 81*, 17–24.

Goodsell, A., Maher, M., & Tinto, V. (1992). *Collaborative learning: A Sourcebook for Higher Education.* University Park, PA: National Center on Postsecondary Teaching, Learning and Assessment.

Hodne, B. D. (1997). Please speak up: Asian immigrant students in American college classrooms. In D. H. Sigsbee, B. W. Speck and B. Maylath (Eds.), *Approaches to Teaching Non-Native English Speakers Across the Curriculum* (pp. 85–92). San Francisco: Jossey-Bass Publishers

Matthews, R. S., Cooper, J. L., Davidson, N. & Hawkes, P. (1995). Building bridges between cooperative and collaborative learning. *Change, 2*, 35–40.

National Science Foundation Advisory Committee to the Directorate for Education and Human Resources. (1996). *Shaping the Future: New Expectations in Undergraduate Education in Science, Mathematics, Engineering, and Technology.* (NSF 96-139). National Science Foundation: Arlington, VA.

Smith, K. A. (2000). Formal small-group learning in large classes. *New Directions for Teaching and Learning, 81*, 25– 46.

Springer, L. Donovan, S. & Stanne, M. E. (1999). Effects of small-group learning on undergraduates in science, mathematics, engineering, and technology: A meta analysis. *Review of Education Research, 69*, 21–51.

Bibliography

Basili, P. A. & Stanford, J. P. (1991). Conceptual change strategies and cooperative group work in chemistry. *Journal of Research in Science Teaching, 28*, 293–304.

National Research Council. (1996). From Analysis to action: Undergraduate education in science, mathematics, engineering and technology: Report of a convocation. National Academy Press: Washington, DC.

Obaya, A. (1999). Getting cooperative learning. *Science Education International, 10*, 25–27.

Smith, K. A. & MacGregor, J. (2000). Making small group learning and learning communities a widespread reality. *New Directions for Teaching and Learning, 81*, 77–88.

Spinger, L. (1997, March). *Relating concepts and applications through structured active learning.* Paper presented at the Annual Meeting of the American Educational Research Association, Chicago, IL.

Towns, M. H., Kreke, K., & Fields, A. (2000). An action research project: Student perspectives on small-group learning in chemistry. *Journal of Chemical Education, 77,* 111–115.

Helpful Web site:

http://www.wcer.wisc.edu.nise (accessed Oct 2002)

12

Your Partner for Successful Teaching: Small Groups

Susan C. Nurrenbern
Department of Chemistry
Purdue University

Abstract

This chapter explores the many aspects one can encounter with efforts to pursue instructional change. Much of the skepticism toward instructional change originates from the normal psychological resistance to any change and will surface within your department, your colleagues, your students, and even yourself. Techniques that the author has found useful and helpful in handling the challenges with colleagues and students are included in the chapter. For example, classroom management and design of tasks and activities for small-group work, informal short-term groups and long-term or fixed groups, are significant factors that can help address the challenges. Knowledge of group dynamics and issues that can arise within groups are necessary for group management. While no one can anticipate all the issues that will arise in any department or classroom situation in advance, being informed about possibilities is an very important key to an instructor's success.

Biography

I began my teaching career as a licensed chemistry (secondary) teacher in Indiana. During my career I have taught junior high general science, high school and community college chemistry courses. I have also spent three years at the Medical College of Ohio as a technician in the hospital clinical lab and in biochemistry research before pursuing my PhD.

Since earning a Ph.D. in science education with an emphasis in chemistry at Purdue in 1979 with Dudley Herron. My teaching experiences in chemistry have been at four-year universities, with 13 of those years at the University of Wisconsin—Stout. At UW–Stout I was promoted to the rank of full professor and was chemistry department chair for five years.

I joined the professional staff as an instructional specialist in the Chemistry Department at Purdue University—West Lafayette in August 1993. Among my varied responsibilities, I coordinate all course activites for the two-semester mainstream freshmen chemistry course having an enrollment of about 2200 students during the first semester and about 1600 students during the second semester. On average, I coordinate the instructional efforts of four to five faculty and 60 to 70 graduate instructors per semester. In this process, I work with graduate instructors to help them develop professional skills and expertise in content knowledge, classroom management, time management, grading skills, recordkeeping, using active learning techniques, and enforcing safety regulations. I handle and coordinate activities and accommodations for students with special needs and issues related to academic integrity. I maintain a course Web site for the mainstream two-semester freshmen chemistry course to provide information about course policies and activities to all stakeholders (e.g., students, parents, academic advisors) in the course at Purdue.

I participate in the Chemistry Department's official TA Orientation Program at Purdue. I serve on the campus-wide Committee for the Education of Teaching Assistants.

My experience in teaching extends into the educational psychology or pedagogical area. I taught the teaching methods portion of summer workshops for high school chemistry/science teachers and middle school science teachers for 10 years at the Institute for Chemical Education at the University of Wisconsin–Madison. I was the laboratory instructor for chemistry advanced-placement workshops at Purdue for four summers. In addition, I have conducted various short workshops and presentations about cooperative learning, concept mapping, conceptual learning, and graduate instructor professional development at 2YC3 Conferences, Biennial Conferences on Chemical Education, and Gordon Conferences.

> *Teaching is what happens outside the head; learning is what happens inside the head. For these students to learn, direct teaching must occur to build these cognitive structures.*
>
> *Ruby Payne (2002), 12*

"I Am A Rock, I am An Island" by Simon and Garfunkel was my theme song during my junior and senior undergraduate years at Indiana State University as I studied to be a secondary chemistry teacher. A course in Group Dynamics that I took while I was studying to earn my master's was an eye-opening reality check about the way most of the world functions. Although other classes and experiences have been very useful and informative, that class has had the broadest impact on my life and profession.

Groups of various types are ubiquitous in everyone's life. Groups vary in nature from the personal and social to the professional. Groups are often organized around a common theme or interest such as family, work, hobbies, or politics. What you learn as you work in the small groups of your daily life can be a significant contributor to the success you have in implementing small-group instruction.

You instantly become a member of several existing groups the moment you accept an offer for a faculty or teaching position. Your department is normally your primary group, but you become a member of the science, the school, and the university faculty. You will not be a member of the clerical or maintenance staff, technicians' group or a student group, but observing and learning how those groups operate can provide values insight into group organization and activity. The more you learn about small groups through personal experience and reflection, the more comfortable you will be using small-group instruction with your students.

> ## The Initial Year(s)
> ## SURVIVE, LEARN, and PLAN
> ## to
> ## Set the Stage for Future Successes

Constructing a solid foundation during the initial years of employment is critical for future productivity. The first year at any job is one of the most stressful experiences in life. With the interview process behind you and your teaching assignment in hand, a significant step toward laying a good foundation and ultimately being successful at implementing small-group instruction involves getting to know your group situations. This involves learning about your workplace: the history, sociology, politics, and culture of the department as well as the philosophies of individuals within the department. Identifying and making connections with potentially supportive colleagues is crucial.

As you progress through these first years, you need to identify things that can be changed to improve student learning, share your ideas with your colleagues, and also plan for changes in the next years.

The department, your colleagues, and instructional change

The usual advice to an instructor teaching a course for the first time is to use the course outline and syllabus from previous terms. While the syllabus is a guideline for content coverage, the techniques you choose to use to present this content is an aspect of your academic freedom.

Incorporating small-group and cooperative learning into a course with defined content coverage requires group tasks that are timed and tightly focused on the content topic and ideas you want students to learn. Think about alternative modes of instruction, such as on-line homework for skill-building exercises. Good classroom organization and time-management skills are essential for implementing any type of effective learning techniques.

One objection to using group work is that it limits the amount of content coverage. Even in my lifetime, not only more content but an increased depth and extent of coverage has found its way into undergraduate chemistry courses. Yet all the research and anecdotal evidence shows that an instructor's lecture coverage of the material does not correlate well with meaningful learning of the material for a majority of students. The approach of using the same, familiar lecture strategies, only with greater intensity, has not been an effective strategy for improving student understanding or achievement. You can "hope that students would learn to *(fill the blank)*, but instructors' hopes have not proved to be an effective motivator for student learning. When I was an assistant professor at the University of Wisconsin-Stout and introduced small-group activities in laboratories and lectures, my colleagues responded with "We'll watch for a couple of years before we comment." It was a little tough going at first, and my colleagues **were watching**! By that time I had learned some things about politics within a department, and during the initial implementation period I shared my trials, successes, and tribulations informally with my colleagues on a regular basis and even asked for their advice. Consequently, I slowly and deliberately educated my colleagues about the process while I maintained a topic coverage schedule that was set by the course syllabus. When students who participated in cooperative learning situations in my class moved to upper-level courses, my colleagues began to observe and comment that the conceptual understanding and creative problem-solving abilities in these students were superior to previous students. By the time I left UW-Stout, I covered somewhat less content (e.g., fewer equilibrium and kinetic computations) but with a different focus (e.g., interpretation of equilibrium and kinetics concepts) yet helped students become better problem solvers while improving their attitudes toward chemistry. Enrollment in upper-level courses increased, and my colleagues introduced cooperative group work in their courses.

If you are debating with yourself whether to venture outside the familiar classroom lecture, individual skill-building labs, and competitive grading format, then give some thought to the type of student you need to reach in your classes. While there are some students who will learn and succeed in the historical style and independent of what the instructor does or does not do, an increasing number of students in our classrooms need a different approach if they are to succeed. You have the opportunity to reach groups that have been marginalized in science and engineering classrooms (Seymour & Hewitt 1997) for many years by using a variety of techniques, including small-group activities. In my experiences cooperative and small-group techniques have been most effective in bringing up the baseline of class performance with a shift of D/F/W grades upward to C and B levels and helping students think more positively about their relationship with chemistry.

Classroom management

Master your general classroom management skills and build your confidence level before launching innovative techniques on a large scale. Among the most valuable classroom skills for an instructor to command are:

- Teacher voice
- Time management
- Visual scanning capabilities

- Listening/hearing skills
- Understanding student body-language

A teacher voice is necessary for maintaining control in any classroom. A teacher voice can be heard by all and has a tone of assertiveness without sounding like a drill sergeant. In small-group work, an effective teacher voice can be important when you want to halt small-group work and bring a class together again as a whole. Conversely, silence can also be an effective management tool.

Planning and conducting cooperative, small-group activities requires attention to the time you will devote to a given topic just as you would do when writing lectures. Set time limits for group activities and stick to them. You do not have to give all the answers to students who choose to be passive recipients in lectures or small-group activities. It does not harm students if they leave class without "the answer." Some students are quite skilled at limiting the amount of material that is discussed or covered in class (thereby limiting what they have to learn for the exam) by asking the same question repeatedly, straying from the task, or sighing with the "I just don't understand this" attitude. Knowing when to tell a student to see you in your office for individual consultation is an extremely critical component of good classroom time management.

Whatever teaching technique you use, the ability to constantly monitor what is happening in your entire classroom or lab is necessary. You need acute visual and listening skills with appropriate filtering mechanisms to be able to differentiate between normal and anomalous classroom behavior, especially when students are working in groups. Your visual scanning skills need to be analogous to a scanning spectrophotometer; your hearing skills analogous to sonar. Sensitivity to odors can help you detect any unapproved activities, particularly in labs.

If in the process of developing classroom management skills you learn that you cannot give up center stage or feel that you will lose control of your class by using small-group instruction techniques, then you can stop reading here. Unless you really believe that small-group instruction, or any other technique, will add value to your students' learning, your attitude and hesitance will be apparent to your students, you will not be able to communicate the value and importance of learning in small groups to them, and ultimately small-group instruction will not be successful for you or your students.

Classroom talk

Student-student classroom talk. Just getting students to engage in productive student-student talk in a classroom can be a challenge, and you may have to demonstrate your expectations. Student-student talk can be initiated by having pairs of students work together in a structured activity where they answer questions or solve puzzles and problems that *do not contain chemistry material*.

A structured pair situation (Whimbey & Lochhead 1979) in which partners take turns being the problem solver and the listener can help initiate student talk. The problem solver reads the problem out loud and then solves the problem while telling the listener what he/she is thinking as he/she solves the problem or puzzle. The listener must remind the problem solver to talk out loud and explain, draw diagrams, words, or numbers to illustrate what he/she is doing or thinking as he/she tries to solve the problem. With a second problem, the partners exchange roles and proceed through the process again.

Figure 1. Initiating Classroom Student-Student Talk: Non-Content Structured Pair Problems (Source: Whimbey & Lochhead 1979)

Instructions: Read and think aloud, explaining your thoughts and your reasoning to your partner as you solve the problems. Take turns with your partner being the problem solver and the listener.

Problem 1) If the circle below is taller than the square, and the cross is shorter than the square, put a *K* in the circle. However, if this is not the case, put a *T* in the second tallest figure.

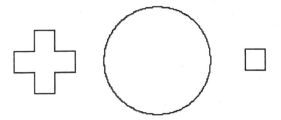

Problem 2) Circle the letter in the name *Anthony* that is 3 letters before the letter that follows the middle letter of the name.

After students learn to talk with each other in class, then you can give them a pair of simple chemistry questions or problems for students to answer or solve in this structured pair mode. As students work with each other, it becomes difficult to avoid talking and helping the other person by hinting at errors being made or the information the problem solver might be overlooking.

Another human characteristic to factor into your design of group work is the fact that most people are very reluctant to participate if there is a risk that they might reveal their lack of knowledge.   Content tasks (Figure 2) to minimize this pitfall can be conceptualized around the idea that it is easier to criticize than to be correct. Tasks where students must identify mistakes in a problem-solving process or answers that you fabricate or recall from commonly made errors in students' work function to reduce risks associated with potentially embarrassing situations. An alternate strategy is to have students evaluate whether answers are correct or incorrect and, if incorrect, then provide the correct response.

Teacher-student talk. All formal and informal messages you give to students must reflect a teaching philosophy and practice that all the students can learn chemistry and succeed in your class. Plan and think about the type and nature of comments and responses you will use as you go around the class, observe, and monitor your students' progress. Comments that recognize student difficulties and frustrations but also reflect your belief that the students are capable of completing the task successfully should be part of your repertoire. Train yourself to use positive comments such as the following when helping students learn in small groups.

- Good job today, everyone!
- I know this can be confusing, but we can get it all sorted out.
- Nice job!
- Having a tough time getting started?
- Let's see what you have done so far.
- Have you thought about ... ?
- Can you draw a diagram or outline of the problem?
- That's an interesting approach. Would you share it with the class?
- Good work. Since we're running out of time, can you help the group next to you while I help the group across the room?

Group activities

Anticipate that students, like some of your colleagues, will resist change to what they have experienced as standard classroom expectations: passive student participation while waiting out the teacher until he/she gives the answer to the class. Expect that when given choices, students and some colleagues will choose a familiar path of least resistance or minimum mental energy and effort. Your ability to counteract that mind-set will depend on your commitment, persistence, and patience.

Figure 2. Getting Started with Small, Informal Groups—Content Problems
Sample Task 1

On a quiz, students were asked to convert 55.5 mg to kilograms and write out the process they used to make the conversion. The following are examples of several answers that students wrote. Your group is to identify the errors in each answer, then write a correct process for the conversion. [Time limit: 4 minutes]

(a) $55.5 \text{ mg} \times \dfrac{1 \text{ kg}}{1000 \text{ g}} = 0.0555 \text{ kg}$

(b) $55.5 \text{ mg} \times \dfrac{1 \text{ g}}{100 \text{ mg}} \times \dfrac{1000 \text{ g}}{1 \text{ kg}} = 555 \text{ kg}$

(c) $1000 / 55.5 =$

(d) $x = \dfrac{55.5}{(1000)(1000)} = 5.55 \times 10^6 \text{ kg}$

The correct process from our group is:

Each group will turn one copy of its work with all group members' name on the paper.

Informal, short-term groups.   The nature of cooperative activities can be beneficial to all your students, but benefits will vary among students. Group activities appears to be most helpful for students who have been intimidated by the traditional, individual, competitive approach (Seymour & Hewitt 1997). This includes many women, minorities, and students who fell through the cracks in high school.

You must establish grading criteria that do not incorporate competition among students for grades. For some students, that will serve as a hook to encourage their participation in small groups. For other students, Skinnerian techniques such as reward for performance (i.e. verification of answers) or other behavior-modification techniques might be necessary to bring students to a point where they recognize the value of learning cooperatively and willingly participate.

Introducing minimal risk–minimal commitment activities with informal groups in a classroom or "lecture" environment is an excellent way to begin small-group instruction (Nurrenbern 1995). Some minimal risk strategies involve combining other techniques with small, informal, short-term groups. For example, small groups can be used in conjunction with:

- Student seat work and problem solving
- Demonstrations
- Concept-map construction

Instead of your working example problems for the class, pose a problem for the students to solve, then stand aside and let them work. Students can work individually and then compare their work with others or approach the problem as a group from the initial stages. They can compare answers with other groups (Figure 3). As you walk around and discover where your students are having difficulties, you can identify teachable moments and readjust your presentation or group activities as needed.

The learning value of classic classroom demonstrations of chemical phenomena can be enhanced by small-group discussion. After a demonstration, small groups of students can discuss the demonstration, identify the main concepts being demonstrated, and list the unanswered questions generated by the demonstration. Get feedback and perform the demonstration again.

Concept mapping has been shown to be an excellent way to help students relate concepts and ideas (Robinson 1999). Concept mapping can be designed as a small-group activity to generate questions and discussion about a topic. After listing a set of related concepts, you can start the concept-map construction on the board by choosing two concepts and linking them together. Then the chalk or marker passes to another person who adds in another concept and link. When all the concepts have been included, shift the focus to adding or editing links. Another method is to have small groups simultaneously construct concept maps with the same concepts on the board or acetate sheets for the overhead. These concept maps can then be compared, discussed, and edited.

Long-term or fixed groups and projects.   Long-term or fixed small groups are commonly utilized in the laboratory component of science courses. The size of groups depends on the scope of the activity and needs to be consistent with the amount of work required. Groups of two, three, or four are commonly used with success. If there is not enough work for each person in a triad to make an individual contribution, for example, then have students work in groups of two.

A traditional lab, such as preparation and determination of the concentration of a base using the titration technique, can be restructured into a suitable group project that incorporates both individual and group responsibilities. A group (or pair of students) can prepare one sodium hydroxide, NaOH, solution. They divide into subgroups (or work as individuals) and each subgroup (or individual) standardizes the NaOH solution. Each subgroup, however, uses *a different acid* for the titration. The subgroups share their results, compare results from different acids, discuss why the concentration values should or should not agree. You can require one report per individual that includes information from the other group members or one report per group. You can factor in both individual and group components for the total lab score in your grading scheme. Additional examples of templates for structuring lab activities can be found in the Appendices.

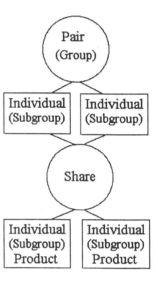

Figure 3.
Think, Pair, Share Model

The type and extent of small-group instruction that you introduce into your courses during the initial years of teaching may well depend on the size of the class. Nevertheless, think "outside the box" when considering small-group instruction. While common knowledge might suggest that board work is suited for small groups only, some instructors have been known to get students to write on the board (eg., balance chemical equations or write the problem-solving process) in a large lecture hall.

Small-group work requires as much planning and preparation as you might expect to spend preparing a lecture. You do not give up control or classroom management skills when students work in small groups. Instead, you help students assume responsibility for their own learning. Managing small-group instruction requires classroom management skills above and beyond what are required for the lecturing or didactic, individualistic learning environment. Since the initial year of teaching is usually characterized as a year of survival, introduce changes slowly and in small steps unless you have a lot of experience with a special technique such as small groups.

Group dynamics and conflicts

Student problems, complaints, and issues arise in any course despite your best efforts to establish rules and guidelines for acceptable classroom behavior. The types of problems that you will encounter will be confounded with the type of teaching technique that you implement. The interactive nature of group work presents challenges different from those associated with the more familiar individualistic approach to learning. You need to be familiar with group processing as well as behaviors and roles of individuals within a group.

The basic development process for long-term groups involves four phases: Forming, Storming, Norming and Performing (Towns 1998). The forming phase can be characterized as relatively peaceful while the students meet each other. The storming phase ensues as students get to know each other better and begin to identify strengths, weaknesses, as well as differences in values, effort, and ability. After the arguing and discussion of the storming phase, the group reaches agreement (i.e. norming phase) and can begin to work together effectively in the performing phase.

Figure 4. Potential Instructor Roles During the Storming Phase

- Jump in immediately and "solve" the problem for the group.
- Be patient and allow the passage of time to help moderate the problem.
- Allow and help the group identify and solve its own problem.

The storming phase can be an intimidating phase for instructors, and mere thoughts of potential conflicts in this phase can be a rate-determining step toward implementation of small-group work. However, this is where your expertise and knowledge about groups will be needed most. If your intervention with group conflicts is needed, you must decide about the nature and extent of your intervention in the group's conflict(s) (Figure 4). You can jump right in and solve the problem for the group, rely on the passage of time to moderate the conflict as it often does, or you can allow and help the group solve its own problems. At first glance, solving the problem for the group may seem to be the most efficient option. However, this strategy has a negative effect on the group's progress and development into the norming and performing phases. The group development process breaks down when members of the group do not have to take responsibility for the group process or their role in the process. Solving the problem for the group can suppress issues and resentments that surface within the group long after the original problem seems to have been resolved.

To allow or help the group solve its own problems, it is often sufficient to give students time to calm down, go away, and put things into perspective. In some situations the group can be assisted with their communication by having an outsider, i.e. the instructor, present. In such cases the process shown in Table 1 is an effective intervention strategy.

Table 1: Helping Groups Through the Storming Phase

- Sit down with the entire group.
- Have the student(s) with concerns restate the concerns to the entire group. If the individual cannot express concerns to the group, you can summarize what you have been told about the group's difficulties.
- Let others respond and tell their side of the story.
- Challenge the group to decide what is a fair or appropriate outcome, as well as what needs to be changed and how the changes will be implemented.

Anticipation of potential group conflicts can generate more anxiety than that caused by actual conflicts. Table 2 identifies other issues about small groups that you need to factor into your thinking as you help groups through the storming phase.

Table 2: Lessons I Have Learned About Handling the Storming Phase

- Problems are usually not as urgent as a student might suggest. Problems often resolve themselves after the initial flare-up. There **is** time to consult with the other group members.
- There is **always** more than one side to a story or situation. OR: Don't believe everything a student tells you no matter how sincere the student sounds or how watery the student's eyes get.
- Never try to solve a group problem with one member of the group. Group problems must be solved with the entire group.

- Never assume that one gender is more likely to be a certain type problem in a group than the other gender.
- The complaining student could very well be the cause of the problems in a group.
- Never deal with saboteurs or bullies alone. As a last resort, the group can divorce the saboteur or bully from the group but then you have a problem of identifying a new group that will take the "problem."

Individual problems in groups

Conflicts in groups can arise from the group process itself, individuals within the group, or some combination of both. A large proportion of conflicts are due to poor communication skills and unspoken assumptions about the operation of a learning group. Some conflicts arise from individuals whose behavior and approach impact the group in a negative way. Jalajas & Sutton (1984–85) identified and characterized the five common types of problem individuals in small groups as Whiners, Martyrs, Bullies, Saboteurs and Deadbeats (see Table 3).

Table 3: Individual Problems in Small Groups

Problem	Characteristics
Whiner	Complains that the group is pulling down his/her grade; usually wants to change groups.
Martyr	Complains that his/her extraordinary work and effort are unfairly pulling up grades for other group members; usually just wants "someone" to know his/her situation when grades are assigned.
Bully	*Active Bully*: Tells the group how things should be done and how dumb or inadequate others are compared to him/herself. *Lazy Bully:* Plays no active role in the group until a crucial decision must be made and then tries to force his/her will on others in the group.
Saboteur	Actively disrupts the group by working "behind" the scenes; "changes or improves" the group's work without their knowledge or approval.
Deadbeat	Totally uninvolved in the group activity, then complains when the group does not carry him/her in the project.

Although using small-group instruction may seem daunting and frightening, many have found it to be worth the effort (Towns, et. al 2001). At Purdue we found that graduate instructors who use group work in recitations receive more positive student evaluations and have fewer student complaints than those who "talk at" their students (Nurrenbern, et.al 1999). The graduate instructors learn to interact with their students and therefore are able to coach students more effectively. While college students may not fall into the socioeconomic poverty levels described by Payne (2002), there are similarities between the learning and educational needs of college students and the groups that Payne describes.

Small-group instruction is a powerful tool that can be very useful in constructing an effective, active learning environment. At the same time, years of experience have given me the wisdom to know that any one teaching technique is not the answer to all learning issues in modern classrooms. In addition, the nature of human being brings me to my broadest observations (see text box) and conclusions about students in classroom learning environments.

Figure 5. Sue's Conclusions about Classroom Dynamics

- It is very difficult to keep students from consulting each other (i.e. work in groups) when it is inappropriate and you want them to work individually or independently.

- If is very difficult to get students to interact effectively in a group when it is appropriate and you want them to work together.

> *Just like organic chemical reactions, you never get 100 percent yield but you keep trying!*
> W. R. Robinson, personal communication

References

Jalajas, D. S., & Sutton, R. I. (1984–85). Feuds in student groups: Coping with whiners, martyrs, saboteurs, bullies, and deadbeats. *The Organizational Behavior Teaching Review, IX*, 94.

Nurrenbern, S. C., & Krupp, A. S. (1995). *Cooperative Learning: A Collection for Chemistry Teachers.* University of Wisconsin-Madison: Institute for Chemical Education.

Nurrenbern, S. C., Mickiewicz, J. A. & Francisco, J. S. (1999). The impact of continuous instructional development on graduate and undergraduate students. *Journal of Chemical Education, 76*, 114.

Nurrenbern, S. C. (2001). Piaget's theory of intellectual development revisited. *Journal of Chemical Education, 78*, 1107.

Payne, R. (2002). Understanding and working with students and adults from poverty. *Eisenhower National Clearinghouse Focus, 9*, 12.

Robinson, W. R. (1999). A view from the science education research literature: Concept map assessment of classroom learning. *Journal of Chemical Education, 76*, 1179.

Seymour, E. & Hewitt, N. M. (1997). *Talking About Leaving: Why Undergraduates Leave the Sciences.* Boulder, Colorado: Westview Press.

Towns, M. H. (1998). How do I get my students to work together? Getting cooperative learning started. *Journal of Chemical Education, 75*, 67.

Towns, M. H., Sauder, D., Whisnant, D. & Zielinski, T. J. (2001). Physical chemistry on-line: Interinstitutional collaboration at a distance. *Journal of Chemical Education, 78*, 414.

Whimbey, A. & Lochhead, J. (1979). *Problem Solving and Comprehension: A Short Course in Analytic Reasoning.* Philadelphia, PA: The Franklin Institute Press.

Appendix

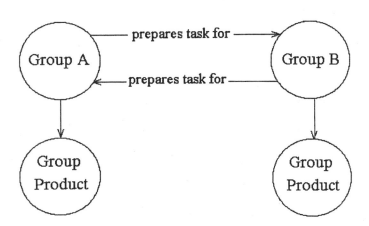

Template A

Example 1   Lab Activity: Introduction to Small-Group Work

<u>Goal</u>   Highlight and emphasize communication skills (mainly writing) as well as working effectively in a group.

<u>Work Plan</u>

Each group gets two plastic bags with identical sets of Lego pieces in each bag. Group A takes one of the bags, constructs a letter of the alphabet with the Legos, and writes down a set of construction instructions for Group B within 20 minutes. Group B gets one copy of the written instructions and the second bag of Legos from Group A. (Group A keeps its constructed letter hidden.) Without talking, Group B distributes the Lego pieces about equally among the group members. Then, without talking and without taking pieces from each other, Group B is to build an identical replica of the letter made by Group A in 20 minutes. Groups then compare their constructed letters and evaluate their work, including their written instructions.

Example 2   Lab Activity: Spectroscopy and Equilibrium

<u>Goal</u>   Establish a standard curve for absorbance versus concentration of $FeSCN^{2+}$; measure absorbance of $FeSCN^{2+}$ in several equilibrium mixtures and calculate the equilibrium formation constant, K_f, for $FeSCN^{2+}$.

<u>Work Plan</u>   Each group:

- establishes a wavelength for maximum absorbance and future measurements; prepares standards and measures absorbance values and constructs a standard curve.

- prepares a set of equilibrium mixtures containing Fe^{3+}, SCN^- and $FeSCN^{2+}$ for a different group to analyze. Groups exchange equilibrium mixtures along with the preparation instructions.

- prepares one report that includes the standard curve they prepared and the analysis of equilibrium mixtures prepared by the other group.

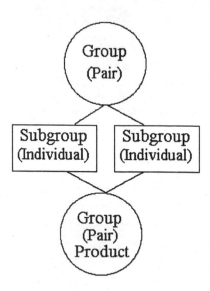

Template B

Example 3   A Lab Project: Equilibrium and Thermodynamics

Goal
- Determine the equilibrium constant, K_{sp}, for borax and the standard enthalpy change, standard entropy change, and standard free-energy change for the process of dissolving borax in water.

Work Plan
- The entire group prepares a saturated borax solution. As the solution cools students take duplicate samples of the solution at five different temperatures.
- Each subgroup titrates ½ of the samples with standardized HCl and calculates the concentration of anion in the solution.
- The subgroups share this information and then calculate a K_{sp} value for borax, and ΔH°, ΔS°, and ΔG° for the dissolution process of borax in water using computational and graphing techniques.
- Each group prepares one report with all the data.

Example 4   A Lab Project: Spectroscopy and Spreadsheet Use

Goals
- Determine the wavelength of maximum absorbance for different food colors.
- Determine which function of %T versus absorbance at 8_{max} produces the best straight line and obtain the equation for the straight line.
- Use the graphing and formatting functions of a spreadsheet to analyze the data.

Work Plan
- Each individual in the group is responsible for collecting and analyzing data for one food coloring.
- Group combines and interprets all the individuals' work into one report.

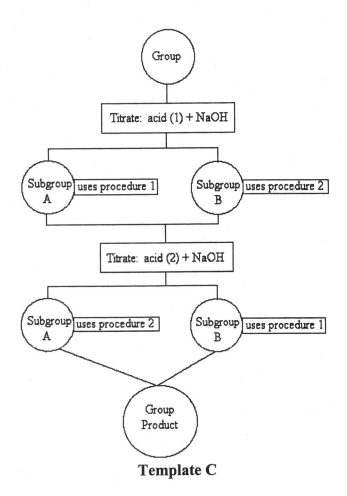

Template C

Example 5   Two-Week Lab Activity: Different Methods, Different Information

Week #1:
Goal
- Collect and compare information obtained from acid-base titrations using an indicator versus a pH titration. Students will use different acids and bases to accomplish this task.

Work Plan
- Subgroup A carries out a regular indicator titration technique of HCl with a strong base.
- Subgroup B carries out a pH titration of HCl with a strong base.
- Subgroup A carries out a pH titration of a weak acid (e.g., acetic acid) with strong base.
- Subgroup B carries out a regular indicator titration technique for a weak acid (e.g., acetic acid) with a strong base.
- The entire group (subgroups A and B) brings all data together to calculate the concentration of the strong base using the two different techniques. Using the pH titration data and graph, they determine the K_a value for the weak acid.
- Group puts together all the data and data analyses for one report.

Week #2
Goals
- Group must design and carry out procedures to determine the following:
  - molar mass and K_a value(s) of an unknown mono- or di-protic acid using a strong-base.
  - concentration and the K_b value for a weak base using a strong acid.

Work Plan
- The entire group must discuss what needs to be done and establish their own work plan.

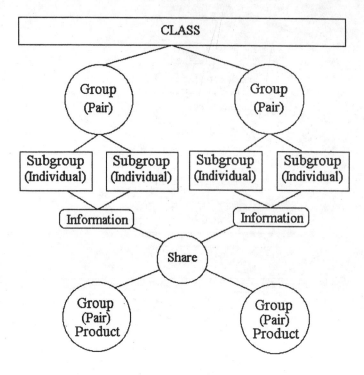

Template D

Example 6   A Lab Project: Analyzing for Iron Content in Food

Goal
- The entire lab has the task of determining whether the iron content differs in broccoli or cauliflower and if the content varies in different parts of the broccoli or cauliflower.

Work Plan
- The entire class decides what parts of the veggie to sample and which parts each group will analyze.

- In small groups, subgroups are assigned different tasks such as:
  - veggie sample preparation.
  - preparation of solutions; cleaning and setup of titration equipment.
  - setup of computer spreadsheet to enter data and graph as the titration data points are collected.

- Each small group calculates the amount of iron per gram of veggie analyzed and shares the results with the entire class.

- Each group prepares a report with its data and data analysis, including the results of all the other small groups.

Section

IV

TESTING AND ASSESSMENT

13

Using Conceptual Questions in the Chemistry Classroom

William R. Robinson
Department of Chemistry
Purdue University

Eunyoung Hurh
Department of Chemistry
Seoul National University

> *The first key to wisdom is constant questioning.*
> *Peter Abelard (1079–1142)*

Abstract

The literature reports that many students do not understand chemistry concepts and have a variety of misconceptions in many areas. Other work has shown that students can solve algorithmic problems but cannot answer questions based on the concepts behind the problems. We suggest that the use of conceptual questions can encourage students to improve their understanding of chemistry concepts. Conceptual questions are questions that a student has not been trained to answer. Answering these questions requires that a student analyze the chemical ideas associated with the question rather than using a memorized answer or algorithm. In this chapter we discuss the nature of conceptual questions, why they should be used, how they can be used, and sources of questions.

Biographies

Bill Robinson is a professor of chemistry and science education at Purdue University, *The Journal of Chemical Education* published his first chemical education article in 1980, and there have been more. Bill or his coworkers present regularly in various DivCHED symposia. He served on the Exams Institute's General Chemistry Examination Subcommittee three times, helped developed the first ACS chemistry conceptual examination, and chaired the committee that wrote the second conceptual exam. He writes a column for *The Journal of Chemical Education* summarizing the science education research literature. He and Sue Nurrenbern developed and tend the conceptual question and challenge problem Web site for the *Journal*. He is chair of the ACS Division of Chemical Education for 2003. Bill has coauthored five editions of *General Chemistry* for D. C. Heath and Houghton Mifflin and a short general chemistry text *Chemistry: Concepts and Models*. In 1993–1994 he was a Project SERAPHIM Fellow at UW-Madison, where he developed tutorial programs for general chemistry and collaborated in the writing of *Teaching General Chemistry: A Materials Science Companion*.

Eunyoung Hurh is an associate professor with responsibility for general chemistry and chemistry teaching laboratories in the School of Chemistry and Engineering at Seoul National University. Her research focuses on chemistry misconceptions, use of conceptual questions, and distance education. From 1999–2001 she was a Korean Organization of Science and Engineering Fellow working with the chemical education group at Purdue University. She presents regularly in various chemical education conferences in the United States and Korea.

Introduction

Conceptual questions serve two purposes. They can push students to expand their thinking by presenting them with problems that are not paraphrases of problems they see in their lecture or text, and they can give instructors better insights into the depth of understanding of their students. This chapter describes the use of conceptual questions in the chemistry classroom. It is divided into four sections:

(1) *What are conceptual questions?* This section describes the features that make conceptual questions different from other questions.

(2) *Why use conceptual questions?* This section presents pragmatic and theoretical reasons for our position that conceptual questions can be helpful in leading your students to a better understanding of chemistry concepts.

(3) *Using conceptual questions.* The effective use of conceptual questions involves more than simply putting them on homework assignments or on examinations. This section suggests ways that they can be used effectively.

(4) *Sources of conceptual questions.* Conceptual questions are difficult to write, but sources of these questions are identified in this section.

What are conceptual questions?

Conceptual questions are questions that a student has not been trained to solve. They are designed to tap into students' understandings of chemical ideas rather than their ability to recall. They also can challenge students to articulate their understanding and, in the process, to evaluate that understanding. Many conceptual questions involve all of the representations used to represent and translate chemical information: macroscopic, particulate, and symbolic representations.

There are various kinds of conceptual questions. But these questions all present a chemical situation and ask students either to predict what happens in a new situation, to explain why something new happens, or to explain how something new happens. These questions address more than simple recall, so what may be a conceptual question for a novice may not be conceptual for a more experienced chemist. What constitutes a conceptual question depends on where you are in your knowledge.

The committee that wrote the first ACS General Chemistry Examination (ACS DivCHED Examinations Institute, 1994) put together a list of characteristics of conceptual questions. They believe that conceptual questions:

> Assess student understanding of the underlying ideas behind phenomena.
> Require students to explain why something occurs.
> Test the transfer of knowledge.
> Require students to adapt an explanation to a new situation.
> Require students to identify the underlying concept in order to recognize which algorithm to invoke.
> Cause a student to visualize a system and use it to reach a conclusion.
> Serve as occasions of learning as well as evaluation.

Any one conceptual question cannot incorporate all of these characteristics, but all conceptual questions have one common characteristic: They are not questions that students have been trained to answer. A conceptual question should have some new twist that requires students to identify which part of their training to use. The following are probably conceptual questions for most students in a general chemistry course.

1. Is 100 milliliters of a solution that contains 20 grams of sugar and 5 grams of NaCl a strong electrolyte, a weak electrolyte, or a nonelectrolyte? Explain your answer.

2. Sketch a qualitative graph of the equilibrium pressure of water vapor above a sample of pure water and above a sugar solution as the liquids evaporate to half their original volume.

3. Describe how the size of 1s orbitals in the atoms change across the second period of the periodic table (from Li to Ne) and down the first group of the table (from H to Fr). Explain.

4. Which of the following 0.10 M solutions in water freezes at the lowest temperature? Assume the molality and molarity are equal in these solutions.

    a. Acetic acid ($K_a = 1.8 \times 10^{-5}$)

    b. Boric acid ($K_a = 5.8 \times 10^{-10}$)

    c. Ammonia ($K_b = 1.8 \times 10^{-5}$)

    d. Methylamine ($K_b = 4.4 \times 10^{-4}$)

    e. Impossible to determine from the information given.

5. What is K_b for the conjugate base of a weak acid if a 0.035 M solution of the weak acid has a pH of 4.14?

6. Ammonium hydrogen sulfide decomposes according to the following reaction:

$$NH_4HS(s) \rightarrow H_2S(g) + NH_3(g) \qquad K_c = 0.011$$

    If 36.2 g of $NH_4HS(s)$ (molar mass = 51.11) is sealed in a 5.2-L container, what is the concentration of $NH_3(g)$ at equilibrium?

The following paired multiple choice question comes from Bowen and Bunce (1997):

7A. A child blows up a balloon to a volume of about 2 L. What happens to the volume of the gas if the balloon is put in a freezer? The volume is

    a. the same as the original volume.

    b. less than the original volume.

    c. greater than the original volume.

    d. impossible to determine.

7B. What is the reason for your answer to #1? The molecules of gas

    e. get smaller when they get cold.

    f. expand when they are cooled.

    g. are not affected by temperature changes.

    h. have a decreased amount of kinetic energy.

    i. have an increased amount of kinetic energy.

The following are probably not examples of conceptual questions except to students who are just starting the study of these topics and who have not practiced the material:

1. How many grams of chlorine react with 12.0 grams of magnesium to form magnesium chloride?

2. What is the freezing point of a solution that contains 12 grams of $C_{10}H_8$ in 100 g of benzene?

3. Explain why the energy of a 2p electron is higher than that of a 2s electron in a carbon atom.

Why use conceptual questions?

Ernst von Glasersfeld's (1995) constructivist model of learning provides a theoretical reason for using conceptual questions. There are three components of his model that are relevant to our discussion:

- Knowledge (understanding) is not passively received but is actively built up by learners.

- Knowledge consists of ways and means of acting that an individual believes adequate in a given situation.

- Learning occurs by testing the fit of knowledge against its environment.

From the constructivist view, our understanding consists of collections of knowledge about concepts as well as actions that we have found to be successful when we encounter a given situation. If our knowledge leads to actions that are successful, we view that knowledge to be valid. On the other hand, we view knowledge to be invalid if it does not produce successful results. If we are always in situations where our knowledge works, we have no need to revise it. Thus, if memorizing definitions and algorithms leads us to a successful result in a chemistry course, then we will have no reason to go further in trying to understand the concepts of chemistry.

In order to change our knowledge we need to experience situations where our knowledge does not work when we expect it to. Conceptual questions can provide situations where students test their knowledge and recognize that they need to learn differently. These questions require students to express their understanding, and by doing that, the students must evaluate that understanding.

There also are pragmatic reasons to use conceptual questions in your classroom. A recent report has shown that a traditional general chemistry course does not enhance students' conceptual understanding (Mulford & Robinson 2002). Most students study those topics they believe will be on an examination. So if we believe that conceptual understanding is as important as recall, then we need to test that understanding. If students have an opportunity to think about chemical concepts in response to conceptual questions and if they are tested with conceptual questions, their learning style will change to include a focus on understanding the concepts. However, to be fair, we should give students experience with conceptual questions before using them in an examination situation. This means using conceptual questions on homework and/or in the classroom.

Several authors (Herron 1996; Barouch 1997; Garratt, Overton & Threlfall 1999; Landis et al. 2001) suggest that classroom use of conceptual questions can increase student understanding. Herschback notes in the preface to *Voyages in Conceptual Chemistry* (Barouch 1997) that concept questions help students improve their qualitative reasoning. Garratt, Overton, and Threlfall (1999) point out that concept questions can reveal differences between those who think of chemistry as a process and those who simply regard it as knowledge to be remembered. Landis et al. (2001) indicate that the use of conceptual questions provides real-time feedback and can be used to invoke peer-instruction. Oral assessments of students' competence demonstrates a higher order ranking for students who take courses that are rich in pedagogical techniques such as interactive lectures and peer instruction provided by the use of conceptual questions in the class room. (Wright et al. 1998)

solving chemistry problems is they do not understand the concepts needed to solve the problem. Students appear to solve problems by memorizing algorithms instead of developing the understanding necessary to solve them. (Gabel & Bunce 1994) For example, most students who memorize how to use dimensional analysis to solve stoichiometry problems generally cannot answer the following question:

Dimethylglyoxime, DMG, is an organic compound used to test for aqueous nickel(II) ions. A solution prepared by dissolving 65.0 g of DMG in 375 g of ethanol boils at 80.3 °C. What is the molar mass of DMG?

K_b = 1.22 °C/m, boiling point of pure ethanol = 78.5 °C

Most students can calculate molality from the freezing-point depression and the freezing-point depression constant. Many can determine the number of moles of DMG in the solution. However, few can determine the molar mass of DMG from the data given. (Robinson, 2002)

A series of reports beginning with that of Nurrenbern and Pickering (1987) have shown that students who can solve quantitative problems may lack understanding of the concepts that underlie the calculation. In their study students solved two types of problems, one quantitative and the other a related conceptual problem. Figure 1 presents one example of a pair of their questions. Eighty-six percent of the students involved in the study correctly answered the quantitative gas law question calculating a pressure of 3.67 atmospheres. Only 16 percent of their sample answered the conceptual question correctly; fifty percent chose answer (b).

Figure 1. A Quantitative Gas Law Problem and a Conceptual Gas Law Problem

1. A sample of 0.100 mol of H_2(g) occupies 600 mL at 25 °C and 4.08 atm. If the volume is held constant, what will be the pressure of the sample at − 5 °C?

2. The figure represents the distribution of molecules in a steel tank holding H_2(g) at room temperature.

Which represents the distribution of H_2(g) molecules at −20 °C?

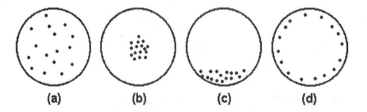

     (a)   (b)   (c)   (d)

Understanding of density provides another example. Most students define density as "mass over volume" and can calculate a value of density from the appropriate data. Some can use density to determine the volume of a substance from its density and mass. However, few students at the general chemistry level understand that a density of 1.37 grams per milliliter for a substance indicates that one milliliter of the substance weighs 1.37 grams.

Finally, experience has shown that using conceptual questions in small-group or whole-group settings during lecture improves interest and attendance. Landis et al. (2001) indicate that the use of conceptual questions increases students enthusiasm for lecture, increases attendance, and decreases attrition. Hurh (2002) has shown the short term use of conceptual questions increases attendance and enthusiasm, although longer interventions appear to be required to improve conceptual understanding.

Using conceptual questions

Conceptual questions can be used on examinations, homework, laboratory reports, and in classroom discussions. One of us (WRR) teaches a large course with exams that usually consist of 20 multiple choice questions. About half of the questions are qualitative and the remainder are quantitative. Depending on the content, two or three of the qualitative questions and two or three of the quantitative questions will be conceptual. Most of the quantitative conceptual questions simply contain extraneous information: For an example see Question 6 in the section *What Are Conceptual Questions?* We also use an answer basket (Binder 1988) with quantitative multiple choice questions such as Questions 5 and 6 in that section. An answer basket is a device that gives a student taking a multiple choice examination a choice of 20 to 25 numerical answers rather than just four or five.

A stand-alone multiple choice conceptual question is graded like any other multiple choice question, right or wrong. We grade each component of paired multiple choice questions separately. We reason that a student may know a behavior but not the reason for it, or may possess a model but may not apply it correctly. Others may choose to give no credit unless both questions in the pair are answered correctly.

Grading free response conceptual questions requires an instructor to assign a weight to the correct behavior and a weight to the explanation. Depending on the importance placed on each part, the weights could be equal or one part of the question could be weighted more heavily than the other. In grading explanations one does need to be careful that the students provide an explanation and not a trend or a restatement of the problem. For a question like "Which is larger, a boron atom or a nitrogen atom. Explain," we would not count as correct the explanation "N is larger because it lies to the right of B in the period" because it cites a trend, not an explanation. Neither would we give credit for "The valence orbitals in N are smaller that the valence orbitals in B" because it is a restatement of the information in the question. We would require an explanation that addresses the effect of increasing nuclear charge on the size of the valence shell for the explanation to be counted as correct.

The use of conceptual questions on exams, homework, and laboratory reports requires no particular changes in these items. However, using conceptual questions in the classroom is best implemented as part of a group activity. Mazur (2000) suggests using conceptual questions as prompts for peer instruction. He intersperses brief mini-lectures with conceptual multiple choice questions designed to illustrate the basic principles of the material. The students work on the questions individually for two or three minutes and commit to individual answers. The commitment can range from a simple show of hands or a colored card to voting on a wireless network. This step allows an instructor to gauge the extent of the class' understanding of the topic. Students then discuss their answers for two to three minutes in groups of three or four. Following the discussion period, the instructor briefly summarizes the answer. Generally a brief explanation is adequate because nearly all students see the correct answer during the group discussion. However, if most of the class members (> 75%) reach the correct answer individually, Mazur skips the group discussion stage, since few students will benefit from it. On the other hand, if very few members of the class (< 30%) arrive at the correct answer individually, there are too few students who understand for the group discussion stage to be fruitful and he goes straight to the faculty discussion.

This approach does require changes in both student and faculty approaches to lecture. Students need to come to class prepared and not expect to see the first introduction to the material during the lecture. Faculty need to revise their lecture presentations to include mini-lectures, conceptual questions, and time for students to work with these questions. There also needs to be some type of feedback mechanism so students can "vote" for the correct answer.

Mazur (2000) and others (Barouch 1997; Garratt, Overton & Threlfall 1999; Landis et al. 2001) report several benefits of this approach. These include increased student satisfaction, immediate feedback to the instructor on student understanding, and higher student performance on both conceptual questions and traditional problems. However, all of these benefits do not occur immediately.

In an introductory college chemistry class in which attendance was not required, Hurh (2002) found that 95 percent of a group that used conceptual questions in the classroom and on homework attended at least three of the five lectures that used conceptual questions, while only 67 percent of the control group using traditional lectures attended three of five lectures over the same material. The instruction did not significantly improve the performance of the treatment group relative to the control group on conceptual questions on an achievement test, but it did not harm performance on algorithmic questions, either. This result might imply that students need to practice more to be comfortable with conceptual questions because these questions are new to them or it could imply that students need a longer exposure to conceptual questions to recognize that their old methods of learning are not completely successful. These students have successful prior experiences learning chemistry and thinking algorithmically. They already have in place a problem-solving model that seems adequate. They may need to experience more dissatisfaction with their performance to be convinced that the old methods will not lead to the necessary understanding.

Several students told Hurh that they enjoyed solving conceptual questions. Others told her that they feel like college students, not high school students, because they were exposed to problems that require higher level thinking. She never heard comments about enjoying the experience from the control group. From the higher attendance and the anecdotal information, it appears that students seemed to enjoy the course more when it used conceptual questions. Improved student attitude could be an important reason to use conceptual questions.

Sources of questions

Additional information about chemistry concept questions is available from a number of sources that include Web sites, journals, and books. A conceptual examination and a blended examination that contains a mixture of conceptual questions and traditional problems is available.

Web sites. The *Journal of Chemical Education* Conceptual Questions and Challenge Problem site, located at http://jchemed.chem.wisc.edu/JCEWWW/Features/CQandChP/index.html, contains a discussion of conceptual questions, sample questions, suggestions for writing conceptual questions, and links to other sites with this type of question.

Additional questions are available at http://www.chem.wisc.edu/~concept/index.html, the ConcepTests web site.

Journals. Research on student misconceptions often involves the use of conceptual questions for diagnosing the misconceptions. The questions are often described in reports in journals that publish science education research. Examples of such journals include *The Journal of Chemical Education*, *The Chemical Educator*, *The International Journal of Research in Science Education*, *The Journal of Research in Science Teaching*, and *Science Education*.

Books. Several books have been published that contain concept questions. *Voyages in Conceptual Chemistry* (Barouch 1997), contains 150 interesting conceptual problems for general and inorganic chemistry. *A Question of Chemistry* (Garratt, Overton & Threlfall 1999) contains five kinds of conceptual problems from all areas of chemistry. Every instructor should be able to find at least a few useful problems in each category. *Chemistry ConcepTests* (Landis et al. 2001) contains many concept questions and examples of ways that these questions can be used in class during a lecture. In addition, many general chemistry books have started to present conceptual questions as part of the end-of-chapter problem sets.

Examinations. A general chemistry conceptual examination and a blended examination that contains a mixture of conceptual questions and traditional problems are available from the ACS DivCHED

Examinations Institute, Chemistry Department, University of Wisconsin-Milwaukee, Milwaukee, WI. The address of their Web site is http://www.uwm.edu/Dept/chemexams/.

References

General Chemistry Examination (conceptual) (1994). UW-Milwaukee Chemistry Department, Milwaukee, WI. [On-line] Available: http://www.uwm.edu/Dept/chemexams/.

Barouch, D. H. (1997). Voyages in conceptual chemistry. London: Jones and Bartlett.

Binder, B. (1988). Improved multiple-choice examinations. *Journal of Chemical Education. 65*, 436.

Bowen, C. W. & Bunce, D. M. (1997). Testing for conceptual understanding in general chemistry. *The Chemical Educator 2*, S1430-4171. [On-line] Available: http://chemed.boisestate.edu/.

Gabel, D. L. & Bunce, D. M. (1994). Research on problem solving in chemistry. In Gabel, D. L. Handbook of research on science teaching and learning (Pages 301-326). New York: Macmillan.

Garratt, J, Overton, T, & Threlfall, T. (1999). A question of chemistry. Harlow, England: Pearson Education Limited.

Glasersfeld, E. v. (1995). A constructivist approach to teaching. In Steffe, L. P. & Gale, J. Constructivism in education (Pages 3-15). Hillsdale, NJ: Lawrence Earlbaum.

Herron, J. D. (1996). The chemistry classroom; formulas for successful teaching. Washington, D.C.: American Chemical Society.

Hurh, E. (2002) Unreported observations.

Landis, C. R., Ellis, A. B., Lisensky, G. C., Lorenz, J. K., Meeker, K., & Wamser, C. C. (2001). Chemistry ConcepTests. Upper Saddle River, NJ: Prentice-Hall.

Mazur, E. (2000). Peer instruction. [On-line]. Available: http://galileo.harvard.edu/galileo/lgm/pi/.

Mulford, D. R. & Robinson, W. R. (2002). An inventory for alternate conceptions among first-semester general chemistry students. *Journal of Chemical Education, 79*, 739-744.

Nurrenbern, S. C. &; Pickering, M. (1987). Concept learning versus problem solving: Is there a difference? *Journal of Chemical Education. 64*, 508-511.

Robinson, W. R. (2002) Unreported observations.

Wright, J. C., Miller, S. B., Kosciuk , S. A., Penberthy, D. L., Williams, P. H., & Wampold, B. E. (1998). A novel strategy for assessing the effects of curriculum reform on student competence. *Journal of Chemical Education. 75*, 986-992.

14

The Testing Trap

I. Dwaine Eubanks
Department of Chemistry
Clemson University

Abstract

Assessment of student knowledge as a basis for awarding grades is a critically important responsibility for new faculty members, who have typically learned less about assessment principles and practice than any other aspect of their teaching duties. Before constructing assessment instruments, instructors must decide what knowledge and skills the student is expected to demonstrate, and at what level. Expectations often involve some combination of recall of basic information, manipulation of formulas and equations, demonstration of conceptual understanding, display of laboratory knowledge and skills, and effective communication of what has been learned. Success with the assessment phase of the instructional process requires instructors to set realistic learning goals and to construct valid test items that measure student achievement of those learning goals. Print sources designed to help instructors learn to write concise, appropriate questions are plentiful. Additionally, new faculty members have access to a large national network of chemistry educators who specialize in student assessment.

Biography

I am currently professor of chemistry at Clemson University. For fifteen years I was responsible for the production of ACS Exams, which seem to be as dreaded by students as they are valued by faculty members. Before coming to Clemson, I was a longtime faculty member at Oklahoma State University. My Ph.D. is in inorganic chemistry from the University of Texas at Austin, and I have experience in industry as well as academe. In addition, I have done a couple of visiting-professor stints (at the University of California at San Diego and at York University in England). Along the way, I have accomplished quite a bit of writing, speaking, consulting, and teacher training in conjunction with ACS projects, as well as in pursuit of my own interests in chemical education. I have served as chair of the Council Committee on Chemical Education, as general chair of a Biennial Conference on Chemical Education, and as chair of the Division of Chemical Education.

The trap

Consider this scenario: You are finishing up your first semester as a new faculty member at Middling University. You have devoted enormous effort to teaching a quality course and have great expectations that your students can demonstrate what they have learned. Much to your astonishment and dismay, your students bomb the final exam. You feel that you have no choice other than to award students the grades they have earned. Fifty percent of the students receive a grade of D or F. Two percent receive a grade of A.

You are called to a conference with your dean and department chair. They have received **many** telephone calls from parents claiming that you are a horrible instructor and teach a terrible course. The dean stresses that Middling U cannot afford to allow you to fail half the students in beginning chemistry. You must change your ways.

Now you are outraged! Only **you** can judge whether your students have learned enough chemistry to be awarded a passing grade. How dare the dean threaten to not renew your contract when you have done your job—and done it well. It's not your fault if the students fail to learn chemistry!

Avoiding the trap—deciding what knowledge is to be demonstrated

As far-fetched as it sounds, the opening scenario is not uncommon. In the preparation of new chemistry faculty members, little is ever devoted to learning how to assess student performance. Left on your own, you—and most new faculty members—reach back to remember what was expected of you at the same point in your career. And, oh! Our memories are *so* unreliable.

The testing trap (and many like it) can be avoided without compromising standards—and without displeasing deans and department chairs. And, without alienating students and their parents. Simply put, when designing any course, ***Begin with the end, and end with the beginning***.

Here is what I mean by that. Begin by making a topical list of every content area to be covered in the course, and consider *what the student must do* to demonstrate his or her knowledge of each content area. Use groupings such as (1) can recall basic information, (2) can manipulate models and equations, (3) can demonstrate conceptual understanding, (4) can demonstrate laboratory skills and knowledge, (5) can communicate results, and so on. A useful way to organize the assessment list is to make a table, such as **Table 1**, for a few bonding topics.

Assessment tables are extremely useful, but they are a lot of work to build. To make a useful table, we really have to focus on what we expect from students. In the remainder of this section, I will explore the ramifications of the *"What the Student Demonstrates"* columns in **Table 1**.

Table 1. Sample Assessment Matrix for Bonding

Topic	What the Student Demonstrates				
	Recall	Manipulate	Conceptualize	Laboratory	Communicate
Ionic Bonding	reason for electron transfer	write electron configurations	account for number of ions in unit cells	determine change in enthalpy	explain Born-Haber cycle
	role of metal and nonmetal	predict formulas	describe anion, cation packing in structure	measure melting point	explain melting points
	relative sizes of ions and atoms	calculate lattice energy	correlate size, charge with lattice energy		explain cleavage planes
Covalent Bonding	role of orbital overlap	write Lewis symbols for atoms	distingiuish core and valence electrons	observe physical properties	explain limitations of Lewis model
	features of "bonding pair" model	write Lewis structures	describe resonance	measure dipole moments	explain bond lengths in structures
	meaning of electronegativity	use VSEPR for structure determination	predict molecular polarity		explain lone *vs.* bound electron pairs in structures
	meaning of formal charge	find formal charges	predict periodic trends		

Recall. Do you expect students to be able to recall vocabulary, definitions, and simple facts? While these are entirely appropriate objectives, they do represent the lowest level of knowledge within any subject. Each of us can recall some facts about things we do not understand at all. When an instructor constructs recall questions, he or she is only testing whether a student has successfully memorized facts, definitions, or whatever. The question of whether the student has integrated the factual information into a broader understanding is unanswered. Some testing of this level of knowledge is necessary, because students must be able to communicate more advanced understanding using vocabulary, facts, and models of the discipline. The good news is that these low-level questions are easy to write.

Manipulation. Do you expect students to use formulas and equations to describe chemical processes and do quantitative calculations? Except for students whose algebra is *very* weak, you can expect students to be able to solve single-step problems using supplied numeric values that they plug into equations that are provided. Algorithmic questions involving simple calculations are easy to write, but you must be aware of when—from the student's perspective—a calculation ceases to be simple. When a calculation problem becomes multistep, you can expect significant numbers of students to be unsuccessful. Success is also diminished when the calculation algorithm is not explicitly given in a word problem. Students also have trouble when numeric values are not given in units that they can plug directly into formulas. Exponential numbers present yet another problem. The list goes on and on.

Every time you write a calculation problem, analyze it carefully. Determine what skills students must demonstrate to be successful, and be sure your instruction has emphasized and reinforced those skills. In dealing with calculation problems, for example, we are always torn between what we want students to be able to demonstrate, and what we can realistically expect. Consider the topics typically included in stoichiometry lectures. Among other things, instructors explain how to do mass–mole–mass conversions and how to deal with impure substances, limiting reactants, side reactions, and percent yield. If a student really understands the material, he or she should be able to do any combination of calculations using an impure substance to react with a limited amount of another reactant to produce less than 100% of the theoretical yield. If, however, we write questions that demand multistep stoichiometry calculations, success is invariably low. My advice is to always begin with the simplest questions possible and build up to the more difficult ones once you know your students' capabilities.

Conceptualization. Do you expect students to demonstrate conceptual understanding? If so, you must write conceptual questions. The downside of testing conceptual understanding is that students tend to have a great deal of difficulty with the questions posed. Consider a simple reaction, such as the electrolysis of water. Many students learn, almost by rote, to write and balance the equation. If, however, these same students are asked to *sketch models* for the products that are produced by electrolysis of water, success plummets. Similar results are found when students are asked to express their ideas using mathematical equations. Many students who have no difficulty with Boyle's law calculations are completely thrown by a question that asks them to draw a line through the points in **Figure 1** that represent the relationship between pressure and volume of an ideal gas. Student success with conceptual questions does improve when the course is taught emphasizing conceptual understanding rather than just algebraic manipulation.

Figure 1. Boyle's Law Plot

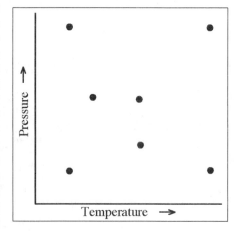

Laboratory knowledge. Why do you have students do laboratory experiments or exercises? Are they expected to master manipulative skills? Are they expected to hone observational skills? Are they expected to design their own experiments to answer lab questions? In each case, the best way to assess laboratory knowledge is to have students demonstrate skills, make observations, draw conclusions, and design experiments *in the laboratory*. Good laboratory assessments are necessarily more subjective and time consuming than recall or manipulation items. On the other hand, laboratory practical tasks are, by far, the most effective way to really find out what students can do in the laboratory. Successful assessment really depends on designing a scoring rubric that emphasizes those things you value in the laboratory experience. Make a list of what you are looking for, and assign a point value to each item on the list. Be sure the assigned point values reflect what you value most. I, for example, place higher value on how students approach laboratory problems than on how skillfully they can perform practical tasks. Suppose we give students the task of finding relative acid strengths of various concentrations of several weak acids. First, they must select a way to approach the problem, such as measuring the pH at the half-equivalence point for each acid. Some students who choose this technique will recognize that equimolar concentrations of each acid are unnecessary. They would receive more credit from me than would those students who go through the labor of adjusting all acid concentrations to equimolarity. Other students might choose an altogether different route, such as testing the acids with pH indicators that change colors in different ranges. For this technique to work, equimolar concentrations of acids are required, and extra points would go to those students who adjusted acid concentrations before testing pH. As you can see, what is really valued is the logic the students demonstrate in analyzing a problem. The particular path they choose to determine the answer is secondary.

Communications skills. Do you expect students to effectively communicate what they have learned? If so, you must give them the opportunity to write and speak. Assessment of communications skills is even more subjective than assessment of laboratory knowledge. The task is made simpler by developing a check sheet (with point values assigned) that addresses various characteristics of the seminar or essay. Here are a few things to consider: Are the ideas expressed clearly? Is the chemistry correct? Is the level appropriate to the audience? Is the organization logical? Are potentially unfamiliar technical terms explained? Are spelling and grammatical constructions correct? Does any supporting graphical material enhance understanding?

Avoiding the trap—writing good exam questions

The merits of various item types (multiple choice *vs.* free response *vs.* short answer *vs.* practical tasks, for example) are often debated in content-free discussions, but each type lends itself best to certain content. There is little point in asking a free response question about something that has a limited, closed set of alternatives, such as choosing the necessary pieces of laboratory equipment from a student locker to perform an acid–base titration. On the other hand, multiple choice items are clearly inadequate if we wish to determine whether a student can successfully standardize a base. For that task, nothing substitutes for actually doing the standardization in the laboratory. On the other hand, if the objective is to determine whether the student can do the required calculations associated with acid–base titrations, a short answer question serves best—particularly if the student is required to show all work.

Beginning with a course-assessment matrix modeled after **Table 1**, each objective that is deemed important enough to occupy a cell must be represented by at least one question on course quizzes and examinations. Sometimes two or more question types will work, but often one type is far superior to the others. Once a question type has been chosen for each objective, the next task is to construct quality items. In the paragraphs that follow, I will consider **multiple choice** items, **short answer** items, and **free response** items.

Multiple choice items. This commonly used format is in widespread use for standardized examinations because it is easy to grade, and the scoring is completely objective. Multiple choice items are, however, the most difficult type of test item to write. They also have the pedagogical weakness that students may be able to *recognize* a correct answer that they would never have been able to devise. Also, students are not usually given the opportunity to demonstrate their thought processes in selecting an answer using this format. These limitations can be largely overcome by careful item construction.

Multiple choice items should generally be designed to address a *single* objective from the assessment matrix. When multiple objectives are embedded in the item, the student who misses the item may have mastered one or more objectives, but not all of them. Unfortunately, it is very easy to end up with an item that appears to be acceptable but that actually focuses on something other than the primary objective of the item. For example, consider the multiple choice item in **Figure 2**, which was intended to determine whether a student understands the notion of percent yield in a chemical calculation.

Figure 2. Two Objectives in Multiple Choice Question (* denotes correct answer)

What is the percent yield if 0.50 mol of ethylene, C_2H_4, is reacted with 0.40 mol of H_2O to produce 0.35 mol of ethanol, C_2H_5OH?

(A) 88%*   (B) 80%   (C) 75%   (D) 70%

As the question in **Figure 2** is written, it tests *both* understanding of percent yield and of limiting reagent calculations. Rewriting the item as in **Figure 3** removes the limiting-reagent aspect of the problem.

Figure 3. Single Objective in Multiple Choice Question

What is the percent yield if 0.50 mol of ethylene, C_2H_4, is reacted with an excess of H_2O to produce 0.35 mol of ethanol, C_2H_5OH?

(A) 88%   (B) 80%   (C) 75%   (D) 70%*

Finding plausible alternatives becomes increasingly difficult as the number of choices increases, and most experienced multiple choice test makers choose to write four-response items. Multiple choice items are often of the *response-to-question* type, as illustrated in **Figures 2** and **3**. If the choices are numeric values, phrases, or formulas, they receive no punctuation. Also, the first word of the choice does not begin with a capital letter unless it is a proper noun. **Figure 4** is an example of such an item. If, on the other hand, the choices are complete sentences, they should be punctuated as sentences.

Figure 4. Phrases in Response-to-Question Multiple Choice Items

Which factor will affect *both* the position of equilibrium and the value of the equilibrium constant for this reaction?

$$N_2(g) + 3N_2(g) \rightarrow 2NH_3(g) \qquad \Delta H = -92\ kJ$$

(A) increasing the volume of the container   (B) adding more nitrogen gas

(C) removing ammonia gas   (D) lowering the temperature*

The choices in multiple choice items may also be constructed to complete a sentence. The *sentence-completion* type of item is illustrated in **Figure 5**. Alternative choices should always end with a period unless the punctuation mark could be confused with a decimal point. The first letter of the first word of each choice is never capitalized unless it is a proper noun.

Figure 5. Sentence-Completion Type of Multiple Choice Question

The fact that $Pt(NH_3)_2Cl_2$ exists in two isomeric forms offers evidence that the geometry is

(A) seesaw shaped.   (B) square planar.*

(C) tetrahedral.   (D) square pyramidal.

Clarity of expression is very important in writing multiple choice items. The sentence structure should be strong and grammatically correct. Students cannot resolve ambiguous language by referring to the larger context as they can in a textbook. Confusing language produces student responses that may not reflect their understanding of the content that you intended to test. Here are a few ideas to keep in mind: (1) Include necessary qualifiers to assure that the question has only one correct response, but beyond that, use as few words as possible. Chemistry items are not usually designed to test reading ability. (2) Place most wording in the stem. The student should be able to understand what is being asked after reading only the stem. (3) Place common elements in the stem, not in the choices. (4) Do not repeat any key words or language from the stem in any alternative choice. (5) Whenever possible, items should be stated in positive form. Negatively stated items are more difficult to understand, and students are more likely to miss them.

Consider the item in **Figure 6**, which was constructed with the intention of determining whether a student understands the basic idea of the Millikan oil-drop experiment. First, note that any question beginning with *"What significant information..."* provides the examinee with little idea of where the question writer is going. In this case, the writer is on the way to producing a stem that is both convoluted and wordy. The student need not worry, however. Choice **(C)** is the only one that even mentions charged oil droplets. A person who had never heard of the Millikan experiment would select it as the intended answer. Even if the construction of the item had not given choice **(C)** away, the question, as written, provides *no* clue to the examiner about whether a student really understands the Millikan experiment. As written, **Figure 6** is purely a recall question. The student only has to distinguish the oil-drop experiment from other experiments of the era that probed the properties of subatomic particles.

Now consider the multiple choice item shown in **Figure 7**. Notice that extraneous elements have been removed. How the droplets were produced, and how they acquired their charges, is not relevant to the question. Nor is Millikan's name, which appeared *five* times in the **Figure 6** example. Also, notice that the rewritten question now briefly describes the experiment in the stem and focuses on whether a student understands the significance of the results.

Figure 6. A Flawed Multiple Choice Item

What significant information about the properties of subatomic particles became available as a result of the Millikan experiment that used oil droplets that were sprayed into a chamber from an atomizer and that were given negative charges by bombarding the droplets with X-rays?

(A) Millikan showed that cathode rays were identical to a stream of electrons coming from an atom.

(B) Millikan confirmed that the neutron and proton were of about the same mass.

(C) Millikan determined the magnitude of the charge on an electron by observing the movement of charged oil droplets in an electric field.*

(D) Millikan proved that the mass of an atom was concentrated in the nucleus.

Figure 7. An Improved Multiple Choice Item

Millikan performed experiments using an electric field to suspend charged oil droplets, countering their tendencies to drift downward under the influence of gravity. In these experiments, the charge on each oil droplet was found to be

(A) the same as the charge on an electron.

(B) an integral fraction of the charge on an electron.

(C) an integral multiple of the charge on an electron.*

(D) directly proportional to the strength of the electric field.

In a multiple choice question, every alternative choice should be plausible and should anticipate likely misconceptions or computational errors. Except for **Figure 6**, the distractors of all the examples cited so far meet this criterion. The choices should be arranged in a sequence that gives no clue to the correct answer. The best advice is to deliberately randomize choices to avoid the tendency to place the correct choice in a preferred position. On the other hand, numeric choices or single letters should always be sequenced in ascending or descending order. Alternative choices should be *parallel in grammatical form*, because non-parallel choices often reveal the correct answer or obviously wrong answers.

The words *always* and *never* are most often used in false statements, and test-wise students key in on these words. Similarly, *"all of the above"* and *"none of the above"* are seldom the intended answer. They allow students to select a choice based on the weakest alternative. Choices are also weakened by *opposite alternatives*. Test-wise students know that one of them is usually correct, which allows them to ignore the remaining alternatives. Finally, be careful to avoid *overlap* of alternatives (<10, <20, <50, <100, for example). The only un-overlapped choice (<100) must be correct, because a value that is, say, <20 is also <50 and <100. **Figure 8** shows an example of an item having overlapping choices. Choice **(D)** was the author's intended choice, but, as the question is written, all four answers must be judged as correct. The item can be repaired by inserting the word "only" after the Roman numerals in choices **(A)**, **(B)**, and **(C)**.

Figure 8. An Item with Overlapping Choices

What product(s) are formed during the electrolysis of a concentrated aqueous solution of sodium chloride?

I $Cl_2(g)$ II $NaOH(aq)$ III $H_2(g)$

(A) I   **(B)** I and II   **(C)** I and III   **(D)** I, II, and III*

The topics included here certainly do not represent an exhaustive discussion of how to construct multiple choice items. Hopefully they have provided a glimpse into the importance of writing good items and have convinced you to read more or seek expert guidance before using multiple choice items extensively in your courses. Several excellent sources are included in the **Bibliography**.

Short answer Items. Good short answer items will channel the student's thinking and provide a clear opportunity to demonstrate relevant knowledge, even though it may not be the knowledge you were seeking. Many of the dictums related to stem construction in multiple choice items are also true for short answer items. The single, encompassing objective is to anticipate all (or at least most) of the ways that both good and poor students will interpret the question. Also, remember that multi-objective or multistep questions will greatly limit student success. **Figure 9** is an example of a question that at least three-quarters of your students are sure to miss, even if they know how to do the individual steps.

Figure 9. A Multistep Question

Dolomitic limestone contains the mineral dolomite, which is a compound of magnesium and calcium carbonates, $MgCO_3 \cdot CaCO_3$. Consider a particular limestone sample that is found to contain 88.3% $MgCO_3 \cdot CaCO_3$. The sample is treated by dissolving it in acid, and subsequently separating the magnesium by precipitating it as $Mg(OH)_2$. In this step, 95.2% of the magnesium in the original ore is recovered. Assuming that all of the magnesium in the $Mg(OH)_2$ sample is then reduced to magnesium metal, what is the theoretical yield of magnesium that can be produced from 100 g of the original ore?

Unless you ask students to show all work, and unless you plan to generously award partial credit for correctly done steps, questions such as the example in **Figure 9** must be avoided. But if you must examine how a student works through a problem, then it is no longer a short answer item.

Well-constructed multiple choice items typically are an excellent source of good short answer items with the supplied choices deleted. Consider the examples that have been cited to this point. Only **Example 6** cannot easily be converted to a good short answer item. For the sentence-completion multiple choice items, the incomplete sentence in the stem must, of course, be converted to a question. **Figure 10** shows the conversion of **Figure 7** to a short answer item.

Figure 10. Constructing a Short Answer Item from a Multiple Choice Item

Millikan performed experiments using an electric field to suspend charged oil droplets, countering their tendencies to drift downward under the influence of gravity. What magnitude of charge was found on the oil droplets?

Free response items. Many instructors consider free response items as being the only viable question type for most situations. Conventional wisdom suggests that they are easy to write but difficult to grade. (Multiple choice items, on the other hand, are purported to be difficult to write but easy to grade.) Conventional wisdom is correct for multiple choice items but not for free response items. They *are* difficult and time-consuming to grade, but they are also difficult to write. If a free response item is not sharply focused, students tend to dump everything they know (and a lot that they don't) onto the page, with the hope that *something* will be judged as correct. You should always be sure that the student understands both the appropriate level of detail and the approximate number of words that characterize a well-constructed response. Consider the two free response items shown in **Figures 11** and **12**. You will recognize these as derivatives of earlier multiple choice items. You can decide which one channels the student response in the most productive way.

Figure 11. First Free Response Item

What significant information about the properties of subatomic particles became available as a result of the Millikan experiment that used oil droplets that were sprayed into a chamber from an atomizer and that were given negative charges by bombarding the droplets with X-rays?

Figure 12. Second Free Response Item

Millikan performed experiments using an electric field to suspend charged oil droplets, countering their tendencies to drift downward under the influence of gravity. Describe the results of the experiment, and explain how the results enabled Millikan to calculate the charge on an electron.

Avoiding the trap—tapping the collective experience

The good news is that you do not have to discover all the minutiae of writing good items and creating good tests all by yourself. Discuss your assessment strategies with experienced colleagues. Show them your questions. Solicit comments and advice. Use resources and ideas from places such as test-item banks, laboratory assessment tasks, and student study guides from the ACS Exams Institute, *J Chem Ed* articles, *JCE Online* resources, other Web-based assessment materials, and conference presentations. Numerous sources are included in the **Bibliography**. Once you have a clear idea about what your students should be able to demonstrate when they leave your course, as well as how to assess their gains, you are prepared to select (or design) instructional materials that help students master the concepts and knowledge that you consider important. And, you can *"teach to the test"* without apology.

Bibliography

Angelo, T. A., & Cross, K. P. (1993). *Classroom Assessment Techniques*. San Francisco, CA: Jossey–Bass Publishers.

Atkin, J. M., Black, P., & Coffey, J. (Eds.). (2001). *Classroom Assessment and the National Science Education Standards*. Washington, DC: National Research Council.

Conceptual Questions and Challenge Problems Home Page. *JCE Online*. http://jchemed.chem.wisc.edu/JCEWWW/Features/CQandChP/index.html (accessed Nov 2002).

Doran, R., Chan, F., & Tamir, P. (1998). *Science Educator's Guide to Assessment*. Arlington, VA: National Science Teachers Association.

Doran, R., Chan, F., Tamir, P., & Lenhardt, C. (2002). *Science Educator's Guide to Laboratory Assessment*. Arlington, VA: National Science Teachers Association.

Eubanks, I. D., & Eubanks, L. T. (1992). *ACS Test-Item bank for General Chemistry*. Stillwater, OK: ACS Division of Chemical Education Examinations Institute.

Eubanks, I. D., & Eubanks, L. T. (1994). *Writing Tests and Interpreting Test Statistics: A Practical Guide*. Clemson, SC: ACS Division of Chemical Education Examinations Institute.

Eubanks, L. T., & Eubanks, I. D. (1998). *Preparing for Your ACS Examination in General Chemistry*. Clemson, SC: ACS Division of Chemical Education Examinations Institute.

Field-tested learning assessment guide home page. http://www.flaguide.org/default.asp (accessed July 2003).

Johnson, D. W., & Johnson, R. T. (1996). *Meaningful and Manageable Assessment Through Cooperative Learning*. Edina, MN: Interactive Book Company.

Kulm, G., & Malcom, S. M. (Eds.). (1991). *Science Assessment in the Service of Reform*. Washington, DC: American Association for the Advancement of Science.

Siebert, E. D., McIntosh, W. J. (Eds.). (2001). *College Pathways to the Science Education Standards*. Arlington, VA: National Science Teachers Association.

15

Assessing Your Students' Understanding of Chemistry

Thomas J. Greenbowe, Department of Chemistry
K. A. Burke, Department of Curriculum and Instruction
Iowa State University

Abstract

Assessment of your students' understanding of chemistry involves more than administering quizzes and examinations. The beginning chemistry instructor must be aware of curriculum decisions, course goals, course level and depth, department and college expectations, and national standards or guidelines. College chemistry instructors are now expected to demonstrate outcomes based on measures other than teacher-made tests. New instructors should be aware of individual differences in student learning styles and in testing. You are sure to encounter students who have special needs or requirements when it comes time for testing. Careful consideration of normative- or criterion-referenced grading systems is at the core of how you will award grades. Even if you are the sole instructor teaching a particular chemistry course, you need to be aware of the history of the course and the general pattern for distribution of grades of the students who enroll in that course. Assessment also involves an evaluation of how the course materials are helping students learn the material and an evaluation of the effectiveness of your teaching.

Biographies

Thomas Greenbowe is currently professor of chemistry and coordinator of general chemistry at Iowa State University. He teaches general chemistry to large sections of science and engineering students. Over the past 20 years he has taught more than 20,000 students. He tries to make his lecture presentations as interactive as possible, employing group work, multimedia, demonstrations, and humor. He works with teaching assistants to help them implement active learning in their recitation and laboratory sections. Before coming to Iowa, Tom was a faculty member at the University of Massachusetts–Dartmouth, the chemistry lecture demonstrator at Purdue University, and a high school physics and chemistry teacher. His Ph.D. is from Purdue University. Tom has served on several ACS General Chemistry Exam committees and is currently the general chair of the 18th Biennial Conference on Chemical Education. Tom is delighted to learn effective teaching and learning techniques from colleagues across the country. He shares what works in his classroom by speaking at ACS meetings and college seminars. He has published papers about chemical education issues and research in the *Journal of Chemical Education, Journal of Research in Science Teaching, Journal of College Science Teaching*, and the *International Journal of Science Education*. He has served as a principal investigator for several curriculum and development projects funded by the National Science Foundation and by the U. S. Department of Education. Assessing students' knowledge of chemistry continues to be a challenge, presenting a moving target.

K. A. Burke has a graduate degree in chemistry from Iowa State University. She has extensive teaching experience at the two-year and four-year college/university level, and has facilitated the direction of two of Iowa's statewide chemical education efforts–the Iowa Chemistry Education Alliance at the secondary level, and the Iowa General Chemistry Network at the post-secondary level. She has served as an NSF evaluator for the Multi-Initiative Dissemination Project, and is currently helping to coordinate adoption of the Science Writing Heuristic at the post-secondary level.

What can go wrong?

Assessment can be defined as the collection of information, both quantitative and qualitative, obtained through various tests, observations, and other techniques used to determine individual, group, or program performance (Doran 1994). Constructing and administering an exam is only one component of assessment. Assessment also involves making decisions about the curriculum, course resources, what is taught, how it is taught, and about the activities you have your students do to help them learn the topics, concepts, principles, and skills that are part of your course. The course grades your students earn should represent an overall assessment of their achievement and understanding of chemistry.

How you go about assessing your students' understanding of chemistry is a responsibility that has far-reaching consequences for your students. As coordinator of general chemistry at two universities, one of the authors of this chapter has seen his colleagues stumble with respect to student protests about testing and grades. Nearly all of these situations could have been avoided if the instructor had taken the time to clearly communicate and fairly implement an effective assessment scheme. Students generally will let you and others know that they feel "cheated" about how the testing and grades are being dealt with after the second exam or after final grades are awarded. Students will demand that the exam questions reflect what is being taught and at the level it is being taught. Students also will demand a certain degree of "fairness" in assigning grades at the end of the course. As an instructor you must strive to strike a balance between awarding too many A's and B's and too many D's and F's. The purpose of this chapter is to provide the beginning chemistry instructor with some basic knowledge about assessment and to provide some practical tips about how to strengthen your resolve about awarding grades.

Questions to ask your colleagues before you teach your course

About a month before you begin to teach a course for the first or second time, you should gather as much information as possible about the course and about course policies and procedures. In most departments there are unwritten policies, and the only way for you to find out what is going on is to ask.

Here are some key questions about assessment to ask your colleagues before you begin teaching a course:

- Is there a standard course syllabus? Is there a strong expectation that a specific number of chapters and topics be "covered" during the course (especially if the course is the first semester of a two-semester course sequence)?

- Are statistical records of all courses taught in the department kept on file?

- Is there a written list of goals for the course? Is there a written list of learning objectives for the course?

- Is group work permitted on homework, on quizzes, on exams, on projects, or on laboratory reports?

- Should homework earn points toward the course total points? If so, what percentage of the total points should homework comprise?

- Are the instructors required to take attendance? Does attendance count for points?

- Is there an expectation of a certain percentage of A's, B's, C's, D's, or F's for the course? Is there an expectation of a certain course grade-point average, within an approved range, for the course?

- Are copies available of previous exams administered in this course?

- Is it common practice to drop the lowest exam score?

- Is it common practice to provide students with appropriate formulas, physical constants, and other pertinent information on each exam?

- Are students permitted to use an information sheet on exams?

- Are graphing calculators, with information storage registers, permitted on the exams?

- What procedures are available for accommodating students who have an "academic disability" and have a Student Academic Accommodation Request (SAAR)?

- Are extra credit or bonus problems allowed on exams? Can students do extra credit projects to make up points for poor performance on an exam?

- What is the policy for students who miss an exam for a good reason? What is the policy for students who miss an exam and do not have a good reason for doing so?

- What is an acceptable average on hour exams? On the final exam?

- Does the department use a common set of questions for the final exam year after year?

- Are the students allowed to keep their final exam booklet?

- Is one of the American Chemical Society Examinations used in this course? If so, how is it used? Many departments use the ACS examinations as part of their "outcomes based" assessment. You can compare the performance of your students to the national average. Or, ACS exams can be used to compare the performance of other sections of colleagues who have taught or who are teaching the course.

- Are laboratory practical exam tasks used to assess students' skills in the chemistry laboratory?

Before you start the course, it is helpful to review previous one-hour exams and final exams. This will provide you with the best indication of the different types of problems, the degree of difficulty of the test problems, and the depth of coverage of topics. If possible, during the semester, have an experienced colleague review your exam before it is printed and administered to the students. Experienced faculty can judge whether or not an exam is too easy, too difficult, too long, or too short for the time allocated. New faculty members should be aware of local conditions that may influence how intense and difficult the course is and the expectations for how the grades are assigned. For example, if you are assigned a "trailer course" (a course taught in the off-semester–i.e. General Chemistry I taught in the spring semester), you can expect to have lower exam averages. You may be expected to assign a lower percentage of A's and B's, and a higher percentage of D's and F's compared to the "on-semester" course.

What to assess?

What you assess and how you assess your students depends on what the goals and objectives are for the course. Angelo and Cross (1993) discuss six broad categories of goals for college courses: higher-order thinking skills, academic success skills, content knowledge and skills, academic values, career preparation, and personal development. You should state in writing the goals and objectives of the course, put the main points on the course syllabus, on the course web site, and keep these in mind when it comes time for constructing assessment activities. The assessment activities should match the course goals and objectives. For example, if one of your goals for the laboratory portion of the course is to have your students design an experiment and control variables, then you should have a laboratory practical exam activity that assesses this skill. If one of your goals is to have students demonstrate problem solving ability in chemistry, then one of your assessments should be a true problem-solving activity.

Most chemistry instructors rely on a cycle of grading homework problems, quizzes, and exams. The instructor allocates points for each graded assignment. In this cycle, students may have the opportunity to solve the same general type of problem three times for points. Instructors generally believe that this is an objective system that places the burden of demonstrating chemistry knowledge on the student. Instructors want to assign grades using an impartial and fair procedure. The assigning of letter grades requires a judgment be made as to what constitutes the difference between an A and a B, a B and a C, etc.

Types of problems on chemistry examinations

Instructor-made tests can include the following types of problems: multiple choice; showing all work of several steps of calculations; writing statements or explanations; justifying a choice; and laboratory practical tasks. Your examinations should include at least one novel problem that requires a transfer of learning. If one of your goals is to have students demonstrate conceptual understanding, then one of your assessments should include paired quantitative and conceptual problems (same structure, same concept). Written explanations require additional time to grade, but they also reveal how well the student understands a topic. We will not debate in this chapter whether or not multiple choice problems are an accurate tool to measure your students' understanding of chemistry (Binder 1988). It is sufficient to say that multiple choice problems are used by many chemistry instructors who have enrollments of over 60-75 students in their course. Most instructors use a combination of multiple choice problems and "show all work" problems on their examinations.

Most often, chemistry instructors are interested in determining wheher students can do a calculation problem. For example, a typical problem might ask the student to calculate the number of grams of precipitate that form when 20.0 mL of 1.0 M $AgNO_3(aq)$ is mixed with 20.0 mL of 1.0 M $NaCl(aq)$. This problem requires students to write a balanced equation, use solubility rules to predict which product will be a precipitate, use stoichiometry to determine the limiting reagent, and calculate the number of grams of AgCl that can form.

Sometimes a simple question can reveal more about the misunderstandings held by your students than a calculation problem. For instance, consider the following conceptual problem. The question is followed by sample data from students enrolled in General Chemistry I for 2001 and 2002. Item analysis data reveal a difference in performance. The item analysis data show the number of students selecting each choice, the percentage correct, and the discrimination index. The discrimination index is a measure of how well the problem discriminates those students who score well overall on the exam compared to those students who score poorly on the exam relative to each individual problem (Mehrens and Lehmann 1978; Bodner 1980). A discrimination index of 0.35 or above indicates that the problem effectively discriminates between students who do and who do not know the material. Instructors can use item analysis to improve the effectiveness of exam problems.

Consider a representation of a small volume of gas in a reaction flask before the start of a reaction between nitrogen gas and oxygen gas to give dinitrogen pentoxide,

_____$N_2(g)$ + _____$O_2(g)$ → $N_2O_5(g)$

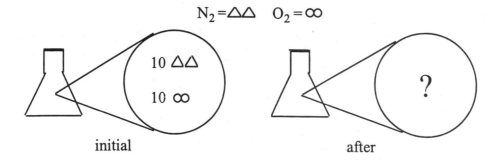

a. Which of the following represents the resulting volume of product after the reaction occurs?

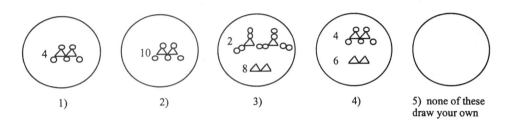

| 1) | 2) | 3) | 4) | 5) none of these
draw your own |

Item analysis (* denotes correct answer)

	1	2	3	4*	5	Omits	n	%	DSCR
2001	13	16	65	354	69	0	517	68	0.40
2002	23	48	89	396	90	1	646	61	0.39

b. What is the limiting reagent in the above problem?

1) N_2O_5 2) N_2 3) O_2 4) both N_2 and O_2 5) none of these

Item analysis (* denotes correct answer)

	1	2	3*	4	5	Omits	n	%	DSCR
2001	0	49	447	23	12	0	517	86	0.32
2002	1	98	529	14	5	0	647	82	0.34

The results of the item analysis indicate that the students have difficulty understanding the fact that some nitrogen remains unreacted. The data show that most students who answered this question could identify the limiting reagent in the problem.

Consider the following problem. It uses a two-tier approach (Birk 1999) to structure a multiple choice question. It assesses factual knowledge—does the student know the definition of endothermic and exothermic—and then assesses whether or not the student can apply this information in a realistic situation.

A sample of baking soda dissolves in water according to the following equation. The initial temperature of the water is 23°C. The temperature of the resultant solution is 18°C.

$$NaHCO_3(s) \xrightarrow{H_2O} Na^+(aq) + HCO_3^-(aq)$$

For the dissolving process described above, the reaction shown is _____ and heat is _____.

1. exothermic, given off by the reaction.

2. exothermic, taken in (absorbed) by the reaction.

3. endothermic, given off by the reaction.

4. endothermic, taken in (absorbed) by the reaction.

5.   cannot tell without knowing the mass of water and the specific heat of the resultant solution.

Item analysis (* denotes correct answer)

	1	2	3	4*	5	Omits	n	%	DSCR
2001	84	2	15	412	4	0	517	80%	0.35
2002	127	36	27	448	8	1	646	69%	0.38

The results of this item analysis indicate that fewer students in 2002 were able to answer this simple question compared to the students in 2001. Both problems focus on assessing students' conceptual understanding of chemistry (Herron and Greenbowe 1985; Nurrenbern and Pickering 1987; Nakhleh 1990). It is desirable to have a variety of different types of problems on your examinations, as well as a range in the degree of difficulty. Most instructors place at least one difficult problem on their exams to ensure that the exam average will be 70 to 75% or lower and to help identify the most capable students.

Maintaining records about the course

One of the biggest challenges a new instructor faces is how hard or easy to make the exam problems. Prior to the start of an academic semester, new instructors should discuss grading standards with other faculty in their department who have taught the course(s) they will be teaching. A record of grades assigned to students in the course in previous semesters may be available in the department for the past five to ten years. This record should include the number of students who started the course, the number of students taking the final exam, (after the drop/add period), the score for the final exam, the total points earned, and the percentage of A's, B's, C's, etc. assigned. The average course grade for the entire course should be calculated. The retention rate should be calculated each time the course is taught and an average retention rate calculated for the fall and spring semesters of the course.

For example, Table 1 displays hypothetical information collected over a five-year period for a General Chemistry I course for science and engineering majors. The course was taught in both the fall and spring semesters. Instructors used a core of similar questions on the final exam. General trends can be spotted from this information. First, the distribution of grades for this course is not consistent from semester-to-semester. Depending when students take the course and who teacahes the course a different percentage of A's and B's will be awarded. Presumably, lower ability students enroll in the spring semester of the "trailer course." Many of these students have failed the course in the fall and are repeating it for a better grade. However, in recent years, these students are earning a higher percent of A's and B's compared to the students enrolled in the fall semesters. A *de facto* limit of 50% A's and B's combined appears to be in place for this department and group of faculty. The same instructor taught the course in the fall of 1997, 1998, 1999, 2001 and 2002. This instructor assigns an average number of A's, B's, and C's compared to other instructors who teach the same course.

Table 1. A record of hypothetical grades issued for General Chemistry I (1997–2003).

Semester	Final exam average	Total points average	Course grade average	%A's	%B's	%C's	%D's
Spring 2003	71	71	2.31	23	21	32	14
Fall 2002	61	74	2.45	15	33	32	12
Spring 2002	45	58	2.07	24	21	21	14
Fall 2001	64	74	2.57	20	35	28	10
Spring 2001	53	60	1.91	21	41	19	22
Fall 2000	67	72	2.20	11	33	34	13
Spring 2000	42	54	1.98	10	22	37	22
Fall 1999	61	72	2.55	22	29	33	12
Spring 1999	50	58	1.85	7	25	32	20
Fall 1998	68	71	2.74	28	27	26	11
Spring 1998	55	64	2.22	18	28	37	9
Fall 1997	58	70	2.40	18	25	39	15

Also, the final exam and course averages for this course are not consistent. There appears to be no correlation between performance on the final exam, the total number of points earned and the assignment of the number of A's and B's in the course. For example, it appears that students enrolled in the fall of 1999 received more A's than students enrolled in the fall of 2001, yet their performance is lower on the final exam and on total points earned. The other instructosr who taught the course in the spring of 2001 and 2002 probably should not have assigned as many A's and B's, because the final exam average and the course average are significantly lower when compared to other semesters.

If you are teaching the same course over a number of years, you should be aware of the statistics of your grading system and how it compares both year to year and to other instructors who are teaching the same course. If your department has not maintained a record of course grades similar to this, your Registrar's Office will have the information on file. The information requested may not be compiled in a useful format when you receive it, but you can format it so that it makes sense to you. You may need only information from the past two or three years to see what the trend is for the students in the course. While there are many variables that can influence the grade profile of a class, the instructor of a course should strive to be consistent from semester-to-semester and year-to-year in the assingment of letter grades.

Assigning letter grades (Cut offs)

Figure 1 displays a graph of the number of students earning a percentage of the course points in a general chemistry course. The average for the course is 60.0%. The number of students is 222. Based on this distribution, how would you assign grades of A, B, C, D, and F? Instructor X might decide the following: 80–100 A; 65–79 B; 50–64 C; 35–49 D; below 34, F. This instructor is using a range of 14% for each grade. Only two students would receive an F using this system. Instructor Y might decide the following: 90–100 A; 80–89 B; 70–79 C; 60 – 69 D; below 60, F. This instructor might have told the students the first day of class that this was the grading scale regardless of what the distributions were on the exams. Half of the class would fail using this system. Instructor Z might decide: 85–100 A; 75–84 B; 60–74 C; 50–59 D; below 50, F. In this system there would be relatively few A's and B's, but many C's, D's, and F's. Any one of these grading assignments may be valid depending on the context of the course and the average on the final exam. How does a novice instructor decide which grade cuts to use?

Figure 1. Distribution of the percentage of total points earned in a general chemistry course

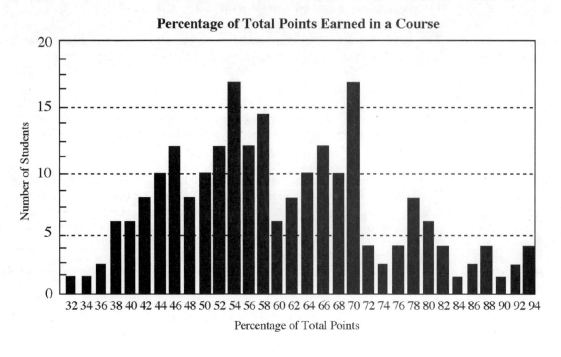

Figure 2. Distribution of the percentage of total points earned in a general chemistry course.

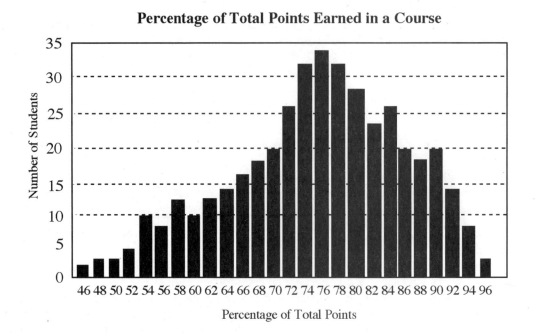

Figure 2 shows a total points distribution for another general chemistry course. The average for the total points earned in this course is 71% (413 students). An analysis of this distribution indicates that the distribution is skewed to the right. Too many students have earned a high percentage of the points. How should an instructor assign grades to this group of students? Should the average grade be a C, C+, or B-?

Instructor Y might use the following grade cuts: 90–100 A; 80–89 B; 70 –79 C; 60–69 D; below 60, F. This instructor might have told the students the first day of class that this was the grading scale regardless of what the distributions were on the exams or the total points earned in the course. Using these grade cuts with this distribution there would be 10.6% A's, 28.1% B's, 34.3% C's; 17.0% D's; 9.4% F's. For courses with an enrollment of 40 to 50 students, the exams usually do not generate a normal distribution. The instructor should look for natural "breaks" in the distribution and assign grades accordingly.

Laboratory practical examination tasks

You should not rely exclusively on the scores of laboratory reports for assessing your students' skills and their understanding of chemistry laboratory topics. Laboratory practical exam tasks can be used to help determine understanding (Rozeiu 1969; Hayes 1972; Jones 1977; Robyt and White 1990; Silberman et al. 1987; Tamir 1998). For example, many teachers have students do a laboratory experiment to determine the concentration of an aqueous solution of hydrochloric acid by performing an acid-base titration with a known concentration of an aqueous solution of sodium hydroxide. To test their understanding, have your students do a short (20 to 25 minute) laboratory exam task that requires them to determine the concentration of an unknown acid. Figure 3 contains an example of an acid-base titration laboratory practical exam task. This task requires students to both think about and actually do chemistry.

There is no limit as to the type of laboratory practical examination tasks that can be developed and administered. Students could be asked to:

1. Determine the ΔH of a reaction by doing a calorimeter experiment.

2. Determine the $E°$ of a half-cell reaction by doing an electrochemical cell experiment.

3. Determine the limiting reagent and the percentage yield of a simple precipitation reaction.

4. Determine the rate law of a chemical clock reaction. Mix two reagents that will achieve an end point at a designated target time.

5. Mix two solutions together that will produce an acidic or alkaline buffer solution that matches a target pH.

Figure 3. A laboratory practical exam task

Your instructor will assign you a sample of acetic acid to analyze. Titrate the acid solution with an aqueous solution of 0.279 M sodium hydroxide. You may use either phenolphthalein or thymol blue to help you determine the end-point.

Record the following information:

Acetic acid sample number	_____	Volume of acetic acid used	_____
NaOH concentration (M)	_____	Volume of NaOH	_____
Acetic acid concentration (M)	_____		

Write an equation for this reaction. Explain whether or not the acid is being neutralized by the base.

We have been administering laboratory practical exams to over 3,000 students each semester for the past 10 years. All of the teaching assistants and instructors for a course meet for about an hour and a half after the exam to establish the grading system for each task. Students receive 20% of the score if they have written a reasonable procedure, 20% of the score for recording clear observations and data, 20% for calculations, 20% for obtaining a reasonable value, and 20% for a correct explanation.

Partial credit

The most common system for assessing and assigning grades for performance in a chemistry course involves the instructor grading problems from homework assignments, quizzes, and exams by assigning points. The problems used by chemistry instructors typically involve the generation of a numerical answer by doing a calculation or involve the student writing a short statement or explanation to a problem. Comparing a student's answer to a correct numerical answer is easy for the instructor to grade because a student cannot dispute the answer. It is either right or wrong. However, instructors typically assign partial credit for work displayed on a problem if a mathematical error leads to an incorrect number, but the procedure is correct. Assigning partial credit to written work is a matter of judgment. As the instructor, you must strive to be consistent in your grading process. Students who exhibit the same work should receive the same credit. Students will compare their graded exams and will demand additional credit if they believe another student received more points for the same or similar work. The development of a written scoring system to assure that the partial credit awarded is consistent, is an essential component of good assessment. If possible, new instructors should develop this scoring system with an experienced instructor. Each instructor should grade the same problem for five or six exams, then stop and compare the partial credit both have awarded. At this stage the graders can make the necessary adjustments to the grading scheme. For a small class, the instructor should grade the same problem on all exam papers before moving on to the next problem. This method can be adapted for grading teams at a larger institution.

ACS examinations and the ACS item test bank

The American Chemical Society's Examination Institute has many different types of examinations that national committees have written, field-tested, revised, and standardized. There are several different types of general chemistry exams: diagnostic, first semester, second semester, full year, as well as exams that focus on conceptual understanding. Exams for general, inorganic, analytical, physical, organic, and biochemistry are available. The examinations use a multiple choice format. There is a national average available for each exam. Some advantages for using an ACS exam can be cited. The exams help you determine whether your curriculum meets what other chemistry instructors deem acceptable. They provide a means to help you demonstrate outcomes from an independent source other than teacher-made exams. If you give an ACS exam as a final exam, then you do not have to write final exam questions. There are some drawbacks to using ACS exams. You will not have addressed between five and six questions on the exam due to differences in the topics you teach and the level and depth of topics you do teach. The exam might be too easy or too difficult for your students. There is a cost involved. You will need to purchase an exam booklet for each of your students. The ACS Exams Institute does not permit anyone to copy an exam. Each exam booklet has a unique identification number printed on the front cover. As a chemistry instructor, you can purchase one review copy of an examination. If your institution purchases a reasonable number of the exams for your students, you may obtain a refund for your examination copy.

The ACS Examinations Institute also offers a Test Item Bank for general chemistry (Eubanks and Eubanks 1992) that consists of questions and problems that have been retired from previous exams. By using the ACS Test Item Bank you can select as many or as few questions as you want on your examinations.

Another piece of the assessment puzzle to consider is the entry-level skills of your students. Figure 4 shows a graph of the mean scores on the ACS California Chemistry Diagnostic Exam (ACS Exam Institute) over a seven-year period for students enrolled in a General Chemistry I course for science and engineering majors. This diagnostic exam consists of 44 questions on basic chemistry facts and skills, algebra, and scientific notation. Practically speaking, the difference in the mean ACS diagnostic score, over the seven-year period, is plus-or-minus one question correct. Based on the results of this exam, we can conclude that since 1995 the mean entry-level chemistry skills of the students enrolled in this course have been about the same. How does this impact the difficulty of exams that can be administered, and how does it impact the final grades assigned to students? If the difficulty of the exams is equivalent to previous years, the instructor might anticipate that the same percentage of A's and B's will be earned in the course.

Figure 4. Mean ACS California chemistry diagnostic score vs. year

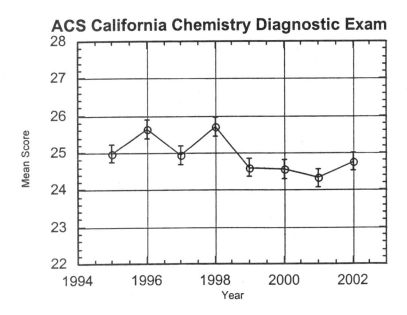

Alternative assessments: portfolios and poster sessions

Some chemistry instructors have their students make portfolios of their work or else present a poster. The instructor develops a grading rubric to grade the students' work. The grade of the portfolio and/or the poster is part of the assessment of the students' understanding of chemistry. The portfolio can contain a variety of documents (Phelps et al. 1997). It can be a paper document or an electronic version that can be presented on a CD-ROM or on the World Wide Web. Poster sessions can be an effective way to evaluate a project on which the student has worked over a two to three week period (Mills et al. 2001). The grading of portfolios and posters can be subjective and time consuming, but it provides the students with an alternative assessment. Vitale and Romance (1999), Edwards (2001), and Popham (2002) provide useful guidelines for scoring nontraditional assessment tasks

Responding to requests for accommodations by students with disabilities

You and your institution are mandated by law (Section 504 of the Vocational Rehabilitation Act of 1973 and the Americans with Disabilities Act of 1990) to provide reasonable accommodation to every student with a disability. Your department and college should provide up to $200 per student per semester to meet the requested accommodation(s) of the student. The student initiates the request to the instructor by showing a Student Academic Accommodation Request (SAAR) to the instructor. With respect to assessment, the accommodations for a student can be extra time, a reader, larger font size, or special materials when taking exams and quizzes. These accommodations have been recommended by your institution's disability officer. As an instructor, you may not inquire about the nature of the disability itself, since the student is not required to explain it. The accommodations are intended to enable disabled students to meet course requirements through an alternative path, with no reductions in standards or quality expected. A problem may arise when a student requests that spelling, grammar, and mathematics errors do not influence the grade on the chemistry quizzes or exams. Or, that because a student has problems with mathematics, the student should have double the time to take the exams. For chemistry instructors, this is at odds with the intention that "no reductions in standards or quality are expected." As an instructor, you can disagree or can ask the student to compromise on any accommodation that you find unacceptable. In such cases, a joint meeting with the disability officer is warranted.

Normative- and criterion-referenced grading systems

You should make a decision to use either a normative-referenced or criterion-referenced grading system (Mehrens and Lehmann 1978) at the start of the course. A normative-referenced grading system determines the achievement of a student by comparing his or her work with the achievement of other students. Students who accomplish a higher level of understanding in an academic course are recognized with a higher grade compared to students who perform at a lower level. Often, a normative-referenced grading system specifies in advance (or *de facto*) that a certain percentage of each grade designation (A's 10-12%, B's 20-25%, C's 30-35%, D's 20-25%, F's 10-12%, Withdraw or drop 10%) will be issued. If the distribution of grades in a course follows a normal distribution over a number of years, a normative grading system is used. A normative-referenced system grading scheme does not encourage students to help each other. If there are only a certain percentage of A's and B's, regardless of student performance, then students realize that by helping another student, they may prevent themselves from obtaining the grade they want. The more students who score ahead of them, the less likely it is that they will receive a high grade.

In a criterion-referenced grading system, student achievement or understanding of chemistry is based upon a pre-determined set of criteria, usually points earned in the course: 90% is an A, 80% is a B, etc. It does not matter how many students earn a particular grade. A criterion-referenced system compares an individual's performance to some pre-specified objectives and or scoring system. A criterion-referenced system encourages students to work in groups and help each other. One student's success does not hinder his or her classmates' ability to earn a grade. Under a criterion referenced grading system there is no limit on the number of A's, B's, C's, D's, and F's that can be earned in the course. Motivation to put forth effort and work in the course can be maintained throughout the semester because there is hope for each student. However, even when instructors tell students that there are no limits to the number of A's or B's, if there is an instructor or department *de facto* limit, students will soon realize this and lose trust in their instructor. Figure 5 represents a typical distribution of letter grades at the end of a general chemistry course with an enrollment greater than 200 students. This distribution could have been obtained using either a normative-referenced or criterion-referenced system. This distribution seems to be the ideal letter grade distribution that most chemistry instructors strive to achieve.

Figure 5. A typical general chemistry course grading profile.

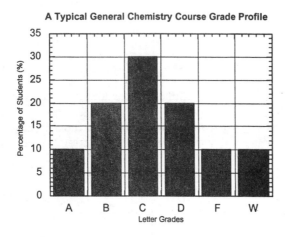

T-scores: an alternative method for grading

If a student earns a certain percentage of the total points i.e. 90%, 80%, 70% 60%, etc., he or she is usually assigned a grade of A, B, C, etc. This approach assumes that all examinations are about the same level of difficulty and that it is valid to simply total the points earned for each exam, for each quiz, etc., to achieve total points earned in the course. Typically, grades are assigned based on the total number of points earned. The flaw in this approach is that chemistry exams and quizzes are not always of equal difficulty. A statistically accurate way to add exam scores is to use T-scores (Mehrens and Lehmann 1978; Agresti and Finlay 1997). Test scores can be interpreted to make decisions about a student's knowledge of chemistry relative to other students currently in the course and other students who have taken the course. Test scores can also be used to make decisions about the degree to which a student has demonstrated knowledge about a topic. If you are using a normative-referenced grading system where there are a limited number of A's and B's to be awarded, then it becomes important for you to accurately compare the performance of students on an exam-to-exam basis. A T-score is generated by calculating a z-score and then transforming the z-score to a T-score by using 500 (or 50) as the mean and 100 (or 10) as the standard deviation.

$$z = (\text{raw score} - \text{mean})/\text{standard deviation}$$
$$T = 100(z) + 500 \textbf{ OR } T = 10(z) + 50$$

Let's compare the scores earned by two students on two exams called "Exam 1" and "Exam 2." Figure 6 shows an example of how raw scores from "Exam 1" are transformed into T-scores. Student X earns a score of 30 points out of 51 points (T-score = 484) on Exam 1 (mean = 31.17, standard deviation = 7.19) and 40 points out of 50 points (T-score = 644) on Exam 2 (mean = 32.59, standard deviation = 5.15). The student's total raw score is 70. The total T-score for the two exams is 1,128. Student Y earns a score of 40 points (T-score = 623) on Exam 1 and 30 points (T-score = 450) on Exam 2. Student Y has the same total raw score of 70 as Student X, but the total T-score for Student Y, 1,073, is lower than the total T-score for Student X. Based on the total T-scores, Student X should earn a higher grade than Student Y. Final letter grades can be determined by adding the T-scores from each graded quiz, exam, or other assessment activity, providing the activities generate a mean and a standard deviation.

Figure 6. An example of how raw exam scores are transformed into T-scores.

Average test score = 61%	Error variance = 9.09
Standard error of measurement in raw scores = 3.01	Standard error of measurement in T-scores = 41.94
Number taking test = 647	Number of scored items = 51
Mean = 31.17	Variance = 51.65
Standard deviation = 7.19	

SCORE	N	CUM	%ILE	TSCORE	SCORE	N	CUM	%ILE	TSCORE
11	1	1	0	219	31	31	326	50	498
12	1	2	0	233	32	29	355	55	512
13	3	5	1	247	33	35	390	60	526
14	2	7	1	261	34	31	421	65	539
15	5	12	2	275	35	35	456	70	553
16	4	16	2	289	36	36	492	76	567
17	6	22	3	303	37	28	520	80	581
18	7	29	4	317	38	21	541	84	595
19	12	41	6	331	39	21	562	87	609
20	8	49	8	345	40	22	584	90	623
21	16	65	10	359	41	15	599	93	637
22	14	79	12	372	42	16	615	95	651
23	16	95	15	386	43	9	624	96	665
24	25	120	19	400	44	11	635	98	679
25	28	148	23	414	45	7	642	99	692
26	30	178	28	428	46	2	644	100	706
27	20	198	31	442	47	0	644	100	720
28	28	226	35	456	48	2	646	100	734
29	29	255	39	470	49	0	646	100	748
30	40	295	46	484	50	1	647	100	762

Summary

The best advice we can provide you with respect to assessing your students' understanding of chemistry is to assess your students on problems and tasks that are consistent with your course goals and objectives. Furthermore, make sure that these problems and tasks are consistent with the manner and level of difficulty with which you taught the course. Use a variety of assessment methods. Be consistent and fair in your grading, especially when you assign letter grades at the end of the course. Keep complete records and compare your course results over five to seven years. Seek advice from your colleagues. At the end of the semester, when you assign grades to your students, you should be confident that you did everything reasonable to provide each student with a fair chance to demonstrate what he or she knows about chemistry.

References

Agresti, A., & Finlay, B. (1997). *Statistical Methods for the Social Sciences, 3rd Ed*. Upper Saddle River, NJ: Prentice-Hall.

American Chemical Society, Division of Chemical Education, Examinations Institute. University of Wisconsin-Milwaukee, WI.

Angelo, T.A., & Cross, K .P. (1993). *Classroom Assessment Techniques: A Handbook for College Teachers, 2nd Ed.* San Francisco: Jossey-Bass.

Birk, J. P. & Kurtz , M.J. (1999). Effect of experience on retention and elimination of misconceptions about molecular structure and bonding. *Journal of Chemical Education, 76*, 124.

Binder, B. (1988). Improved multiple-choice examinations. *Journal of Chemical Education, 65*, 436.

Bodner, G. M. (1980). Statistical analysis of multiple-choice exams. *Journal of Chemical Education, 57*, 188.

Denyer, G. S., & Hancock, D. (2002). Graded multiple choice questions: Rewarding understanding and preventing plagiarism. *Journal of Chemical Education, 79*, 961.

Doran, L., & Hegeson, J. (1994). Assessment. In D.L. Gabel (Ed.), *Handbook of Research on Science Teaching*. NY: MacMillan.

Edwards, M. (2001). Pedagogical assessment activities in a middle school life science classroom. In D.P. Shepardson, (Ed.), *Assessment in Science: A Guide to Professional Development and Classroom Practice*. Norwell, MA: Kluwer.

Erickson, G. L., & Meyer, K. (1998). Performance assessment tasks in science: What are they measuring? In B. J. Fraser & K. G. Tobin (Eds.), *International Handbook of Science Education*. Boston: Kluwer.

Eubanks, I. D., & Eubanks, L. P. (Eds.). (1992). *ACS Test-Item Bank for General Chemistry*. Clemson, SC: American Chemical Society Division of Chemical Education Examinations Institute.

Hayes, D. (1972). A laboratory practical for a first-semester chemistry course. *Journal of Chemical Education, 49*, 710.

Herron, J. D., & Greenbowe, T. J. (1986). What can we do about Sue: A case study of competence. *Journal of Chemical Education, 63*, 528.

Jones, M. M. (1977). Simple practical lab test for freshman students. *Journal of Chemical Education, 54,* 178.

King, M. M. (1974). A practical laboratory examination for organic chemistry. *Journal of Chemical Education, 51,* 125.

Mehrens, W. A., & Lehmann, I. J. (1978). *Measurement and Evaluation in Education and Psychology, 2nd Ed.* New York: Holt, Rinehart, and Winston.

Mills, P. A., DeMeo, S., Sweeney, W. V., Marino, R. & Clarkson, S. (2000). Using poster sessions as an alternative to written examination—the poster exam. *Journal of Chemical Education, 77,* 1158.

Nurrenbern, S. C., & Pickering, M. (1987). Concept learning versus problem solving: Is there a difference? *Journal of Chemical Education, 64,* 508.

Nakhleh, M. (1992). Why some students don't learn chemistry. *Journal of Chemical Education, 69,* 191–196.

Nakhleh, M. B., & Mitchell, R. C. (1993). Concept learning versus problem solving. *Journal of Chemical Education, 70,* 190.

Nakhleh, M., & Krajcik, J. (1994). Influence of levels of information presented by different technologies on students' understanding of acid, base, and pH concepts. *Journal of Research in Science Teaching, 31,* 1077.

Phelps, A. J., LaPorte, M. M. & Mahood, A. (1997). Portfolio assessment in high school chemsitry: One teacher's guidelines. *Journal of Chemical Education, 74,* 528.

Popham, W. J. (2002). *Classroom Assessment: What Teachers Need to Know, 3rd edition.* Boston: Allyn & Bacon.

Rozeiu, A.M. (1969). Practical exam for a multisectioned engineering chemistry laboratory. *Journal of Chemical Education, 46,* 120.

Robyt, J. F., & White, B. J. (1990). Laboratory practical exams in the biochemistry lab course. *Journal of Chemical Education, 67,* 600.

Silberman, R., Day, S., Jeffors, P., Klanderman, K. Phillips, M. G., & Zipp, A. (1987). Unusual laboratory practical examinations for general chemistry. *Journal of Chemical Education, 64,* 622.

Tamir, P. (1998). Assessment and evaluation in science education: Opportunities to learn and outcomes. In B. J. Fraser and K. G. Tobin (Eds.), *International Handbook of Science Education.* Boston: Kluwer.

Vitale, M. & Romance, N. (1999). Portfolios in science assessment: A knowledge-based model for classroom practice. In J. J. Mintzes, J. H. Wandersee, and J. D. Novak (Eds.), *Assessng Sceince Understanding: A Human Constructivist View.* New York: Academic.

Section

CAREER AND PROFESSION

16

JCE: A New Teacher's Best Friend

John W. Moore, Elizabeth A. Moore, Jon L. Holmes, and Mary E. Saecker
Journal of Chemical Education
University of Wisconsin–Madison

Abstract

The *Journal of Chemical Education* (*JCE*) is an excellent companion and mentor for a beginning teacher. It is a peer-reviewed journal published by the American Chemical Society Division of Chemical Education, a nonprofit organization. It is a resource of many dimensions and specialties. *JCE* always looks to the future, but everything it does is based on 80 years of experience building a community of chemists who teach.

Using current monthly issues and the resources on *JCE Online* will enable anyone, from first-year teacher to experienced faculty member, to go further and deeper—to try more than could be done using individual, or even institutional, resources. Through *JCE* a new teacher can draw on the entire chemical education community for help and guidance.

Biographies

John W. Moore is Professor of Chemistry at the University of Wisconsin-Madison and was appointed the seventh editor of the *Journal of Chemical Education* in 1996. Elizabeth A. Moore, Jon L. Holmes, and Mary E. Saecker are associate editors of the *Journal*.

Why should a new teacher read *JCE*?

For us to tell a new (or even experienced) faculty member how useful *JCE* can be might seem immodest. However, our readers have impressed upon us that what we know to be a high-quality, refereed publication is always worth their time to read and is often invaluable. Consequently, we will use unsolicited comments from readers—members of the chemical education community and your colleagues—to help us present a clear, succinct, and meaningful statement of the benefits to be derived from *JCE*.

Richard Stolzberg from the University of Alaska, Fairbanks, has an interesting method for getting his new colleagues to read *JCE*. He tells us "Every time we hire a new faculty member, I saunter down to the departmental offices and ask the administrative assistant if the department could possibly spare the price of a year's subscription to *JCE*. There is always money available, and I think that the new faculty have actually read some articles and get to thinking good thoughts about undergraduates."

JCE's aims have been stated well by one of its former editors, W. T. Lippincott: "To provide chemistry teachers with information, ideas, and materials for improving and updating their background and their understanding of the science, and for helping them in their teaching and in their effectiveness in developing the talents of students. The central idea here is that this should be not only a 'living textbook of chemistry' as one of the early editors put it, but a perpetual and dependable learning source for chemists who teach."

Both college and high school teachers have told us how much they rely on their *JCE* collection for checking their chemistry as well as teaching it. Evan Genest, a teacher at NEHS High School in Taiwan, says it this way: "As a new teacher I find *JChemEd* more useful than any other single source of information on how to teach. Sometimes I go to Xerox some articles from it and end up Xeroxing more than half of the issue. The wide-ranging, super-eclectic selection of articles, everything from ivory-tower Piaget pedagogy to hands-on stuff; new school to very old school, is great."

JCE consists of several components: print, on-line, software, and books (such as the *Handbook for Teaching Assistants*). Each of these provides information and ideas that will help a first-time teacher.

What does a subscription to *JCE* provide?

JCE mails monthly issues of approximately 130 printed pages to its subscribers, but this is only a fraction of what a subscription brings. Each subscriber also has full access to *JCE Online*, the Web-based portion of *JCE*, which reproduces everything that we print and contains much much more.

The content of an issue of *JCE* (both print and online) is divided into these topical sections:

- **Chemical Education Today** (news, commentary, reports, reviews of books and media, letters to the editor)

- **Chemistry for Everyone** (applications, history, interdisciplinary activities, public understanding; *JCE* Classroom Activities)

- **In the Classroom** (teaching tips, methods, demonstrations, content, principles)

- **In the Laboratory** (experiments, microscale, safety)

- **Research: Science and Education** (science education research papers, review papers that interpret a specific aspect of chemistry for teachers)

- **Information/Textbooks/Media/Resources** (chemical information, textbook forum, technology and multimedia applications, information technology)

- **Supplementary Material** (found on the Web on *JCE Online*)

What will I find in *JCE*?

There is a wealth of information in *JCE*, and articles span a broad range of ideas and topics that represent the breadth of chemical education today. What we publish represents what our authors submit and our reviewers recommend be accepted. Here is a closer look at some important categories that you will find in nearly every issue.

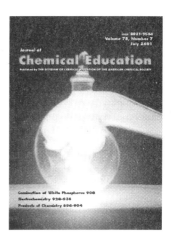

Tested Demonstrations. Chemistry is inherently interesting—even exciting. Chemical demonstrations have been popular with students and the general public for nearly two centuries. If you want to bring this excitement to your students, find a new demo or a new variation on an old demo in *JCE*, practice it and use it in your next class. Every demonstration that is published has been tried and tested by peer reviewer/testers, so you can be confident that it will work. You will find a description of the procedure and what the students will see, warnings of potential hazards, and information about the pedagogical value of each demo.

Laboratories. Suppose you have been asked to develop a new laboratory exercise or to revise an existing lab for one of the courses you teach. In *JCE* you will find a wealth of labs developed by other chemistry teachers and tested by those teachers through use with typical students. Before any lab is published, it is peer reviewed by several reviewers. Since 1998 nearly every lab has included supplementary materials, such as the handout that was given to students who performed the lab in the author's classes, notes for the instructor, and a list of chemicals required. These handouts are made available on *JCE Online* in standard word-processor format. They may be downloaded, modified as necessary, and used free of charge in any *JCE* subscriber's classes. With the aid of *JCE*, the process of finding and implementing a new laboratory is simple, quick, and successful. Some of our subscribers, such as Greg Dodd, are so enthusiastic about the labs that they are willing to be quoted: "If you get one lab a year, it is worth the subscription price."

Chemical education research. Research in chemical education has produced results that can be very helpful to a beginning teacher. *JCE* publishes such results as a regular Chemical Education Research feature. Some articles will help you get started applying chemical education research methods to your own teaching; others present the results of chemical education research studies so that you can benefit from what has been learned. Authors of chemical education research articles are asked to describe how their work can be applied to day-to-day pedagogy, providing a clear message that you can put to practical use. Georgios Tsaparlis, editor of CERAPIE, got his introduction to science education research in the pages of *JCE*. Here is how he put it: "I am a subscriber since 1979, as well as author in three papers. Your journal is for me not only a continuous source of precious chemical knowledge, but also the source of my first readings of chemistry/science education papers—actually the cause that turned me into a science-education researcher."

Up-to-date summaries of chemical research. In 1998, *JCE*'s 75th year, we initiated Viewpoints: Chemists on Chemistry, a series of articles that reported on various areas of chemical research in terms understandable to upper-division undergraduates. Articles were written by pioneers in each field, and those pioneers provided perspective on past developments and projections for the future. Review articles that are accessible to undergraduates and to teachers who are not experts in the field are an ongoing feature that provides an excellent means for keeping up to date with chemical research and bringing the excitement of the latest research to your students.

Real-world applications of chemistry. Do you need examples of chemistry in action to use in class that students can quickly relate to? *JCE*'s Products of Chemistry column provides a broad range of information about how chemistry is used in the real world: dental-filling materials; pharmaceuticals from plants; lab-on-a-chip technologies; gas hydrates; humic acids and soils; photochemotherapy; genetic modifications; and many others.

Safety information and awareness. As a beginning teacher, you may be wondering how to find out what you need to know about safe handling of laboratory chemicals and how to make your teaching labs safe for students to work in. Chemical Laboratory Information Profiles provide the information a busy teacher needs to know about hazards of substances commonly used in teaching laboratories. The Safety Tips column includes a variety of safety-oriented material. Laboratory experiments and demonstrations that are not safe are not published, and every laboratory has a Hazards section so that you can evaluate whether it is safe enough for your teaching situation.

Interdisciplinary connections. Like all other chemistry teachers, you will find that many of your students are interested in related disciplines such as biological sciences or materials science. To help you keep up with what is happening in other disciplines, *JCE* provides many articles on the latest interdisciplinary or multidisciplinary research. Also, there are regular reports from *Nature*, *The Physics Teacher*, *The Science Teacher*, science education research journals, and more.

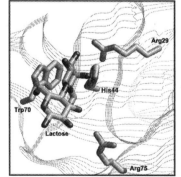

Biochemistry. The ACS Committee on Professional Training's guidelines for ACS certified degrees recently added the requirement that the curriculum for chemistry majors must include biochemistry. As a new faculty member, you may be called upon to incorporate biochemistry into existing courses or to teach a new course in this area.

JCE has a regular feature, Concepts in Biochemistry, that will help a lot. In addition to articles about biochemistry, you will find many new biochemistry experiments. Since 1965 more than 300 biochemistry experiments have been published in our pages.

Classroom activities. New faculty members are often asked to participate in National Chemistry Week or other outreach programs. An invaluable resource to help make such programs successful is *JCE* Classroom Activities. These are simple hands-on experiments that use household chemicals and will fascinate young students (and their parents as well). They can also provide take-home or dorm-room assignments for college students. A complete list of the more than 50 *JCE* Classroom Activities published to date can be found in *JCE Online*. Topics range from acid rain to fingerprints to LEDs to zeolites.

If you are already involved in an outreach program, *JCE* can help make it more successful. Our *Journal* Ambassador program can provide you with free copies of our materials (such as *Journal* issues) to hand out at workshops, short courses, teacher conferences, award nights, seminars, or ACS Local Section meetings.

Book and media reviews. Are you debating about what textbook to use when you teach your first class? Do you need to decide whether the rather hefty purchase price for a new multimedia learning tool is actually worth paying? *JCE* Book and Media Reviews can provide the information you need. Several extensive reviews written by experienced teachers are published in each issue. Reading the reviews will keep you up to date on what books, computer software, and other teaching materials are available, and provide you with the best possible information about how useful and effective these materials are.

News and announcements. Do you need to know the deadlines for submitting proposals to the NSF, the Dreyfus Foundation, or the Research Corporation? You will find this information in *JCE*. You will also know when conferences, short courses, and other opportunities for personal development are available, and you will learn who has won awards in chemical education and major research awards, such as the Nobel Prize.

To summarize, you will find in *JCE*—in an issue, a volume, or a collection—a wealth of information over a broad area. As David Adams of the University of Massachusetts, Amherst, says, "The only journal I have on my office shelves is *J. Chem. Ed*. I refer to it constantly and would not be without it."

What is available in *JCE Online*?

If you are like most new faculty members, you use the Web for literature searching and for finding useful information. *JCE* recognizes the value of 24-7 availability of information, and so we have developed a Web site that will serve your needs effectively. *JCE Online* includes abstracts of all papers published in print, the papers themselves in Adobe Acrobat PDF format, and all supplemental materials, such as data, lab handouts, and spreadsheet templates. Laboratory handouts are provided as computer-readable files that can be modified to suit your local needs. Color graphics appear online even though they were monochrome in print. Spreadsheets are live and ready to download and use. In some cases digitized

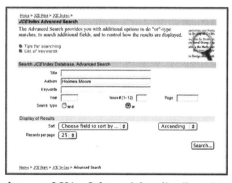

videos or animations are provided to illustrate a point. Currently over 35% of the articles distributed in print have supplements in *JCE Online*.

As a new member of the teaching profession, you will be expected to contribute to the profession in a variety of ways. Publication of results of your efforts is the most obvious of these, but reviewing manuscripts also benefits both you and the discipline. And as a reviewer you will learn how manuscripts are structured and revised into publishable form. *JCE Online* includes information about *JCE*, such as our Guide to Submissions, Reviewer Questionnaire, Supplemental Guidelines for Lab-Experiment Manuscripts, and much else. If you are thinking about writing a manuscript, reviewing manuscripts, or just contacting the editorial staff, here is where you can find out how.

In addition, there is *JCE* **Index**. Using this popular on-line feature, you can search *JCE* from 1924 until the present to find articles by any author, or articles with any word or words in their titles. For articles published since 1995, you can also search by keyword. There is a wealth of useful information in back issues of *JCE*, and the *JCE* Index on-line is an indispensable tool that provides easy access to it. Since most *JCE* readers continue to refer to issues for many years, this is particularly useful. Gail Horowitz of Yeshiva College is really enthusiastic about this feature: "The next greatest thing I discovered years after having discovered the *Journal* is the online index. This is a terrific invention. I cannot tell you how useful it has been to me as a laboratory instructor."

Only@JCE Online is a special section that appears only on the World Wide Web. Here you will find papers that cannot be published in print because they include live spreadsheets, animations, and other nontraditional components that require information technology for their delivery. You will also find these columns:

Mathcad in the Chemistry Curriculum. Edited by Theresa J. Zielinski, this feature should be bookmarked by anyone who is using Mathcad in teaching (or is considering its use)! This type of symbolic mathematics software allows students to engage in complex numerical analysis and to explore mathematical models for chemical systems. The Mathcad documents and the editorial commentary of this column serve as excellent examples of using "Mathcad in the Chemistry Curriculum."

Conceptual Questions and Challenge Problems. Edited by William R. Robinson and Susan C. Nurrenbern, this is a source of questions and problems that can be used in teaching or assessing conceptual understanding and conceptual problem solving in chemistry. Included are examples, along with hints for writing your own questions and problems.

Biographical Snapshots of Famous Women and Minority Chemists. This column, edited by Barbara A. Burke, includes more than 50 brief biographies that aim to inspire and enlighten by means of personal information about women and minorities who have made important contributions to chemistry.

Project Chemlab database. This database is the product of a committee chaired by Carolyn B. Allen and is a significant aid for those looking for good labs. Project Chemlab has teamed up with *JCE* to offer an on-line searchable annotated database of laboratories published in *JCE*. At this writing the database includes 5,038 laboratory experiments that have appeared in *JCE* between 1955 and the present—and the number of experiments grows every month.

The Project Chemlab database and the supplementary materials that are on-line are especially appreciated by those who want to develop new labs or revise existing ones. Juliette Bryson of Las Positas College in Livermore, California, is an example. "I really enjoy access to *JCE Online*. I have downloaded the additional materials that accompanied two experiments and have already tried one of the experiments in Organic Chemistry. Other additional materials have also been useful."

Reviewed WWW Sites. Edited by David B. Shaw, this on-line column consists of active links to sites that have passed muster with our WWW site reviewers. For chemistry education WWW sites that make the grade, start your surfing here.

Chemical Education Resource Shelf. Edited by Hal Harris, this on-line compilation of sources for textbooks, laboratory manuals, reference books, software, molecular models, and other tools of the trade is particularly useful for new teachers who have not yet developed their own collection of helpful sources.

Hal's Picks of the Month. Edited by Hal Harris, this column recommends readings for teachers of chemistry and related sciences. Hal maintains a file of articles, pictures, and references coordinated with the topics in his curriculum. Examples from that file make up this eclectic list of items.

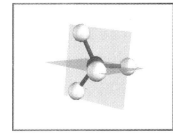

JCE WebWare. Edited by William F. Coleman, *JCE* WebWare publishes articles that are Web-based active-learning tools for use by students in the classroom, laboratory, dorm room, or home. Some examples may help to define what WebWare is about. Currently included are a VRML viewer that shows symmetry elements in methane and allows students to rotate and examine the molecule, an application that calculates concentrations of species in aqueous equilibria, and an application that integrates and smoothes data. This column also includes the Featured Molecule of the Month: a molecule, selected because it is related to an article published that month, is made available on-line in Chime format so that it can be viewed and manipulated on a computer screen.

How will my students benefit from *JCE*?

Students obviously benefit indirectly whenever their teachers read and learn more about chemistry and chemical education. However, *JCE Online* and especially *JCE Software* publish a wide variety of materials that are intended for use by students, and these help students much more directly. The *JCE* WebWare applications mentioned above are one example. There are many more in *JCE Software*.

When *JCE Software* was founded in 1988, it was the first science journal to be published in electronic media. Today *JCE Software* includes digitized video, multimedia software, and Web-ready publications. Some are aimed toward teachers, others are intended for students, and many serve both audiences. All have been developed by chemistry teachers, tested in classrooms and laboratories with typical students, thoroughly evaluated by peer reviewers, and carefully edited and produced in electronic format. At present *JCE Software* is distributed almost entirely on CD-ROMs.

Many new faculty members are developing lectures in PowerPoint format. If you are thinking of doing this, the Chemistry Comes Alive! (CCA) Series is exactly what you need. CCA currently consists of six CD-ROMs loaded with video clips and animations that are intended to be pasted into your classroom presentations. CCA videos and animations can also be incorporated into multimedia materials that you prepare for your students.

If you are looking for materials that your students can use on their own, then *JCE* Software's General Chemistry Collection, Advanced Chemistry Collection, ChemPages Laboratory, General Chemistry Multimedia Problems, and Periodic Table Live! are just what you need. Each of these CD-ROMs is available from *JCE Software* for classroom adoption. To help you learn more about what is available, all of the *JCE Software* publications are described—usually with illustrations and a program demonstration—at the *JCE Software* Web site: http://jchemed.chem.wisc.edu/JCESoft/index.html

Chemistry Comes Alive! Users consider this collection of clip videos and pictures to be spectacular. It currently includes six volumes showing chemical reactions, atomic-scale animations, laboratory techniques, and much more. Chemistry is shown close up and is the focus of the action. The videos have been digitized and compressed for Web delivery. They are easy to present in a classroom with a computer and LCD projector, and they can be incorporated into PowerPoint presentations using simple techniques described on *JCE Online*. Video clips have been keyed to course topics and popular textbooks, so if you are teaching Chapter 4 and want to show a relevant reaction, you can find it quickly and easily.

- **CCA! Volume 1** includes combination reactions, decomposition reactions, double-exchange reactions, electrical properties of matter, gases, single-exchange reactions, and stoichiometry.

- **CCA! Volume 2** includes bonding, electronic structure/periodic table, solids/liquids, solutions.

- **CCA! Volume 3** includes electrochemistry, enthalpy and thermodynamics, and oxidation-reduction.

- **CCA! Volume 4** contains two main topics: Reactions in Aqueous Solution, which shows mixing and subsequent reaction, if any, of aqueous solutions of inorganic compounds; and Reactions of the Elements, which shows elements reacting with air, water, acids, and base.

- **CCA! Volume 5** contains several hundred movies dealing with organic chemistry and biochemistry—nearly two hours of video.

- **CCA! Volume 6** contains more than 600 QuickTime movies and more than 3600 still images that illustrate laboratory procedures and techniques. The laboratory equipment and techniques demonstrated include those that students typically need to learn in general chemistry, analytical chemistry, and organic chemistry courses. The CD-ROM is organized around four topic areas: manipulating and transferring samples; measuring; separating and purifying; and safety. For those teaching quantitative analysis, all techniques related to quantitative volumetric analysis are grouped in one part of the table of contents.

There is unquestionably a lot of wonderful chemistry in the CCA! Series—both stills and movies. When there were just four volumes in the series, Mike Horton sent us this unsolicited statement: "As the host of the Southern California Science Teachers' Idea Exchange, I have personally reviewed hundreds of science software titles. If you want a good chemistry program, check out *JCE Software*. The 'Chemistry Comes Alive' products are among the best I've seen. The 4-CD series contains a collection of hundreds of videos for chemical demonstrations that are too expensive, dangerous, complicated, time consuming to do yourself. Your students will be mesmerized by videos such as touch explosives, ferromagnetic fluid, ice bomb, 5-stage colorized ammonia fountain. It's obvious that *JCE* is not 'just in it for the money'."

The Periodic Table Live! This CD-ROM is intended for direct use by students and can also be used for classroom presentations. It uses the periodic table as a navigation tool and contains a large database of information about the elements (descriptive text, physical properties, and atomic-level properties). Each property is hotlinked to its definition and to the source for the data. There are graphics and animations to illustrate solid-state structures, typical uses of the elements, and other properties. Digitized videos show elements reacting up close so that every detail can be seen. A graphing and sorting function allows more than a dozen

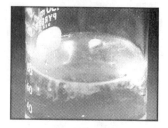

numeric properties (such as density, ionization energy, or atomic radius) to be graphed in real time. Sorting provides for both numeric and alphabetic sorting of elements' names and properties. This CD-ROM provides an interactive experience with the periodic table suitable for students at all levels of chemistry, especially in courses focusing on introductory, inorganic, and solid-state chemistry. Maria McLennan of Rochester, Michigan, sums it up in just a few words: "The Periodic Table Live is awesome!"

General Chemistry Collection (GCC) and *Advanced Chemistry Collection (ACC).* These CD-ROMs are collections of programs intended for hands-on use by students. Like Periodic Table Live! GCC and ACC are available for classroom adoption. Volume discounts are available and arrangements may also be made for custom publishing of subsets of these collections. Each CD-ROM has a collection of software that has been designed and peer-reviewed by teachers. The advanced collection is useful to students in analytical, inorganic, organic, and physical chemistry courses and biochemistry courses.

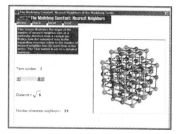

ChemPages Laboratory. This CD-ROM is a multimedia encyclopedia of laboratory techniques and apparatus that first-year students are likely to encounter. It is excellent for pre-lab preparation and also can be used as an in-lab reference. Coupled with online pre-lab quizzes it can help your students prepare for laboratory, just as Marv Bunch of Corning Community College found it did his: "I love the ChemPages Laboratory CD-ROM. It really fills in the gaps in the varied high school chemistry backgrounds of my general chemistry students. Almost every lab we perform now includes a "page" from ChemPages Laboratory as part of the pre-lab assignment."

Where does *JCE* stand today?

JCE is the world's most important repository for papers on chemical education. It is the recognized leader in the community of chemical education, and has 80 years of experience in back of it. There is no other journal like it. Many people begin reading *JCE* in their undergrad or grad student years. And they keep reading and referring to is throughout their teaching career. Barry Coddens of Northwestern University is an example. "I've read the *JCE* since I was a freshman in 1971. I started reading the *Journal* because back then it was the only journal a freshman could understand. I'm still reading the *Journal* twenty-nine years later."

JCE is a recognized leader in the community of chemical education. *JCE* is a place where teachers who investigate new pedagogy, content, or curricula can share their efforts. *JCE* is a reporter of opportunities for teachers within ACS and other organizations. *JCE* is an important source of information on chemical education research. *JCE* is a major resource for both high school and college teachers of chemistry. *JCE* is an international journal with respect to authors, reviewers, readers.

JCE's influence goes beyond the boundaries of chemistry, at least according to David McConnell of the Department of Geology at the University of Akron. "Without the papers I can read from journals like *J Chem Ed* I would not be aware of much of the excellent work that has been done to reform classroom teaching and learning. Just yesterday I came across Donald Paulson's 1999 paper on active learning in organic chemistry in *J Chem Ed*—great stuff. Just to show that your articles have a wide audience, Paulson's paper was recommended to me by a colleague in communications."

JCE hopes it can help you make a strong and confident start as a chemistry teacher. This is something that the editorial staff feels strongly about, and it is something that *JCE*'s readers have always believed in. *JCE* does more than report on happenings in the discipline, its pages have always led the discipline. *JCE* does more than adopt the latest technological advances for publication, it pioneers them. *JCE* is an active leader in the chemical education community. *JCE* readers, reviewers, and authors have a sense of ownership and stewardship. They rely on *their* journal: "As a chemistry teacher, I don't know how you can get along without it." This is what Ron Fedie of Augsburg College in Minneapolis has told us, and he thinks that he is fairly typical.

How can I contribute to *JCE*?

You can become a reader, a reviewer, an author, or all of these.

As a new faculty member, you may not feel ready to become a reviewer or an author, but don't be daunted. Think of these as opportunities to learn and to grow professionally and personally. The best possible time for professional growth is when you are young and new to the job, so take advantage of the opportunity.

As a reviewer, you will learn a lot about how manuscripts are revised and edited from relatively rough drafts into the polished versions that appear in print. Several reviewers are assigned to each manuscript, so if you miss something, the responsibility is shared. Reviewers tell us that they learn a lot when they review. The reviewing process provides an opportunity to enhance your mastery of chemistry content, of chemical pedagogy, and of how to write about and explain chemical concepts.

Lest you think that urging you to review for *JCE* is self serving, we will let Joseph Beatty (now a science education consultant and formerly a teacher at Roseberg Senior High School) tell you of his experience. "I have enjoyed being able to review articles. The insights I have gained from the review process were shared with my students as they were writing and rewriting reports of their laboratory work. The fact that I could talk from personal experience about both the writing and reviewing of papers for publication helped them understand that adults also write and rewrite words for publication."

As an author, you will learn that it is impossible to think of everything that will help readers understand a topic, and it is very difficult to anticipate the various meanings readers will draw from your words. Writing about something is an excellent way to learn the subject more thoroughly, and so writing will contribute to your ability to teach chemistry and to do chemical research. You will also learn that there are many members of the reviewer community who are willing to go the extra mile to help you create the best possible version of your manuscript for publication. And there are always experienced editors to help and advise you.

You will benefit from each of these activities, and so will *JCE*. You can involve your colleagues, your students, and local teachers in the *JCE* community; that is a *JCE* tradition. You can begin by giving us your ideas and your feedback. Check out *JCE Online* (http://jchemed.chem.wisc.edu), send us an e-mail (jce@chem.wisc.edu), or use the postal service to mail your comments to *JCE*, University of Wisconsin-Madison, 209 North Brooks Street, Madison, WI 53715-1116. We are looking forward to hearing from you, and so are your colleagues.

17

Getting a Job in Academia: Tips from a Recent Candidate

Dawn Del Carlo
Department of Chemistry and Biochemistry
Montclair State University

Abstract

Finding a job can be a daunting enough procedure when one knows what to expect; for the first-time candidate, it can be downright intimidating. This chapter will outline how to search for positions, put together a curriculum vitae (CV), write a cover letter, and write a statement of teaching philosophy. It discusses the basic interview protocol for a typical academic position, what types of questions a candidate should ask, and what things to look for on a campus visit. Finally, it highlights negotiating the job offer and discussion of start-up funding. The emphasis is on applying to positions at four-year institutions not heavily focused on research. While the job hunt can still be intimidating, it is not nearly so overwhelming when one is prepared for what lies ahead.

Biography

I am currently in my second year as an assistant professor at Montclair State University in Upper Montclair, NJ (the position I attained going through the process outlined in this chapter). As I looked for my job, I was completing my doctorate in chemistry education at Purdue University and did not have a really good idea of how much time went into searching for a job or what to expect at each step of the process. I took what advice I could from my adviser and others in the same boat as myself, but I still felt relatively unprepared as I went through the process. I think I did a pretty good job in the end (after a year I'm still happy with the position I have), but I learned a few things along the way and also now have the benefit of hindsight on things I would have done differently. My goal for this chapter is to share what I already know about searching for jobs, what I learned along the way, and what I would change if I had known more. I cannot promise automatic success for anyone who follows my path, but I can at least offer the reader a good place to start.

When should I start looking for a job?

The very first decision that needs to be made in the process of finding an academic position is when you should start looking for your job. For those people who are still in the throws of graduate school, the decision becomes one of when you and your adviser predict you will be finished. It is possible to accept a position ABD (All But Degree) and write your dissertation in absentia, but every graduate student has heard of the trials and tribulations that await that option. I knew enough about myself to know that I would be unable to start a career and finish a degree at the same time, but everyone is different, and you might find that this is not the case with you. You may also want to consider looking for a postdoctoral fellowship. My field of specialization is chemistry education, and there aren't many postdoctoral opportunities in that field. However, several institutions advertising for a "traditional" field in chemistry look for applications with this experience. Although you may know you want to ultimately enter academia, a postdoc may help you in this endeavor.

Another decision to be made is the kind of position you are looking for: tenure track or temporary. If you are at a point in your life where you can afford to be relatively mobile, a temporary position may not be a bad option. It gives you a taste for what a permanent position is like, and if you have only minimal teaching experience, a temporary position is an opportunity to refine your teaching before you find yourself in the tenure track marathon. Since I was fresh out of graduate school and still pretty mobile, I applied for both permanent and temporary positions. Temporary positions that start in the fall of an academic year are usually advertised as early as January all the way up to the first day of the fall semester. For those positions starting in January, expect to see them advertised the previous fall.

Permanent positions typically have a starting date in the fall semester and are advertised at varying points of the year, depending on the position. Major research institutions start their hiring processes early. Expect to see advertisements in August for a position starting the following August. Other institutions will start advertising anywhere from six months to a year ahead.

Where do I look for an academic position?

There are an incredible number of places to look for a job, but as far as I can tell, there are four main sources that inform you of just about any job available in science academia. The first is *Chemical and Engineering News*. If you are a member of ACS, you already get the paper copy, but you also have access to their on-line database at http://pubs.acs.org/cen/cenwelcomepage.html. I found the on-line database much easier to search for positions because it allows you to quickly scan the titles of the advertisements. The ACS also has a new career Web site available (www.jobspectrum.org). This site was not in operation for my search, but from what I have seen, it looks fairly comprehensive.

The next resource to look into is the *Chronicle of Higher Education*. Their classified section is available on-line (http://chronicle.com/jobs) for free with a one-week lag time from when the ad was first published. The most recent advertisements are available both on-line and in print for those who have a subscription. Again, I find the on-line postings much easier to read and sort.

Finally, the last resources to tap are other faculty in your field. There were several position announcements that members of my committee passed along to me simply because they knew I was looking for a position. Get the word out that you are trying to find a job, and ask faculty in the field to keep an eye open for you.

How do I know if I want to respond to a job announcement?

As you browse all of the advertisements, you need to determine what kind of job it is that interests you. I have already discussed the option of temporary versus permanent, but the decision goes beyond that one choice. What kind of institution are you looking for? You may not want to work at a major research institution, but there are several levels of institution besides that one. How big of an institution do you want to work at? What level students are you willing to work with? Undergraduate? Masters level? Ph.D.? Where in the country do you want to work? Are you looking for or avoiding institutions with a particular religious affiliation? Keep in mind that there are several levels of religious affiliation that schools maintain from seminary to state school. The best way to learn about an institution and the chemistry department is to check out their Web sites. Look at the mission statement, history, and general facts, and think about whether this is the type of institution where you might want to build your career. On the departmental level, look at the faculty and their research, the instrumentation, and available facilities. Many times you can get a feel for how well you will fit into a department by just doing a little research first.

I wanted a job at a primarily undergraduate institution, focused on teaching and undergraduate research, with a student population around 10,000 or less, and located in the northern part of the country (I become incredibly irritable in hot weather). I was interested in both inorganic and chemistry education at this research level and consequently applied to positions in both disciplines. Even with these stipulations, I was able to apply to over 30 positions, so do not be afraid to be somewhat selective in your search. If you know, based on the advertisement and your research interests, that you would never be happy at that particular institution, there is no reason to send them an application.

What goes into a Curriculum Vitae (CV)?

I will be perfectly honest and come right out and say I lifted the format of my CV from another member of my research group. The example CV in Appendix A is the one I used for my applications, but there are several ways to organize a CV, and most of them are perfectly acceptable. Some things that can be done differently include using reverse chronological order, putting the dates on the left, including references (some announcements require this), and changing the font. For more ideas, there are quite a few books available on writing CV's (refer to the references at the end of this chapter) or look up the Web pages of faculty at different institutions and see if they have their CV's posted. The goal is to make your CV clean and easy to read. Once you have yours drafted, give it to someone else to look over. If they have difficulty following the information, then you need to re-work it.

What is a statement-of-teaching philosophy?

Just about every position you apply for will request your statement-of-teaching philosophy. This is the institution's way of screening how reflective a particular candidate is on their teaching. Due to the personal nature of this topic, I cannot tell you how to write your statement-of-teaching philosophy. There are, however, several topics that you should consider discussing as you write your teaching philosophy.

First and most important, you must address your basic philosophies of teaching. This includes discussing why students need to take chemistry classes at all, how you are motivated to teach, how you motivate your students to learn, what different learning styles you have observed, and how your teaching style is affected by these factors. Discuss how these things may be different for different classes (majors vs. non-majors), and use examples from past teaching experiences, even if it was only as a teaching assistant in graduate school, to illustrate your points. Do you prefer a formal classroom or something a bit more casual? Lecture- or interactive-based classroom? Independent or collaborative work? Remember, there are no "right" answers here. This is simply a reflection of who you are as an educator.

Other topics to include in this document pertain mostly to curriculum issues. How do you pick out a textbook for a particular course? How does it fit in with your lecture or other teaching approach? What is the basic course structure you aim for in terms of number of tests, assignments, and classroom activities? What is the role of the laboratory in your science classes? How should that be structured? What educational role does the research laboratory have in your approach to teaching? Again, give examples from your past experiences to illustrate your points. One last topic to discuss is how you plan to assess your students. What kinds of assignments do you employ (homework, quizzes, lab reports, exams), and what are they like? What assignments will be graded and how heavily will they play in a student's overall grade? How many exams do you feel are appropriate for a semester-long course? What is the basic format of these exams?

Finally, at the end of the document, you should write a concluding paragraph to give the reader an overview of your teaching philosophy. It is easy to get lost in the details of your philosophy so you want to be able to supply a "take away" message at the end that sums up the main themes. The length of this document varies greatly from person to person; mine is about six and a half double-spaced pages. Some institutions will ask for a specific page length, and I found mine was typically near the upper limit, so I do not recommend going much longer than that. Your statement of teaching philosophy is also something that will and should change as you build teaching experience. As discussed previously, it is a self-reflection of who you are as an educator, so it should not be tailored to any one particular institution. In addition to the fact that it would be unbearably tedious to write a new statement for each application, you would be too concerned about trying to match the institution's philosophy rather than paying enough attention to your own. If a potential employer does not agree with your teaching philosophy, you would be miserable at that institution, and unable to reach your students in the way you believe to be most effective. Write one statement-of-teaching philosophy and send it with any application that requests it.

What should I say about my research interests?

The answer to this question is solely dependent on the type of academic position to which you apply. Because I did not apply to major research institutions, a simple five-page statement of my research interests was sufficient. If, however, you apply for a research-based position, be prepared to submit at least two to three full-length research proposals, including how you anticipate funding them. Temporary positions usually do not request anything about your research.

Regardless of the institution you apply to, two things must be clear when you write about your research. First, you must explain where you are and how you got there. The only way you can explain what you want to do is to explain where you have been. Give a little background on your past research and what the results were. Second, and more important, you need to explain how you intend to grow. This is the time for you to explain your potential as a researcher. What are your ideas, and how do you intend to implement them? Why are they good ideas to implement? How can your research plans be integrated into an already existing department? Like your statement of teaching philosophy, this should not be written to be specific to any one institution. Your research proposals/statement should describe your research plans, not the plans you think a potential employer wants to hear.

Should I include a cover letter?

The simple answer to this question is "yes." Unlike your statement of teaching philosophy and research interests, this is where you tailor your strengths to the institution. There should be three things included in your cover letter: 1) Why are you perfect for this job? 2) What can you offer them? and 3) Show that you care about this specific position (even though you have probably applied to a dozen others). The cover letter I sent to the institution that hired me is included in Appendix B, and there are a few references on cover-letter writing listed at the end of the chapter. The first paragraph of my letter simply outlines which position I am applying for (many times institutions are hiring for more than one position at a time), and what other materials are included in the envelope. The middle two paragraphs explain why I believe I would be perfect for their job and what my expertise can offer to their department. Finally, the last paragraph shows that I want to make sure they have all of the materials they need and that I am anticipating some sort of notification from them acknowledging receipt of my application. Each cover letter sent out should be unique to the institution you apply to. You may use a similar paragraph structure, but each letter should include information gleaned from individual department websites, the job advertisement, and your expertise. The cover letter is where you sell your talents and try to convince the search committee that you are the one for the job. It is the most personalized and institution-specific aspect of the application and also the reason why an application should never be without one.

When will I start hearing from college/universities?

Shortly after you start sending out applications, you will start receiving letters of receipt, affirmative-action cards, and possible requests for additional information. The affirmative-action card is simply a way for human resource offices to keep track of who is applying for the position. The information you supply cannot be used for qualifying or discriminatory action, and you have the option not to return the card if you are uncomfortable with the idea. However, the letters of receipt are definitely pieces of information that need to be checked. These usually indicate what information is still missing from your application file. Whether the missing material is something you left out of the envelope, academic transcripts, or a letter of recommendation that never made it to its destination, your application will probably not be reviewed until it is complete. I had one university tell me in their letter that I had not included my statement of research interests, but when I looked back at their advertisement, they never requested one. After a quick call to the secretary of the department, the matter was straightened out, and the department chair saw that I cared enough to take the time to check.

Beyond that initial letter, you may never hear from an institution again. I'm still waiting to hear from some, and I did my search in the fall of 2000! This is generally considered poor practice, and if it is a position you are highly interested in, you may want to call or e-mail the contact person to inquire about the status of your application. If the position is one among a sea of others you would be interested in, I found it best to leave well enough alone. Also during this time, you will receive rejection or "ding" letters. As hard as it may be, try not to take them personally. The search committee had to draw the line somewhere, and it often will not include you. They know what type of person they need to fill that position, and only a few people will fit the bill. It can be frustrating to know you did not make the cut, but hang in there. There are several other applicants receiving very similar letters to yours.

For those institutions that DO want you (and there will be some), they will make first contact either via e-mail or phone, so if you are not in the habit of keeping up with your messages, you need to start. There is nothing like missing out on an opportunity because you only check your e-mail once a week. The first thing they will ask is if you are still interested in the position. It sounds like a stupid question (why else would you have sent in the application), but they need to make sure that your circumstances have not changed and that interviewing you is going to be worth their time. From here they will either ask you to set up a phone interview or a campus visit. I will get to phone interviews in the next section, but if they request a campus visit, establish when you are to visit, the number of days you will be interviewing, and what materials you should prepare for the visit. You will most likely set up your own flight or transportation and then be reimbursed by the institution after the fact. Consequently, make sure your credit cards are not too overloaded so you will have the available credit line to make these purchases.

What do I do about phone interviews?

Phone interviews are becoming more popular especially as school budgets are cut. When I did my job search, I was not asked to do any phone interviews, but several of my graduate school colleagues participated in them, and I learned from their experiences. The phone interview is a great way for a search committee to narrow a pool of six or seven applicants down to only one or two to invite for a campus visit, so a phone interview should not be taken lightly. Set up a time when you know you will not be rushed between classes or experiments. Ask them to call you at a phone number where you have little chance of being disturbed. If you are working in a large, noisy lab, with several people walking in and out all day, have them call you at home or in another office where you can close and lock the door. Although it is an option, I do not recommend having the committee call you on your cell phone. The first problem is ensuring that you get a signal wherever you decide to situate yourself; there is nothing worse for your potential career than to have your cell phone lose its signal in the middle of your interview. Second, most interviews are conducted by a committee on a speaker phone. I have yet to encounter a system where speaker phones and cell phones work with perfect auditory response. The second worst thing for your career is not to hear the interview because the reception cut out as someone else started talking.

Before the interview, set yourself up in your space. Have on hand notes about the school and department, the advertisement to which you responded, your cover letter, a glass of water, a pad of paper and pen, and any questions you might have about the position or institution. When the committee calls, the first thing they should do is introduce themselves. When this happens, write down each person's name and their position (dean, department chair, organic faculty, etc.) so you know who you are speaking to as the interview progresses. From here you are on your own. The interview can last anywhere from 30 to 60 minutes. Answer their questions honestly and openly and try to relax!

What happens during a campus interview?

After the initial phone call or the phone interview, you may be asked to participate in a campus visit. While you are there, you will probably eat all your meals with various members of the department, take a tour of the facilities, give a seminar on your research, teach a class (either to real students or faculty pretending to be students), talk to several people individually as well as the search committee, and miscellaneous other activities depending on what may be happening in the department at the time. For example, on one interview my host was an active member of the local ACS chapter, and so one evening we attended a local meeting. This list is by no means exhaustive but it covers the basic activities of an interview. There will always be some campus interview that surprises you. One institution I interviewed with wanted me to present my research to a class of general chemistry students in the same way that I would teach that class. Consequently, this is also a time when you may have to be creative. One thing to keep in mind is that fact that whatever it is you are doing, no matter how casual an event may seem, you are still on an interview, and you need to maintain a certain level of professionalism as a result.

What kinds of questions will they ask me?

Some of the people you may meet include the department chair, the dean of the college, the members of the search committee, other members of the department and staff, and possibly some students. Each of these groups will have their own set of questions for you, and these will vary greatly. Some of the most common questions I have heard include:

- Why did you choose "Such-and-So University"?

- Tell me why I/we should hire you?

- What would you do about John/Suzie Student who…?

- How do you plan to… (this can be with regards to teaching, research, or curriculum development)?

- What are your expectations of us?

I realize that these are pretty vague questions, but all you can do is roll with the punches and be honest. Some of these questions reflect things that you have already stated in your cover letter, teaching philosophy, or research plans, and they may be asking for clarification or elaboration. Sometimes they just want to see how you think on your feet. I had a friend who interviewed at a school that was highly interdisciplinary, and they wanted to know how he would teach a chemistry class to art majors. I was asked the question why I chose to apply to "Such-and-So University" at every interview, and my response varied from place to place because I chose to apply to each institution for different reasons. Just like everything else, there are no right answers. Take your time answering questions, and be thoughtful in your answers. The people questioning you are not out to get you as much as they are attempting to learn what you have to offer their department.

What sorts of things should I be thinking about during the interview?

Now that you know what your interviewers are going to ask, you need to figure out what information you want to obtain from them. Remember, the interview is a two-way street. Not only are they figuring you out but you need to figure them out as well. Some things that you should at least be considering as you proceed through the interview include:

- Do they have reasonable expectations of what the job entails? You have a pretty good idea by this point in your academic career what one faculty member is capable of doing. Make sure they are not asking you to do the work of three people.

- Is it clear how tenure and promotion work? Some campuses are unionized and therefore have very specific procedures to follow. Others are not and may have procedures of their own. A friend of mine went on an interview to an institution where faculty do not come up for tenure for 10 years. Be sure you know how the system works and what you will be expected to do in order to make it through the system.

- Do their philosophies on education agree with yours? If there are glaring discrepancies between these two areas, no one will be happy with the teaching style you are able to implement at that institution.

- Do you get along with the department chair? Your future colleagues? The Dean? These are the people that you will be working closely with; if you do not get along with the department chair in the interview, chances are it will only get worse once you start working there.

- What do you think of the community in which the institution is located? Could you make a home for yourself there or would you have to live elsewhere and commute? Are you willing to do that?

- Last but not least, ask yourself if it "feels" right. I admit this is a qualitative measurement, but many times your gut tells you something; you should listen.

If these issues are not clear from what you are able to observe, you should ask for clarification. There are several other questions pertaining to things like health benefits and retirement funds that I consider to be "secondary" questions. This is not to imply that they are not important issues but instead, that they are issues that should be considered after the above issues are resolved. Regardless of how good their retirement plan may be, if the job is not what you are looking for, it is going to be a long way to retirement.

What happens after the interview?

After it is all over several different things can happen and it depends on where you were in the institution's interview timeline. If you were their last candidate, they probably have a good idea of where you stand and may let you know before you leave—although if they extend an offer, be wary of it until it is in writing, because verbal offers are easily misunderstood and can by withdrawn. They should be able to give you an idea of when they will make their final decision, so you know when to expect to hear from them. On the other hand, if you were their first candidate, you will have to wait until they have had the chance to interview everyone on their list. In either case, a thank-you note is in order after returning from the interview if you are still interested in the position. Unfortunately, the next steps in the process are not as clear-cut as they have been so far. A lot of what happens now depends on how long it takes the institution to finish interviewing, get their preferences filed through the appropriate administrative levels, and extend the offer to you. On your end, you may still be interviewing with other institutions and may have an offer extended to you before you have finished interviewing everywhere. If this is the case, explain your situation (assuming that you are interested in the offer at all) and see if you can buy yourself some more time. If you have one or two offers on the table, you may have to let one or two go before knowing anything. Try not to wait too long for one position that seems to be dragging its feet, but in the same vein, do not jump at the first offer you get simply because it is there. This is probably the hardest part about finding a job, and there are no easy solutions or hard and fast rules to follow.

They want me; I want them. Now what do I do?

You've made it. They have officially contacted you and extended an offer. You want to be ready for the next step in the process which is negotiation. It makes things go much smoother for both parties if you have an idea of what you want before they even extend the offer. Two things to keep in mind as you approach negotiations: 1. If you've made it to this point, you can ask for anything and you will probably get it, and 2. Ask for whatever you think you may need and then round up. You are essentially bargaining for the added extras in your job, so you want to aim high and then come down if you have to.

So what things are considered negotiable?

There are many things to consider in terms of what you can negotiate. The following list is nowhere near complete, but it gives you a good place to start.

- Salary—Some people claim that the offered salary is somewhat negotiable. From what I have seen, it really depends on the institution and the position. Many times, there is only one salary range budgeted into the fiscal year's account. If that is the case, the salary probably cannot be altered much. However, it never hurts to ask if you feel they are offering an amount grossly under either your qualifications or the job description.

- Start-up funding—On the other side of things, what you ask for pertaining to start-up money for your research can be extremely flexible. Many temporary positions will not offer start-up funding, but any position that expects research to be performed should allocate a certain amount of money for that purpose. This is where you can really have fun. Obviously, try to keep your requests under control and check to see what sort of facilities the department already has before you start negotiations. If you ask for a 400 MHz NMR, and the department already has one, it shows that you have not been paying attention. At the same time, you may need very specific equipment and chemicals depending on what your research entails. Making a list of what you think you may need takes some time and effort, especially if you never had to purchase large pieces of equipment before. Have it all in writing before the job offer is made. That way you can give them a grand total right off the top of your head and actually have some information to back it up. The other thing to clarify is how long you have to spend this money. I thought I had a full academic year when in actuality my time ran out at the end of the fiscal year in June.

- Teaching load—Many institutions reduce your teaching load in your first year to allow you the extra time to get adjusted and set up. If your future employer does not, and you are concerned about being able to live up to all of your responsibilities, asking for a reduced load may be the way to go.

- Relocation costs—If you are moving across the country to take this job, you may want to consider how you are going to find a new place to live and how you are going to get there from where you are now. Expenses in this category also include the trips to the area to look for a place and moving expenses once you find a place.

- Travel money—If you plan to be attending or presenting at a number of conferences your first year, you can ask for compensation for those trips since you will be traveling on behalf of the institution. This is something you can include in your list for start-up funding.

- Summer stipend—For those positions that involve only a 10-month contract, you may want to ask for funding to carry you through your first summer so you can get your research established without having to worry about how you are going to support yourself financially. Many times it is not until your first summer that you are able to get things going anyway, so why not make that your primary focus? This is also a good thing to include as part of your start-up requests.

- Family needs—More and more institutions are beginning to realize that candidates have lives other than their work, and in order to persuade the candidate, they may need to lend a helping hand toward their family. This may include help in relocating a spouse's career or setting up daycare for your children. At the very least, they should be able to offer some names of people you can contact.

- Scheduling requests—Some candidates are in a position to need several days off in a row either to travel back to finish their dissertation, visit with family that could not relocate, or for research and collaboration purposes. If you find yourself in this situation, you can request a teaching assignment that excludes Monday or Friday classes to allow you a few extra travel days.

Remember, these are just ideas to get you started. The main idea is to sit down and really figure out your priorities. What things are the most important to you, and how can you make them work in your new job?

Are we done yet?

YES! After you and your future employer agree upon the details of your contract, you will receive an official letter in the mail extending an offer of employment and outlining your requests. A formal written acceptance is expected, so do not forget in your excitement to send one. Congratulations! You are now gainfully employed. Let the fun begin, and good luck!

References

Forme, D. M., & Reed, C. (1998). Job Search in Academe: Strategic Rhetorics for Faculty Job Candidates. 1st ed: Stylus Publishing LLC.

Gutmann, J. (2000). How to Write a Successful CV. Sheldon Press.

Heiberger, M. M., & Vick, J. M. (1996). The Academic Job Search Handbook. 2nd ed: University of Pennsylvania Press.

Jackson, A. (1996). How to Prepare Your Curriculum Vitae. 2nd ed. NTC Publishing Group.

Ryan, R. (2002). Winning Cover Letters. 2nd ed: Wiley, John, and Sons Incorporated.

Yate, M. J. (2000). Cover Letters that Knock 'em Dead. 4th Complete revised and expanded ed: Adams Media Corporation.

APPENDIX A – Curriculum Vitae

Dawn I. Del Carlo
Department of Chemistry
Purdue University
West Lafayette IN 47907-1393
(555) 555-5555
dawnd@purdue.edu

Birthdate: 3 April 1973
Birthplace: Suburbia, IL

Education

B.A.   Chemistry/Math minor, Augustana College, Rock Island IL, May 1995

M.S.   Chemistry (Inorganic), Purdue University, West Lafayette IN, May 1998

Ph.D.   Chemistry (Chemistry Education), Purdue University, West Lafayette IN, expected August 2001

Research Theses

M.S.   "Competitive Incorporation of Dyes into Potassium Dihydrogen Phosphate Crystals"

Ph.D.   "Academic Dishonesty in the Context of a Classroom Laboratory"

Professional Experience

Research Experience

Research Assistant for the GE Initiative   1998-1999

Teaching Experience

Undergraduate Lab Proctor   1992-1995
    General Chemistry
    Organic Chemistry
    Department of Chemistry
    Augustana College

Private Tutor   1992-1995
    General Chemistry
    Organic Chemistry
    Department of Chemistry
    Augustana College

Private Tutor   1995-2001
    General Chemistry–various courses (engineers/majors, non-majors)
    Organic Chemistry
    Department of Chemistry
    Purdue University

Graduate Teaching Assistant   1995-1998
    General Chemistry–various courses (engineers/majors, non-majors)
    Department of Chemistry
    Purdue University

Course Supervisor	Spring 1997
General Chemistry for non-majors	
Department of Chemistry	
Purdue University	

Course Supervisor   Spring 1997
 General Chemistry for non-majors
 Department of Chemistry
 Purdue University

Tutor Coordinator   1997-1998
 Women in Science and Engineering Program
 Purdue University

Graduate Teaching Assistant   Fall 1999
 Introduction to Inorganic Chemistry
 Department of Chemistry
 Purdue University

Assistant Course Supervisor   Spring 2000
 General Chemistry for engineers and majors
 Department of Chemistry
 Purdue University

Instructor of General Chemistry   Fall 2000
 General Chemistry for engineers and majors
 Department of Chemistry
 Purdue University

Course Supervisor   Spring 2001
 General Chemistry Chemical Engineers
 Department of Chemistry
 Purdue University

Professional Societies

Phi Lambda Upsilon–National Honorary Chemical Society
American Chemical Society Division of Chemical Education
National Association for Research in Science Teaching
American Association for the Advancement of Science

Publications

1. Bodner G., Oakes, W., Lowrey K., Del Carlo, D., White, S, & Samarapungavan, A. (2000). "The Freshman Engineering Experience: The Student Voice." Accepted for publication in the Proceedings of the 2000 ASEE Annual Conference, Session 3653.

Meetings Attended

2. 210th American Chemical Society Meeting, Chicago IL, August 1995

3. Midwest Organic Solid State Chemistry Symposium VIII, Lincoln NE, June 1996

4. 14th Biennial Conference on Chemical Education, Clemson SC, August 1996

5. 15th Biennial Conference on Chemical Education, Waterloo Ontario, Canada, August 1998

6. 34th Midwest Regional American Chemical Society Meeting, Quincy IL, October 1999

7.   73rd National Association for Research in Science Teaching Meeting, New Orleans LA, April 2000

8.   16th Biennial Conference on Chemical Education, Ann Arbor MI, August 2000

Papers Presented

1.   Del Carlo, D. *Relative Adsorption of Azo Dyes into KDP Crystals*. Presented at Departmental Seminar, Purdue University, March 1997.

2.   Del Carlo, D. *Relative Adsorption of Azo Dyes into KDP Crystals*. Presented at Departmental Seminar, Augustana College, April 1997.

3.   Del Carlo, D. *Playing with NUD*IST: It's not what you think; It's a way of analyzing qualitative data*. Presented at Departmental Seminar, Purdue University, October 1999.

4.   Del Carlo, D., Lowrey, K., Bodner, G., Oakes, W. *The Freshman Engineering Experience at Purdue University*. Presented at 34th Midwest Regional American Chemical Society Meeting, Quincy IL, October 1999.

5.   Del Carlo, D., Lowrey, K., Bodner, G., Oakes, W. *The Freshman Engineering Experience: The Students' Perspectives*. Presented at 16th Biennial Conference on Chemical Education, Ann Arbor MI, August 2000.

APPENDIX B – Cover Letter

PURDUE UNIVERSITY

DEPARTMENT OF CHEMISTRY   October 11, 2000

Dr. ███████
Chair
Department of Chemistry and Biochemistry
Montclair State University
Upper Montclair, NJ 07043

Re: Chemistry Education position starting Fall 2001

Dear Dr. ██████,

I was pleased when I saw your advertisement in the October 2nd issue of C&EN. My CV, statement of teaching philosophy, statement of research interests, and academic transcripts are enclosed for your review and I have asked three references to send letters of recommendation.

I believe I would make a good addition to your faculty for two reasons. First, my PhD will be in Chemical Education and while I don't have any direct experience with teacher education, I believe my graduate training has prepared me with a strong background in educational research to be able to approach new fields with enthusiasm.

Second, I have a MS in Inorganic Chemistry and therefore feel prepared to work within that field as well. While I am applying for the science education position at MSU, my experience in inorganic chemistry has prepared me to teach an introductory or advanced level inorganic chemistry course as well as conduct research in this field. Consequently I have included potential inorganic research that I am prepared to conduct.

In closing, I feel that my graduate experiences in education made me an ideal candidate for this position. Please feel free to contact me for any additional information. Thank you for your consideration and I look forward to hearing from you.

Sincerely,

Dawn Del Carlo

18

Teaching at a Community College: The Best of Both Worlds

Richard F. Jones
Liberal Arts and Sciences
Sinclair Community College

Abstract

Community colleges are an American invention in higher education that has experienced phenomenal growth and has become an important part of the United States higher educational system. Community colleges combine many of the best features of colleges and high schools. In this chapter, the philosophy and background on the students and the teaching experience at community colleges are described, as well as some tips on how to get a job at a community college.

Biography

I earned my Ph.D. from Purdue University in inorganic chemistry. After teaching five years at a private high school, I joined the faculty at Sinclair and have taught there for 25 years. I was chair of a 12-member chemistry, geology and geography department with nine chemists for 20 years. After a year as Interim Dean of Liberal Arts and Sciences, I became Dean of Liberal Arts and Sciences. I am a past chair of the Two Year College Chemistry Consortium ($2YC_3$), a recipient of Chemical Manufacturers' Responsible Care ® Award in 1997, and Alternate counselor of Division of Chemical Education.

So you want to teach at a community college?

I personally think that teaching at a community college is the best-ever teaching position. We have close interactions with our students, like high school teachers and faculty at small colleges. We have resources such as instrumentation, technology support, and sophisticated teaching facilities common to large universities. But we do not have the high school teachers' "cafeteria duty" or the "publish or perish" pressures of research universities. Community colleges are an important part of the American educational system. They are exciting places to work and provide a great platform to launch a professional career. I want to help you become a member of one of these great institutions.

What are community colleges?

Community colleges are an American invention that began with the first community college, Joliet Junior College, which opened around 100 years ago. The United States faced major challenges in the early twentieth century. At the same time a more educated workforce was needed, three-fourths of the high school graduates were not continuing their education, partly because they were reluctant to leave home to attend college. High schools stepped into the void and offered curricula beyond the traditional high school level. At the same time, Vincennes University had built a successful model of higher education on the premise of small classes and close faculty/student interactions. Vincennes University became one of the first community colleges and was the model for both private and public community colleges (American Association of Community Colleges 2002).

The community college movement gained momentum in the 1960s when many public community colleges were established. Many of these were technical colleges, but recently the trend has been for all two-year colleges to offer a comprehensive curriculum. This represents a movement comparable in importance to establishment of the land grant colleges. The fundamental concept is to provide affordable education within a reasonable commuting distance of everyone, regardless of wealth, heritage, or previous academic experience. My institution, Sinclair Community College, Dayton, OH, has a mission statement that is typical: "Help individuals turn dreams into achievable goals through accessible, high quality, affordable learning opportunities." Most community colleges are open admission, requiring only a high school diploma or GED to attend and having a national average tuition of $1518 per year (American Association of Community Colleges 2002).

Two-year colleges are among the fastest-growing institutions in the United States. The 1171 community colleges now enroll 10.4 million students and account for 44% of all U.S. undergraduates. When branch campuses of community colleges are included, there are approximately 1600 community college campuses. That 65% of all new healthcare workers in the country get their training at community colleges demonstrates that two-year colleges are a major influence in workforce development. Many students use a community college as their start toward a baccalaureate degree, with 25% of community college students transferring to four-year colleges. In the fall of 1992, community colleges accounted for over 40% of all undergraduate science, math, engineering, and technology course enrollments. It is estimated that more than 40% of K through 12 teachers completed some of their science and math courses at community colleges (National Science Foundation 1999).

Emphasizing accessibility, community colleges represent the rich diversity of our society. Since 46% of African American, 55% of Hispanic, 46% of Asian/Pacific Islander, and 55% of Native American students attend community colleges, community colleges play a significant role in bringing minority students into higher education (Community College Press 2000).

What are the students like at a community college?

The national average age of community college students is 29, but this is likely to drop as more and more recent high school graduates attend community colleges. In my county, Montgomery, OH, 30% of graduating high school seniors attended Sinclair Community College within a year of graduation in June of 2000 (Sinclair Admissions Office 2002). Many of our students are women returning to college after suspending their college career to raise a family. Many attend a community college to retrain after a job loss or to train for a change in careers. The result is that many community college students are part-time. Many of our students are the first from their families to attend college. These students have a higher level of angst about attending college than the traditional student. They have not been in the classroom for a lengthy period of time, and they often require remediation in basic learning skills.

A growing trend is for students to come to community colleges with the intent of transferring to a four-year institution. They receive two years of high-quality education at a very low expense and transfer to a four-year college. At a greatly reduced cost, they still get a baccalaureate with the name of a four-year institution on their diploma. In 2001 25% of community college students transferred to four-year colleges (America's Best Colleges 2003). Many students at community colleges are enrolled concurrently at four-year colleges. This is especially true as they complete their studies at a community college. It is common for Sinclair Community College chemistry students working in our stockroom to be taking classes at Wright State University a few miles up the road. Not only are these students interested in transferring credit to Wright State University but they often will transfer Wright State University courses back to Sinclair Community College to complete their Associate of Science degrees. A counselor from an affluent suburb tells parents of students who have a strong academic record but a low level of maturity to go to a community college. To paraphrase her advice, "Sending Johnny away to a four-year residential college or university will almost certainly result in his flunking out. He can attend Sinclair Community College and by staying at home and maturing an extra year, he will be able to transfer to the four-year institution of his choice and not lose a year. He will receive excellent instruction in small classes at half the tuition rate."

Most community college students are commuters. Many of them are underprepared; consequently, our developmental/remedial departments have large enrollments. Increasing numbers of our students have a goal of continuing their education at a four-year institution, and last year community college graduates transfering to four-year institutions in Ohio had a junior-year GPA of 2.9 compared to a junior-year GPA of 3.0 for students who started at the four-year college (Ohio Board of Regents 2002).

What is it like to teach at a community college?

If you want to teach at a community college, you must have excellent teaching skills, and your first priority must be to teach. Many of our students are fragile: They lack confidence in their academic abilities, they often do not have a support system that helps them through difficult times, and they may have competing family and job pressures. To elevate these students to a level where they can compete equally with their peers who are juniors at a four-year college requires the teachers to be dedicated, hardworking, and have expertise in their academic discipline.

The typical community college chemistry faculty member will teach about 15 to 20 contact hours, or two to three lectures, and three to four laboratories as a base load. This includes teaching labs as well as lecturing. In fact, some of the most effective nurturing of our students takes place in the lab. Community college faculty share this common experience with our colleagues at small colleges. We also have in common with them the expectation of close contact with students by maintaining office hours and by doing our own grading. While community colleges do not have graduate assistants to help with the teaching, many do have part-time instructors who teach about half of the lectures and labs. Part-time instructors typically come from industry or high school teaching faculties. Community college chemistry faculty also spend a lot of time mentoring part-time faculty. Part-time instructors employed in industry usually have a doctorate degree but need assistance with teaching skills, while the high school faculty may need assistance in content. While the typical high school teacher working part-time as an instructor may have a masters degree in chemistry, he/she may not have had time to keep up with recent developments in chemistry, especially those dealing with instrumentation. As a result, community college faculty mentor part-time instructors to help maintain the high standards of teaching excellence that community college students need.

Teaching a student population with an average age of 29 is different from most teaching jobs. There is a popular phrase used in beginning chemistry labs: "You will have to pick up after yourself; your mother is not enrolled in this course." I often use this as a means to lighten up a class of tense and unsure students. One time, however, I got the response, "Yes, she is. She is right over there." The student who said that was 34 years old. (I never found out the age of the mother.) Typically, older returning students are very motivated as they have experienced firsthand in life the costs of not having a college degree. However, they have strong competing-time priorities related to their responsibilities as wage earners, parents, and homeowners.

The typical minimum degree for the faculty at a community college is a master's degree, although in the chemistry departments, one-third of the faculty usually have a doctorate in the discipline. While teaching is the first and most important priority of community college faculty, there is also a strong expectation of service outside of the classroom. This can include, but is not limited to, being involved in the development of innovative curriculum and pedagogical approaches, participating actively in discipline organizations, and contributing to the college life through committee participation in discipline-related professional growth or through outreach to the community.

The size of the community college varies just as it does with four-year institutions. However, in small community colleges, it is common for the Chemistry Department to be part of a Physical or Natural Science Department rather than an independent department. This has numerous advantages and disadvantages that a prospective faculty member at a community college must evaluate for herself or himself. Sinclair Community College is one of the larger community colleges, with a single urban campus fall enrollment of around 12,000 FTE. We have nine full-time chemistry faculty in our Chemistry, Geology and Geography Department. Community colleges are equally divided among urban, suburban, and rural campuses, but most community colleges are much smaller than Sinclair Community College. About two-thirds of community colleges have only one or two chemists on their faculty.

During the summer session many of the students enrolled in courses at the community college are from four-year colleges or universities. At Sinclair Community College these students comprise about three-fourths of our summer student population. These students are getting a "leg up on their peers" or making up "a momentary lapse in academic excellence." The rest are typically Sinclair Community College students or high school students who have just graduated and are "trying on a college class for size." Students are typically impressed by our community college's facilities and have often remarked that the facilities "are much better than we have at our home institution." Of course, many of these students are freshman and therefore are not familiar with the upper-level labs and instrumentation of the chemistry departments at their home college. However, at a community college, the infrared, atomic absorption, gas chromatograph, NMR and GC/MS instruments are used by students in general and organic chemistry. The community college chemistry professor must be able to design experiments using these instruments as well as maintain the instruments himself. Usually these instruments are obtained by funding from outside sources such as the National Science Foundation or other competitive funding sources.

One of the greatest rewards in teaching at a community college is the small class size. At Sinclair Community College we limit our lecture sections to 34 students in a lecture and 17 in a laboratory. It is common to have 25 to 35 students in lectures and 15 to 30 students in laboratories at community colleges. Teachers can be a more innovative with a small class than they can with a large class. Faculty are almost unlimited in employing novel teaching methods and techniques at a moment's notice. Applying the latest idea from *The Journal of Chemical Education* requires only an hour or two of preparation! Since faculty teach both lecture and laboratory sections, the interaction between teacher and student is very close. Community college teachers know their students very well and are often involved in counseling these students outside the classroom. Of course, the time that a former student comes up to you to thank you for his or her position at EPA or an equally prestigious job, and you remember him to be the struggling student that you spent an extra hour helping master stoichiometry problems, is priceless.

Because Sinclair Community College is a large community college, we have separate courses for chemistry classes that support science, engineering and premed, and other courses for nurses and technicians. About two-thirds of Sinclair Community College chemistry students are in our majors course with career goals in medicine, biology, chemistry, and engineering. The remaining students are looking for positions as technicians in the allied health fields. It takes a teacher with solid content knowledge and exceptional teaching skills to effectively teach these students. For these practical-minded people, a theory must have an immediate application.

How do I get a job at a community college? A view from the inside.

Since teaching is the function of community colleges, providing evidence of good teaching is a must for applicants. It is easy to demonstrate good research potential through prior research grant support, publications, and a research proposal. It is a lot harder to prove that you are a great teacher. Search committees at community colleges have a very difficult job. The easiest qualification to identify is technical competency. The resume and transcripts quickly eliminate those not qualified. The trick is to identify those individuals who can effectively support the fragile student and raise him or her to a level where the student can compete on an equal basis with juniors either at a four-year college or in the workplace. In a resume and cover letter, a sincere dedication to the art of teaching must be evident.

A typical mistake for people applying for a job at a community college is to include a research proposal. This is often the "kiss of death" for the aspiring applicant. It sends a signal that the applicant is really looking for a job at a research institution but will "settle for a job at a community college until an opportunity presents itself." Wastebaskets of search committees at community colleges are littered with applications like these.

Often, a "sample" lecture will be required as part of an interview. Even then, one clever lecture with supporting pedagogical "tricks of the trade" is often not enough. Lecturing is not teaching at a community college.   Effective communication is assumed, but it is not sufficient.   Community college search committees often ask for prior teaching experience. Graduate school teaching experience, unless very different from the usual, is often dismissed as "no real experience." If you are in graduate school and looking for a position at a community college, you would be wise to investigate the possibilities of teaching part-time at a local community college. High school teaching with good references is highly praised, but even better is part-time teaching at a community college (with good references).   The best way to demonstrate "teaching excellence at the community college level" is to teach part-time at a community college. Mentor evaluations, student evaluations, and your ability to speak from first hand experience is invaluable. Because it is so hard to evaluate good teaching from a cover letter, resume, and interview, many "new hires" at community colleges come from the ranks of part-time instructors.

References

American Association of Community Colleges, About Community Colleges. Date revised. (15 October 2002).<http://.aacc.nche.edu/Template.cfm?section=AboutCommunity Colleges>

Ease the leap to a university. (2002). *A U.S. News and World Report 2003 Edition, America's Best Colleges*, 42-43.

Community College Press. (2000). *Pocket Profile of Community Colleges: Trends and Statistics, 1995-96* (3rd ed.).

National Science Foundation. (1998). *Investing in Tomorrow's Teachers*. (National Science Foundation Publication 99-49).

Ohio Board of Regents. (2002). *The Performance Report for Ohio's Colleges and Universities 2002: Profile of Student Outcomes,Experiences and Campus Measures.* http://www.regents.state.oh.us/perfrpt/2002HSindex.html

Sinclair Admissions Office. (2002). *Top Feeder High School Summary for 2000-2001.*

19

Professional Development and Expectations

Philip S. Bailey
Dean, College of Science and Mathematics
Christina Bailey
Department of Chemistry and Biochemistry
California Polytechnic State University—San Luis Obispo

Abstract

Combining a successful teaching career with a rich, professional development program is a lifelong endeavor for a faculty member. For the newly appointed instructor, it is a maze of responsibilities and expectations that may be explicit but is more likely implicit. Successful negotiation of the maze leads to tenure and promotion. The following paper contains the comments and advice of two tenured full professors at a leading undergraduate teaching institution, one of whom is also the dean of a college.

Biographies

Phil and Tina Bailey have been a team both professionally and personally for more than 36 years. Phil has been dean of the College of Science and Mathematics at Cal Poly for over 20 years. He is the only dean at Cal Poly who teaches every academic quarter. Together Phil and Tina have written an organic chemistry textbook for survey/short courses that is currently in its 6th edition and has been translated into Japanese, Spanish, and Korean. Tina, although a biochemist, has developed a unique approach to teaching general chemistry for engineers in the studio classroom integrated lecture-lab courses she coordinates. Both have been recognized by students and staff as dedicated teachers who care about the quality and personal attention that are the hallmarks of an excellent undergraduate teaching institution like California Polytechnic State University.

Perspectives

Each institution and each department within an institution has its own culture and requirements. It is important to find out just what the climate is at your institution. Both teaching and research universities have the same ultimate goal as far as undergraduates are concerned: to successfully educate and graduate students. However, approaches for achieving this goal and the attitudes, priorities, and expectations of the faculty can be dramatically different. Research institutions have the responsibility to make new discoveries and expand the frontiers of knowledge. Teaching institutions do that also, but their primary purpose for doing research is to provide special learning experiences for students and enhance the professional competency of the faculty so they will continue to be excellent teachers and mentors. Faculty at teaching institutions may be relieved of the emphasis and output of publishable research expected of their colleagues at research institutions, but in turn they bear an increased responsibility for teaching and learning at the undergraduate level.

Cal Poly, San Luis Obispo, is one of the 23 campuses of the California State University System (CSU). It is a comprehensive, polytechnic institution of 18,000 students. The focus is undergraduate teaching, and admission is highly selective. The College of Science and Mathematics is one of six in the university (the others are Liberal Arts, Engineering, Architecture and Environmental Design, Agriculture, and Business).

The Department of Chemistry and Biochemistry usually has about two dozen tenured and tenure track faculty members, three to five lecturers on two-year appointments, several emeriti professors who teach part-time, and a half dozen or so part-time faculty members. In any year, there are 250 to 300 chemistry and biochemistry majors in the program. Hiring of tenure track faculty members is carried out according to present and projected needs not only in the two major degree programs but also in the essential support areas.   More than 80% of our teaching loads are in "core" courses required by most of the programs throughout the university. There are only a few large lecture halls on campus; by large we mean 100-140 seats. Most lecture rooms have 24, 48, or 72 seats. Regular faculty teach both lectures and laboratories; we have no graduate teaching-assistant population.   The teaching loads are fairly heavy, averaging 12 "weighted" teaching units per quarter (10-week term). A typical teaching assignment would be two lecture sections (three one-hour lectures each) and three lab sections (three hours each).

Hiring is one of the most important responsibilities of the tenured faculty.

What qualities are considered in hiring a new faculty member?

They are the same qualities expected on a continuing basis from all faculty members:

- Ability to convey information in written and oral forms

- Teaching experience and interests or teaching potential

- Enthusiasm, initiative, work ethic

- Proposals for involving undergraduate students in a research program, including outside sources of funding

The terms and timetable for earning tenure should be clearly defined by the department, college, and university. As a new faculty member, one should look for clear standards and procedures as well as a system that allows for evaluation each year in the probationary period.

In most institutions the probationary period leading to a tenure decision is six years. Probationary faculty must submit annual reports for evaluation by the tenured faculty. In some places, a probationary faculty member may apply for early promotion without waiting for tenure. There is also an option to apply for early tenure. Both are best discussed with one's senior colleagues, department chair, and the dean before the decision to apply is made.

Evaluation of probationary faculty

This again varies by institution, but in most cases a peer review committee is constituted at a specified time before evaluation. In our department, every tenured faculty member serves unless he or she requests an exemption for a substantive reason (e.g., absence because of a sabbatical leave). Our department chair and the elected chair of the tenured faculty serve at separate levels of review.

Evaluation involves the reading of a working personnel file (professional portfolio) submitted by the probationary faculty member as well as classroom visitations and individual consultations with members of the peer review committee, if desired. A meeting of the peer review committee is held to discuss the junior members. This is followed by formal written and signed evaluations submitted by all members of the peer review committee. At a specified time, copies of the evaluations are given to the candidate who has a period of time for rebuttal before the evaluations and department vote for retention are passed onto the college committee and dean. The college committee reviews materials and makes recommendations for tenure and promotion to the dean.   The dean reads the working personnel file, considers the recommendations of the department, department chair, and college committee and then makes his/her recommendation to the provost and president.

Professional portfolio for peer-review committees

At a minimum we would recommend the following components:

- current resume

- statement of teaching philosophy and pedagogical approach

- courses taught with salient comments and sample course materials (syllabus, exams, special efforts)

- summary of student evaluations and grading patterns

- professional development plan

- overall five-year plan for teaching and professional development

As you prepare these materials, be sure to include your course repertoire. Focus on professional and teaching accomplishments and development. No teacher springs from the womb as a Socrates. Even Socrates had to work at it and really wasn't appreciated in all sectors.

Seek out and mention opportunities for collaborative efforts with colleagues both on and off campus, intra- and interdepartmental. Comment on your interpersonal relationships with colleagues, especially the staff. Use senior faculty members as mentors. There is a reason that your department has arrived at its current position. Find out the positive aspects of the teaching in your department and emphasize how you are emulating these traits. Seek advice from those you respect.

KEEP YOUR MATERIALS CURRENT! As you finish a term, add to your portfolio as you put materials away. Having a current file saves time when preparing for imminent tenure and promotion in terms of gathering the supportive information.

It is useful to construct a table to summarize the courses you have taught, the terms in which you have taught them, the class GPA, the final grade distribution, and the student evaluation ratings for the course and instructor.

Here are some ideas for describing your teaching philosophy and approach:

- What role do you play in the teaching and learning process?

- How do you encourage critical and creative thinking as well as genuine understanding and learning?

- Are your courses an intellectual experience and reasonable in terms of level, rigor, and time required by students?

- How do you engage students both in and outside of class?

- What guidance and incentives do you provide to promote studying and learning outside of class?

- How do you promote student success?

- What special approach or effort do you make to help new freshmen understand how to study, learn, and be successful in your courses and in college in general?

In describing your professional accomplishments:

- Was the work done before you joined the current institution or was it done at the institution?

- Identify student coworkers and other coworkers.

- Describe your relative role in the work and the significance of your work and accomplishment. If the accomplishment has produced a publication, indicate if the paper was refereed and consider how the journal is regarded by your professional colleagues.

Senior faculty review of your materials

As a tenured faculty member, I would consider the following as my responsibilities:

- to read and comment on all materials supplied

- to consider teaching progress (see Socrates comment above)

- to help the junior member develop a focus in teaching and professional development especially by the 4th year of probationary status

- to expect an undergraduate research program of reasonable scope to have been established

- to meet with any junior faculty member on a one-to-one basis to discuss the evaluation and comments

Dean's role in professional development

Consider these factors:

- The president/provost will focus the greatest attention on the dean's recommendation because of the personal time constraints of the senior administration and closer professional relationships of the dean with his/her faculty.

- The dean is a single voice, not a mixture of ideas as may come from recommendations of the tenured faculty members. There can be differences among the faculty members in a department as to the directions a probationary faculty member should emphasize in the areas of research, teaching, and service. Sometimes this advice is conflicting and difficult to navigate both for the junior member being evaluated as well as the upper levels of administration making decisions about the quality and improvement of the institution. The dean has the responsibility of coalescing and prioritizing many opinions into one coherent recommendation.

- The dean may have personal guiding statements on retention, promotion, and tenure that are consistent with personnel documents and reflect university expectations. If he or she doesn't have such personal guidelines, it is important for the probationary member to know it.

- The faculty members working towards tenure are among the dean's most important priorities. The quality of the faculty is crucial to a university. It is important that the probationary faculty develop in teaching, professional development, and in understanding the priorities and values of the university.

Important issues in tenure and promotion

Teaching is absolutely the most important aspect of your career to emphasize.

- How do you present your courses?

- How do you promote student engagement, learning and success?

- How do you evaluate student progress?

- How do you evaluate your progress as an instructor?

- What have you done to improve your teaching?

Almost equally important is your growth as a scientist.

- What is your plan for professional development?
- Are you supervising student research projects?
- Are you involved in collaboration?
- Have you spent summers doing research either at home or elsewhere?

A tenured faculty member is expected to maintain a career-long, creative professional development program that is capable of occasional external validation. Collaborative efforts involving students are especially valued. External validation can take many forms including refereed publications, receipt of competitive grants, invited and competitively accepted papers/presentations, national publication of educational materials such as textbooks and software, leadership activities in professional societies, and productive collaborations with the public or private sector.

Service is included in the descriptions of materials to be supplied in personnel packages. For the assistant professor, service per se is not as important as teaching and professional development. There will always be opportunities to serve on committees, help out in local schools for science projects, or hold a position on the academic senate. Preparing for tenure has a set time period, usually six years, and establishing your teaching and professional development during this period is critical. You have to focus on your career at its most formative stages. However, that said, you have to be involved with your department and indicate your potential for the future. The university and surrounding areas depend upon an academic center to be part of the community.

What does tenure mean?

In terms of teaching: A tenured faculty member is an effective instructor, one who models and inspires curiosity, imagination, creative and critical thinking, and true engagement in learning. A tenured faculty member demonstrates a deep responsibility for the curriculum and its pedagogical delivery and makes meaningful contributions to its evolution. A tenured faculty member believes in students, promotes student learning and success, and is respected by students and colleagues alike.

In terms of professional development: A tenured faculty member is expected to maintain a career-long, creative professional development program that is capable of occasional external validation. Collaborative efforts involving students are especially valued.

The following are some excerpts from this dean's evaluation letters to junior faculty.

Tell me and I will forget.   *Show me and I will remember.*   *Engage me and I will understand.*   **A Lakota Sioux Saying**

I hear and I forget.   *I see and I remember.*   *I do and I understand.*   **A Chinese Proverb**

Comments concerning teaching

"American higher education has done well with the lecture method of instruction. It, however, in many cases, represents the show (some) and tell (a lot) parts of the

quoted Lakota Sioux saying. Encouraging student involvement outside of class by inspiration (quality of presentations, intellectual stimulation) and incentive (frequent graded assignments, quizzes, exams) is crucial to successful learning."

"Your submitted materials show that you understand the importance of engaging students outside of class as well as in class. Your homework assignments, six quizzes, two exams, term project, and final provide plenty of incentive for students to keep up with the course, become personally involved in the learning process, and receive frequent feedback on meeting your expectations. Very important, it is clear you are providing a substantial intellectual experience at an appropriate level."

"I greatly appreciate your taking the challenge as an instructor to coordinate technology in an active learning environment, a less controlled educational environment than chalkboard lecturing, and developing pedagogy in an older facility that is not ideal for innovation. The studio concepts have generated both excitement and controversy within the college. Understand that what you are doing is important, valued, and is having an influence on our educational methods."

Comments concerning professional development

Professional development in traditional research

"Your approach to undergraduate research as a creative opportunity for your students and a vehicle for your own professional development exactly fits a priority of the College of Science and Mathematics strategic plan. The weekly group meetings, opportunities for students to collaborate and communicate progress and results, and the culmination of the student experiences with a presentation at a scientific meeting are key ingredients of your well-designed program. It appears that you recognize undergraduate research as a very special form of teaching."

"I am especially excited about the paper you and Dr. _____ are submitting to the journal _____. It has several student co-authors; this is a very important and special experience for them."

Professional development in the area of K-12 teacher education

"You are clearly showing an interest in teacher education. You are already conducting meaningful senior projects and in-service activities for teachers. The $----- grant you received from --- not only provides special opportunities for teachers in the area but also serves as a form of external validation."

Professional development in the area of undergraduate pedagogy

"I appreciate your courage and persistence in teaching in the ... It offers many exciting opportunities but can be challenging because of the uniqueness of the pedagogy. Not only are you influencing the way we teach, but your curriculum and pedagogy development activities are an acceptable form of professional development that are capable of external validation."

Is there life after tenure?

Tenure is the most important of all personnel actions. It is an expression of confidence in a faculty member's intellect, creativity, initiative, work ethic, and career-long value to the university. It presumes a loyalty and responsibility on the part of the faculty member to the institution, the students, and the curriculum. With tenure comes the expectation that a faculty member will, during his or her career, accomplish a body of work in teaching, professional development, and service that is of recognizable value and importance and which constitutes a meaningful contribution to the mission of the university. Tenure expresses a belief in the future and the role of the tenured faculty in shaping it. Achieving tenure is an honor and a privilege, an accomplishment of tremendous significance.

Tenure is a beginning, a new stage of your career—one with greater responsibilities, opportunities, and expectations.

Conclusion

As in all professional careers, the first years as a faculty member are crucial to establishing oneself as a productive member of the institution. The criteria for evaluating progress towards this goal need to be clearly delineated, achievable, and understood by all those involved from the probationary faculty member to the president (provost). Evaluations by senior members of the faculty and administration have to adhere to these guidelines and be completed in a timely and professional manner. The granting of tenure is the most important of all personnel actions. It is also a step to a fruitful career in academia.

References

A fundamental source for the modern-day paradigm of university scholarship is Ernest Boyer's Carnegie Foundation Report "Scholarship Reconsidered: Priorities for the Professorate" (1990), Princeton: Carnegie Foundation for the Advancement of Teaching.

An Annotated Bibliography produced by the National Academy for Academic Leadership lists several other sources of information – http://www.thenationalacademy.org/Resources/facrewardbiblio.html

The National Education Association Web site presents a list of myths and realities concerning tenure at http://www.nea.org/he/truth.html

The AAUP (American Association of University Professors) is also an excellent source of information at http://www.aaup.org

One Last Word

Okay, so you have read the book. Now what? Well, it's probably time to select your textbook and talk to people in the department about expectations for course organization and grading. Don't worry if no one has told you anything yet. Just ask. You will find the answers you need. Once you have done that, think about what teaching methods you want to use in your course—demonstrations, small groups, technology both in and out of class, etc.—and plan accordingly. It is always best to start small and work up to a complete course revamping. Take one innovation that you sincerely believe in, and use it on a regular basis. As you determine its effectiveness and make modifications, branch out and include more of the same or introduce other innovations. Keep this planning in mind as you write your syllabus and determine your grading policy. Allow for midstream corrections or modifications.

Don't think you have to go through this alone. Talk to others in your department as your course progresses. Explain what you are trying to accomplish and your estimation of how things are going. Share your successful and your not-so-successful stories. Pursue other advice by taking advantage of the references listed in the chapters in this book to explore topics in more detail. Pick up a recent copy of the *Journal of Chemical Education* or peruse the on-line version of the *Journal* (http://JChemEd.chem.wisc.edu) to look for interesting and pertinent articles and activities. Join a professional society, whether it is a local organization or a national one like the American Chemical Society (http://www.chemistry.org), the National Science Teachers' Association (http://www.nsta.org), or the Two-Year College Chemistry Consortium (http://2YC3.vinu.edu). Attend local and national meetings of some of these societies to learn more of what is going on in chemistry teaching. Read their journals. Talk with peers. Join chemistry teaching listservs such as (http://jchemed.chem.wisc.edu/ChemEd/ChemEdL). Get involved first as a participant and soon after as a presenter. If you can afford to attend only one national meeting, try the Division of Chemical Education's Biennial Conference on Chemical Education, known as the BCCE (http://divched.chem.wisc.edu/CHED-meetings.html). This conference offers insights and reports on innovative teaching in high school, two-year colleges, four-year colleges and university chemistry courses. If you attend one of these biennial meetings, you are guaranteed to meet chemistry teachers at all levels of chemistry teaching who are excited about teaching and more than willing to share their ideas.

And when you have one of those teaching days from hell, go back and reread some of the chapters in this book. They will renew your courage and resolve to keep going. Welcome to the chemistry teaching community. We are glad to have you as a colleague and look forward to meeting you soon.

Sincerely,
Diane M. Bunce
Cinzia M. Muzzi